revise

GCSE

Geography

David Jones

with Tony Buzan

Hodder & Stoughton

A MEMBER OF THE HODDER HEADLINE GROUP

ISBN 0 340 66386 3

First published 1997
Impression number 10 9 8 7 6 5 4 3 2 1
Year 2001 2000 1999 1998 1997

The 'Teach Yourself' name and logo are registered trade marks of Hodder & Stoughton Ltd.

Designed and produced by Gecko Ltd, Bicester, Oxon
Printed in Great Britain for Hodder & Stoughton Educational, a division of Hodder Headline Plc, 338 Euston Road, London NW1 3BH by Scotprint Ltd, Musselburgh, Scotland.

Mind Maps: Helen Whitten
Illustrations: Joe Little, Andrea Norton, Mike Parsons, John Plumb, Stephen Ramsay, Chris Rothero
Cover design: Amanda Hawkes
Cover illustration: Paul Bateman

Contents

Key to symbols

As you read through this revision guide, you will notice symbols which occur frequently throughout the book. These are to help you identify specific sections of text quickly and easily while you revise. This is what they mean:

Syllabus check: check the syllabus you are studying to make sure you have all the information you need.

Project ideas.

Look at other parts of the book that are relevant to the topic you are studying. The text tells you where to find them.

Test yourself: questions to answer to help with your revision, based on the section you have just read.

Review: ideas to help you review and revise a topic.

Exam tips or important tips to remember.

Revision made easy

The four pages that follow contain a gold mine of information on how you can achieve success both at school and in your exams. Read them and apply the information, and you will be able to spend less, but more efficient, time studying, with better results. If you already have another *Hodder & Stoughton Revision Guide*, skim-read these pages to remind yourself about the exciting new techniques the books use, then move ahead to page 5.

SUCCESS

This section gives you vital information on how to remember more *while* you are learning and how to remember more *after* you have finished studying. It explains

- **how to use special techniques to improve your memory**
- **how to use a revolutionary note-taking technique called Mind Maps that will double your memory and help you to write essays and answer exam questions**
- **how to read everything faster while at the same time improving your comprehension and concentration**

All this information is packed into the next four pages, so make sure you read them!

Your *amazing* memory

There are five important things you must know about your brain and memory to revolutionise your school life.

1. **how your memory ('recall') works *while* you are learning**
2. **how your memory works *after* you have finished learning**
3. **how to use Mind Maps – a special technique for helping you with all aspects of your studies**
4. **how to increase your reading speed**
5. **how to zap your revision**

1 Recall during learning – the need for breaks

When you are studying, your memory can concentrate, understand and remember well for between 20 and 45 minutes at a time. Then it *needs* a break. If you carry on for longer than this without one, your memory starts to break down! If you study for hours non-stop, you will remember only a fraction of what you have been trying to learn, and you will have wasted valuable revision time.

So, ideally, *study for less than an hour*, then take a five- to ten-minute break. During the break listen to music, go for a walk, do some exercise, or just daydream. (Daydreaming is a necessary brain-power booster – geniuses do it regularly.) During the break your brain will be sorting out what it has been learning, and you will go back to your books with the new information safely stored and organised in your memory banks. We recommend breaks at regular intervals as you work through the *Revision Guides*. Make sure you take them!

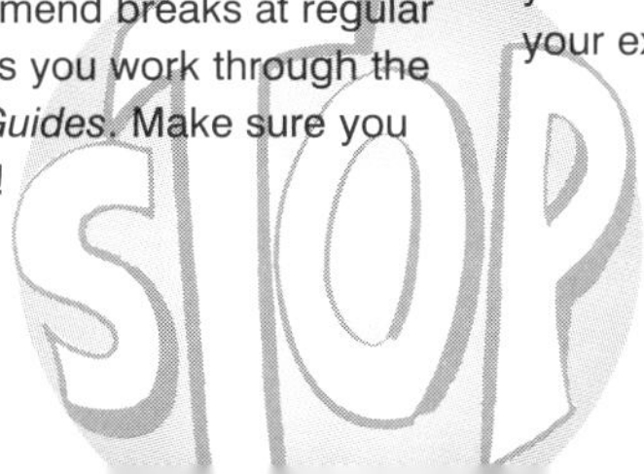

2 Recall after learning – the waves of your memory

What do you think begins to happen to your memory straight *after* you have finished learning something? Does it immediately start forgetting? No! Your brain actually *increases* its power and carries on remembering. For a short time after your study session, your brain integrates the information, making a more complete picture of everything it has just learnt. Only then does the rapid decline in memory begin, and as much as 80 per cent of what you have learnt can be forgotten in a day.

However, if you catch the top of the wave of your memory, and briefly review (look back over) what you have been revising at the correct time, the memory is stamped in far more strongly, and stays at the crest of the wave for a much longer time. To maximise your brain's power to remember, take a few minutes and use a Mind Map to review what you have learnt at the end of a day. Then review it at the end of a week, again at the end of a month, and finally a week before the exams. That way you'll ride your memory wave all the way to your exam – and beyond!

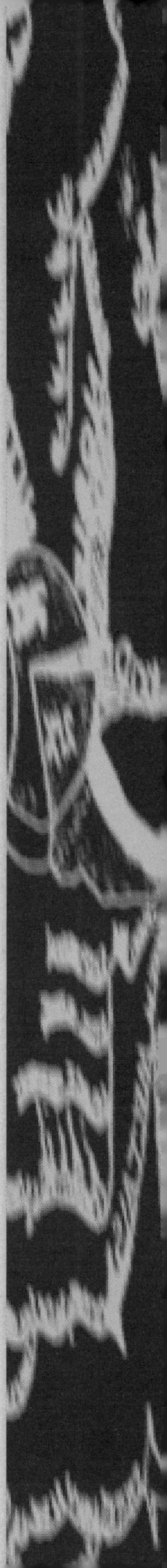

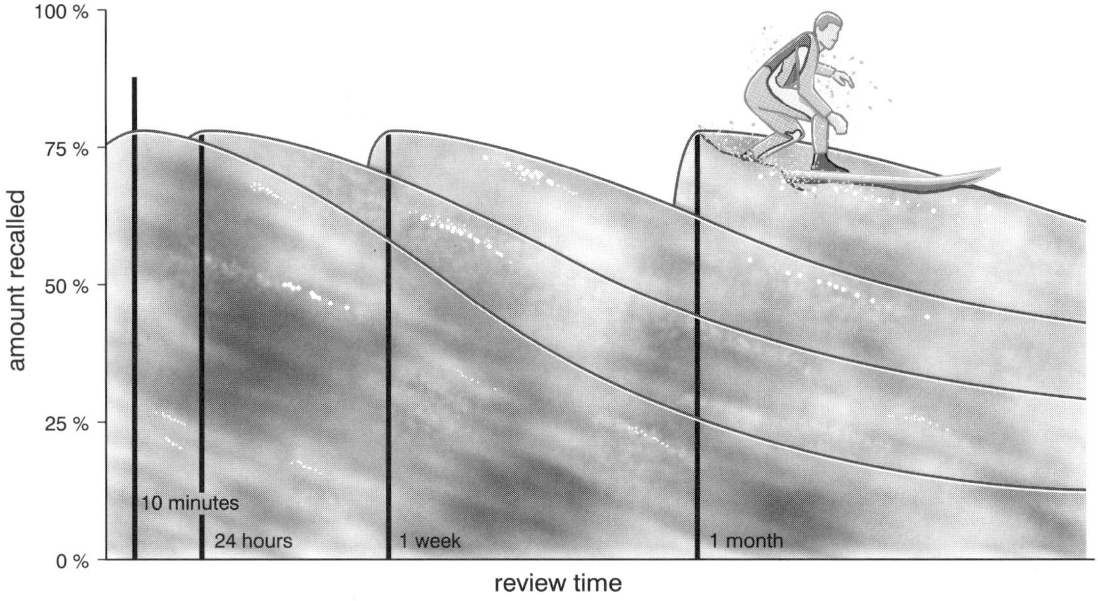

Amazing as your memory is (think of everything you actually do have stored in your brain at this moment) the principles on which it operates are very simple: your brain will remember if it (a) has an image (a picture or a symbol); (b) has that image fixed and (c) can link that image to something else.

3 The Mind Map® – a picture of the way you think

Do you *like* taking notes? More importantly, do you like having to go back over and learn them before exams? Most students I know certainly do not! And how do you take your notes? Most people take notes on lined paper, using blue or black ink. The result, visually, is *boring*! And what does your brain do when it is bored? It turns off, tunes out, and goes to sleep! Add a dash of colour, rhythm, imagination, and the whole note-taking process becomes much more fun, uses more of your brain's abilities, *and* improves your recall and understanding.

A Mind Map mirrors the way your brain works. It can be used for note-taking from books or in class, for reviewing what you have just studied, for revising, and for essay planning for coursework and in exams. It uses all your memory's natural techniques to build up your rapidly growing 'memory muscle'.

You will find Mind Maps throughout this book. Study them, add some colour, personalise them, and then have a go at drawing your own – you'll remember them far better! Put them on your walls and in your files for a quick-and-easy review of the topic.

How to draw a Mind Map

- Start in the middle of the page with the page turned sideways. This gives your brain the maximum room for its thoughts.
- Always start by drawing a small picture or symbol. Why? Because a picture is worth a thousand words to your brain. And try to use at least three colours, as colour helps your memory even more.
- Let your thoughts flow, and write or draw your ideas on coloured branching lines connected to your central image. These key symbols and words are the headings for your topic. The Mind Map at the top of the next page shows you how to start.
- Then add facts and ideas by drawing more, smaller, branches on to the appropriate main branches, just like a tree.
- Always print your word clearly on its line. Use only one word per line. The Mind Map at the foot of the next page shows you how to do this.
- To link ideas and thoughts on different branches, use arrows, colours, underlining, and boxes.

How to read a Mind Map

- Begin in the centre, the focus of your topic.
- The words/images attached to the centre are like chapter headings, read them next.
- Always read out from the centre, in every direction (even on the left-hand side, where you will have to read from right to left, instead of the usual left to right).

Using Mind Maps

Mind Maps are a versatile tool – use them for taking notes in class or from books, for solving problems, for brainstorming with friends, and for reviewing and revising for exams – their uses are endless! You will find them invaluable for planning essays for coursework and exams. Number your main branches in the order in which you want to use them and off you go – the main headings for your essay are done and all your ideas are logically organised!

GOVERNMENT
CLIMATE
FARMING
INFRASTRUCTURE
RELIEF
SOIL
MARKETS
FARM

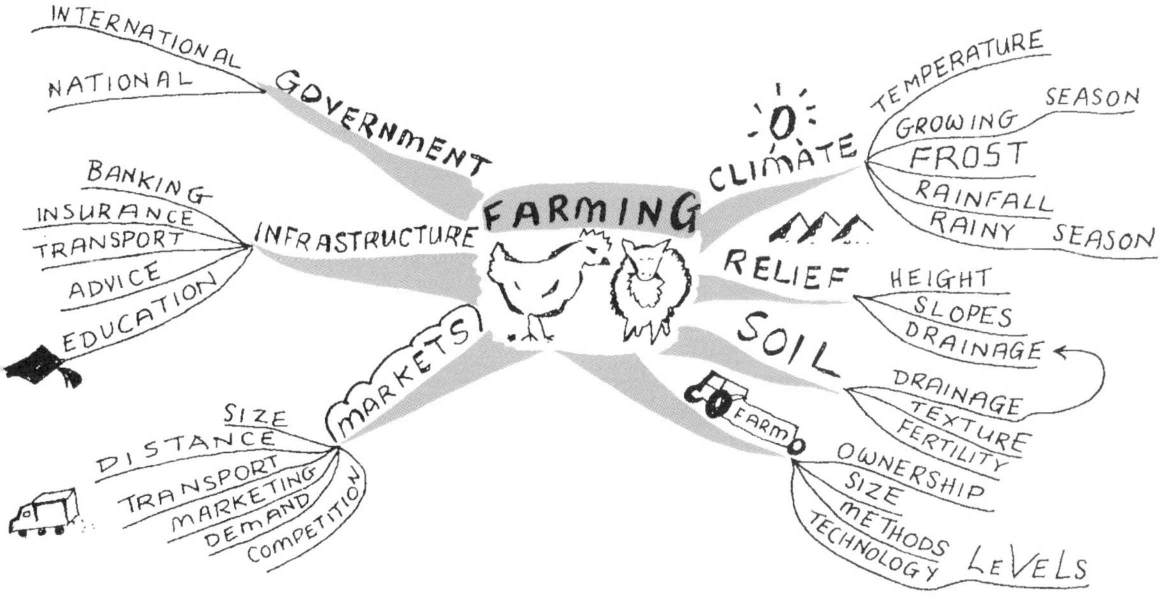
INTERNATIONAL
NATIONAL
GOVERNMENT
TEMPERATURE
GROWING
SEASON
FROST
RAINFALL
RAINY
SEASON
CLIMATE
FARMING
BANKING
INSURANCE
TRANSPORT
ADVICE
EDUCATION
INFRASTRUCTURE
RELIEF
HEIGHT
SLOPES
DRAINAGE
SOIL
DRAINAGE
TEXTURE
FERTILITY
MARKETS
SIZE
DISTANCE
TRANSPORT
MARKETING
DEMAND
COMPETITION
FARM
OWNERSHIP
SIZE
METHODS
TECHNOLOGY
LEVELS

4 Super speed reading

It seems incredible, but it's been proved – the faster you read, the more you understand and remember! So here are some tips to help you to practise reading faster – you'll cover the ground more quickly, remember more, *and* have more time for revision!

- ★ **Read the whole text (whether it's a lengthy book or an exam paper) very quickly first, to give your brain an overall idea of what's ahead and get it working. (It's like sending out a scout to look at the territory you have to cover – it's much easier when you know what to expect!) Then read the text again for more detailed information.**
- ★ **Have the text a reasonable distance away from your eyes. In this way your eye/brain system will be able to see more at a glance, and will naturally begin to read faster.**
- ★ **Take in groups of words at a time. Rather than reading slowly and 'carefully' read faster, more enthusiastically.
Your comprehension will rocket!**
- ★ **Take in phrases rather than single words while you read.**
- ★ **Use a guide. Your eyes are designed to follow movement, so a thin pencil underneath the lines you are reading, moved smoothly along, will 'pull' your eyes to faster speeds.**

5 Helpful hints for exam revision

Start to revise at the beginning of the course. Cram at the start, not the end and avoid 'exam panic'!

Use Mind Maps throughout your course, and build a Master Mind Map for each subject – a giant Mind Map that summarises everything you know about the subject.

Use memory techniques such as mnemonics (verses or systems for remembering things like dates and events, or lists).

Get together with one or two friends to revise, compare Mind Maps, and discuss topics.

And finally...

- *Have fun while you learn* – studies show that those people who enjoy what they are doing understand and remember it more, and generally do it better.
- *Use your teachers* as resource centres. Ask them for help with specific topics and with more general advice on how you can improve your all-round performance.
- *Personalise your* ***Revision Guide*** by underlining and highlighting, by adding notes and pictures. Allow your brain to have a conversation with it!

Your brain is an amazing piece of equipment – learn to use it, and you, like thousands of students before you will be able to master 'B's and 'A's with ease. The more you understand and use your brain, the more it will repay you!

Learning Geography

Your syllabus

Start by filling in the name of your examination board and the syllabus (Figure 1). Most boards have more than one syllabus; make sure you know which one you are doing.

If there are options within the syllabus check which options you are doing.

There are also different papers to sit at the end of the course. Make sure you know which ones you are doing and write them in on Figure 1.

Figure 1

Exam board .... Syllabus ....

Option ....
(if applicable)

Exam papers ....

....

Coursework

Coursework is mainly worth 25% of the total marks. You have to do one or two pieces of work. One has to be a fieldwork-based geographical investigation. If there are two, the second one can use secondary or library sources. There are ideas on possible projects throughout the book.

Before you go any further...

Have you skimmed through the whole book yet?
Have you looked at the last page?
Have you seen the photographs?

Have you found any maps or diagrams that look like ones you have seen before? Have you found topics or places you have already studied?

If you haven't skimmed through the book – do it now!

Figure 2

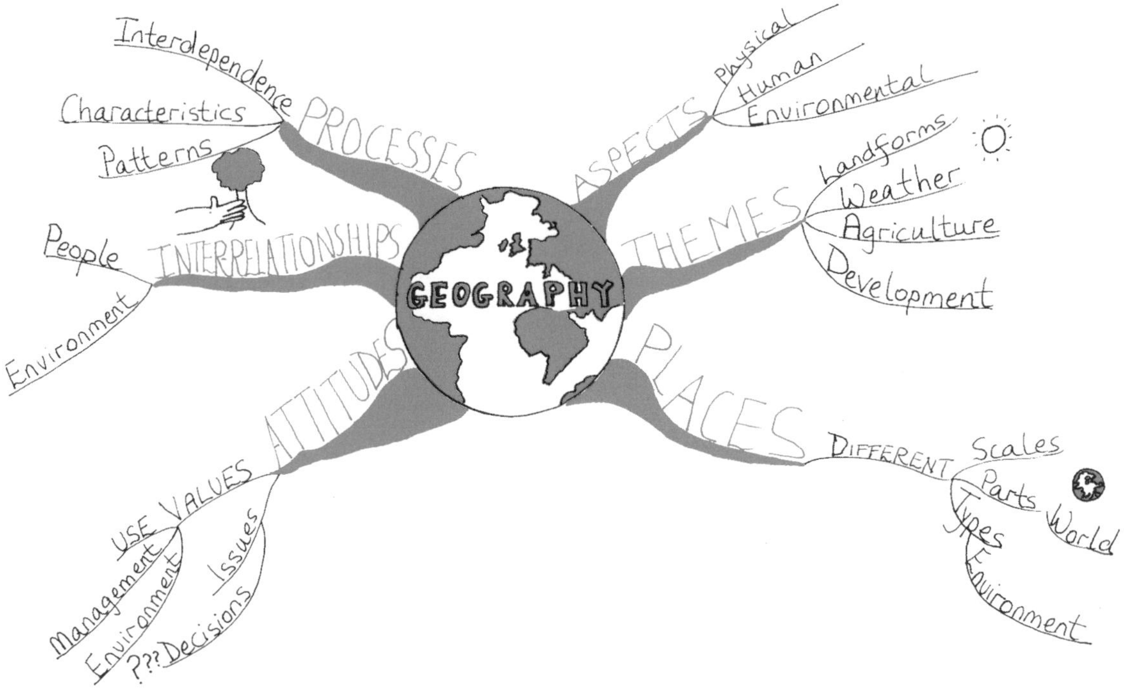

Task 1

What is the plan for the whole of your GCSE course? If you don't know, find out from your teacher. Colour in the relevant sections of the Mind Map (Figure 2). If you have sections left over, find out why. Remember, different names might be used for the same topics.

Task 2

Use a large sheet of paper and make a Mind Map of your own geography course. Do a rough version first.

Now you have a Master Plan for the course. Use it to help you keep track of your work. It will give you a plan for revising your work regularly.

Task 3

How does the book match your geography course? Add page numbers to each section on your Master Plan diagram.

Ideas, processes and case studies

Much of the book is concerned with general points or the **ideas and processes** to do with a topic. But there are case studies as well.

Each of the 17 chapters in this book is divided into 'units' or topics. The units vary.

- Some give you just general points about topics.
- Others have general points with brief case studies.
- Others are mainly case studies with general points based on them.

Examinations

All syllabuses are examined by two written papers and by coursework. The topics covered by the two examination papers vary from one syllabus to another. Make sure you know your syllabus.

There are two tiers of examination paper: the Foundation Tier (Grades C–G) and the Higher Tier (Grades A*–D). Questions on Foundation and Higher papers generally cover the same topics and issues. They usually use the same resources, like maps, statistics or photographs. The layout and wording of the questions may be different so make sure you see examples of questions for your tier.

General tips

1 Read the rubric (the instructions on the front of the paper) to check:

- how many questions you have to answer;
- if any questions are compulsory;
- how many questions you have to answer from each section (if the paper is divided into sections).

2 Take time to decide which questions to answer. Read the questions carefully. Questions which look difficult often become your best questions after you have thought for a while.

3 Work out how much time to spend on each question and stick to it. Don't spend extra time on a 'good' question. You will lose more marks than you gain by not finishing your last question.

4 Most question papers are also the answer papers. The spaces give you an idea of how much to do on each part of a question. Otherwise use the number of marks for each part as a guide. For example, if part of a question is worth half the marks then spend about half the time allowed for the question on it.

5 Follow the instructions in the questions. If a question says 'For a named example…' you must name the example.

6 Answer every part of each question you attempt.

7 Make a plan for any part of a question which asks for extended writing. Mind Mapping is a good way to brainstorm a set of points, and it's easy to add to.

Sample exam questions are included throughout this book, and each has suggested answers, but try to answer the question yourself before you read them.

What to learn and when to learn it

Figure 3 on the next page is a review and revision grid. It is a timetable for reviewing and revising your work, based on this book. Modify it to fit your particular needs.

Stick to your review plan and you will have to do far less work than you thought! Each review will take just a few minutes, as you will see.

It takes time to make the plan, but it is worth it. You only have to do it once. Make as large a copy as possible. Stick it on the wall if you can and mark off reviews as you do them.

Brainstorming

Wherever there are lists of points about topics try to add a few more of your own. Start by jotting down *anything* connected to the topic. Some ideas will be good, some won't be. Use only your good points. Brainstorming works best with two or three people, so get together with some friends if you can.

Review timetable

1 First review – after only ten minutes. If you have spent half an hour revising a topic in this book, have a ten-minute break then review the topic. Spend five to ten minutes on this first review.

2 Next day spend five minutes.

3 After one week spend two to three minutes.

4 One month later spend two to three minutes.

5 Two months later another two or three minutes.

By now you will really know the work.

Further reviews depend on how much time you have before the exam, but every two months should be more than enough.

Figure 3

Worksheets				Topic done	Reviews 1	2	3	4	5	6
PHYSICAL	Landforms	1. 2. 3. 4. 5. 6. 7.	Include titles of each section. The title should be enough to remind you of a lot about the topic.	Either put a tick or the dates of starting and finishing.	Either tick when done or put the date.					
	Weather and climate	1. 2. 3. 4. 5. 6. 7.								
	Vegetation and soils	1. 2. 3.								
HUMAN	Population	1. 2. 3. 4.								
	Settlement	1. 2.								
	Towns and cities	1. 2. 3. 4.								
	Transport	1. 2. 3.								
ECONOMIC	Agriculture	1. 2. 3. 4.								
	Industry	1. 2. 3.								
	Tourism	1. 2. 3.								
	Trade	1. 2.								
	Development	1. 2.								
ENVIRONMENT	Resources	1. 2. 3. 4.								
	People and environment	1. 2. 3.								
	Issues and problems	1. 2. 3.								

Make a note of **anything** special about the topic – if you find it difficult or if you have seen a good case study in a magazine or on TV, for example.

COURSEWORK **Starting date**
Add other important dates e.g. interviews with your teacher, data collection deadline.

Completion date
Coursework varies but in most cases your teacher should give you a booklet of guidance notes. This will be geared to your specific course and will be much more useful than general guidance.

1 Landforms 1

preview

What you need to know

- Plates and plate boundaries
- Volcanoes and volcanic landscapes
- Earthquakes
- Hazards of earthquakes and volcanoes
- The effect of rocks and rock structures on landforms and landscapes
- Types of weathering
- Limestone scenery
- Screes, soil creep and landslides
- Types of glaciers
- Features of glaciers
- Processes of erosion, transport and deposition by ice
- Landforms of glaciated uplands
- Landforms of glaciated lowlands

Plates, volcanoes, and earthquakes

The Earth's crust is broken into rigid **plates** which move about over time. The plate boundaries are marked by zones of **volcanoes and earthquakes** (Figure 1).

The pattern of earthquakes and volcanoes matches the plate boundaries very closely. Places with volcanoes are also likely to have earthquake activity.

Volcanoes

Volcanic features include:

- ash cones
- composite cones
- volcanic shields and domes
- caldera
- lava flows or plateaus
- geysers and hot springs
- fumaroles (steam and gas vents).

Volcanic eruptions produce ash, gas and lava in different proportions. They can be explosive or continuous. Volcanoes can have a single, central vent, or activity can be along a fissure or crack.

Earthquakes

Earthquakes are movements of the surface as a result of events in or below the crust. The movements are usually linked to movements of the plate boundaries (Figure 2). The location of the movement is the focus. The place which receives the greatest shock, immediately above it, is the epicentre.

Figure 1

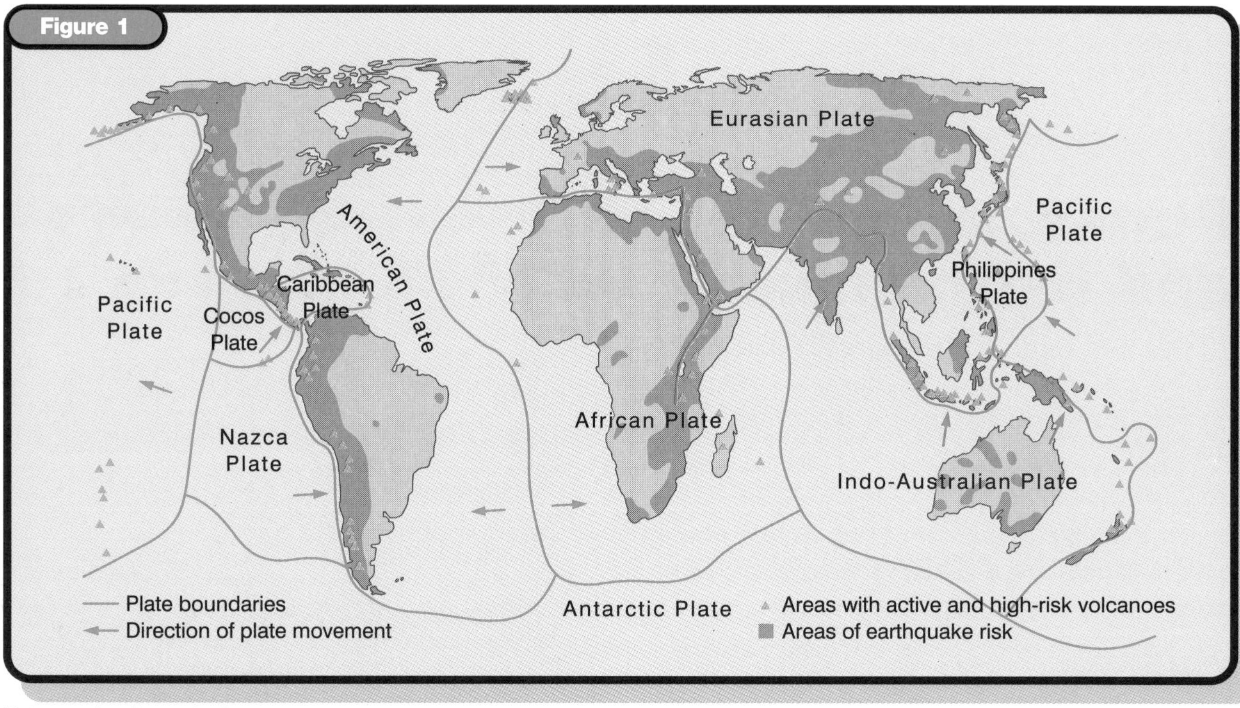

Plates, earthquakes and volcanoes

Earthquakes affect the landscape. They:

- produce the rise or fall of areas of land
- create fault scarps
- offset streams and other features
- cause landslides.

Tsunamis or tidal waves are set in motion in the oceans when earthquakes make the sea bed rise and fall.

Effects on people

Volcanic eruptions

Volcanic eruptions have different effects depending on the kind of eruption and the precise events. Major explosive eruptions can cause many deaths. With most eruptions there is usually enough warning for people to evacuate the areas of greatest risk. However, ash may cover fields and built-up areas so people have to leave eventually.

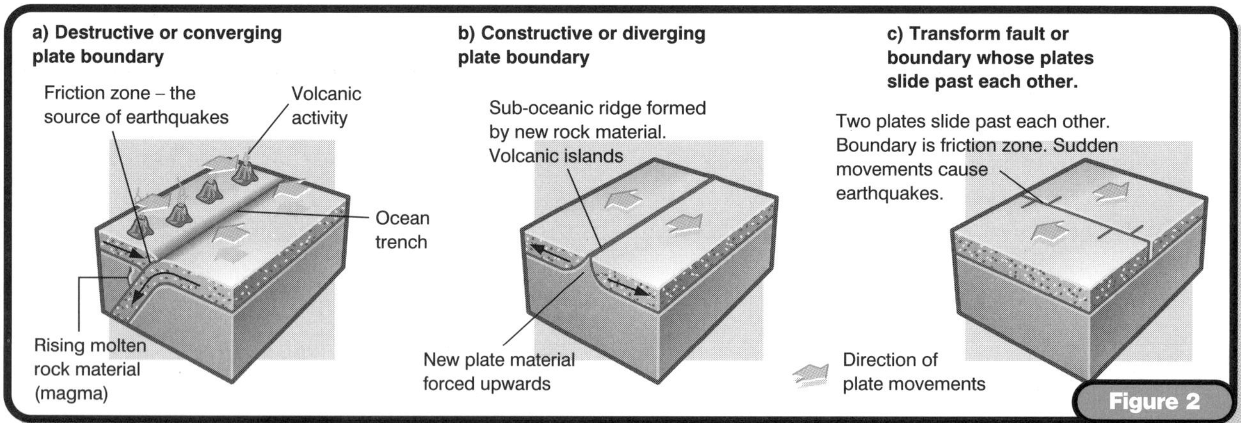

Figure 2

Types of plate boundaries

Figure 3

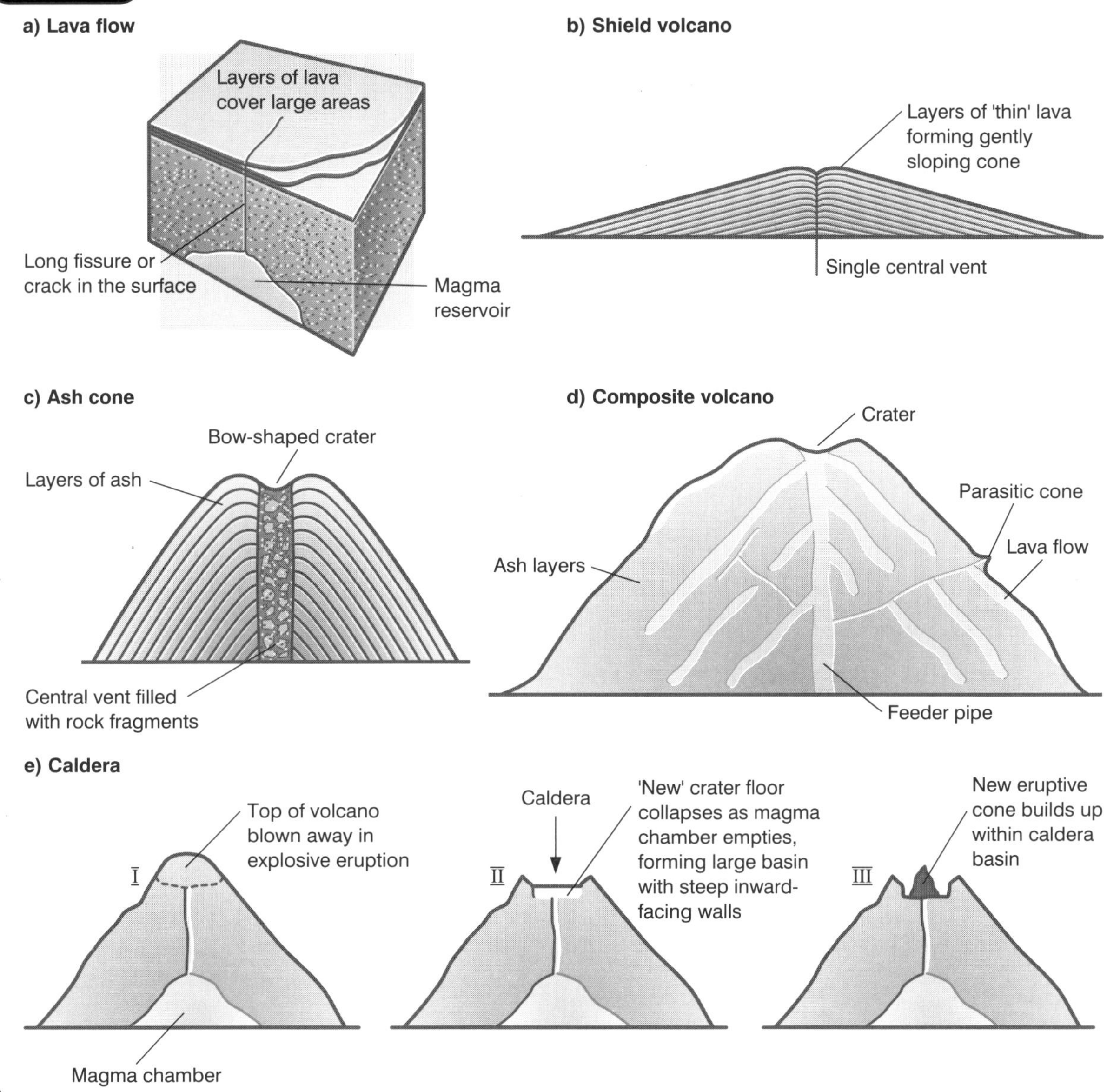

Volcanic landscapes

Mud flows are a major hazard. They occur when the eruption causes snow and ice on the volcano to melt. The melt water rushes downslope picking up all the loose soil and rock debris.

Earthquakes

Earthquakes can be devastating. Collapsing buildings can kill large numbers of people. This is worse where buildings are of a poor standard and unable to withstand the shock of an earthquake. This is a bigger problem in less developed countries but it also applies to places in the developed world.

In cities, the aftermath of the earthquake often causes the greatest damage and loss of life. Gas from broken gas mains catches fire and large areas can be devastated because water supplies are also disrupted by damage.

In hilly or mountainous areas the earthquake can trigger landslides making it difficult to get help from outside. This is a major problem in isolated areas especially in less developed countries.

Test yourself

1 What is a crustal plate?

2 Name the different kinds of plate boundary.

3 What is a composite volcano composed of?

4 What sort of landform is produced by a large fissure eruption?

5 What are the effects of earthquakes?

6 What or where is the epicentre?

review

Summarise what you know with a Mind Map using these four themes:

The relationship between plate boundaries, volcanic activity and earthquake activity

The types of volcanic activity and landforms

Where and why earthquakes occur

The effects of earthquakes

Rocks, landforms and landscapes

Rock features

★ **Resistant** rocks, like granite, are slower to erode than less resistant ones, like shale.

★ **Permeable** or **pervious** rocks allow water to pass through along joint and bedding planes, like limestone, or through pore spaces.

★ **Porous** rocks have spaces between the rock grains (e.g. sandstone).

★ **Impermeable** or **impervious** rocks do not allow water to pass through (e.g. clay).

Landforming processes

1 **Weathering** breaks up rock.

2 **Mass movement** causes rock waste to move downhill.

3 **Erosion** by ice, rivers, sea and wind wears away the rocks of the crust. The rock is broken up and carried away.

4 **Transport** by the agents of erosion moves rock material away from its original site.

5 **Deposition** happens when transport comes to a halt. Often this is temporary, like gravel on a river bed, but the ultimate destination is the sea.

These features affect:

- rates of erosion
- water supply and storage
- the hydrological cycle.

Rock structures

Small- and larger-scale structures affect landforms.

Rock structures are important because:

- **joints** and **faults** create lines of weakness which can be eroded more easily;
- faults bring less resistant rocks against more resistant rocks, producing rapid erosion of the less resistant rock and leaving the more resistant rock as higher land;
- **anticlines** stretch and crack rocks making them easier to erode;
- **synclines** compress rocks making them stronger.

Scenery

Where layers of dipping rocks are eroded they produce important landforms. Less resistant rocks are eroded leaving the more resistant ones as high ground. The edge of the higher ground forms a **scarp**. This is a steep slope marking the eroded edge of more resistant rock. It often forms a prominent feature running across country for a great distance.

Figure 4

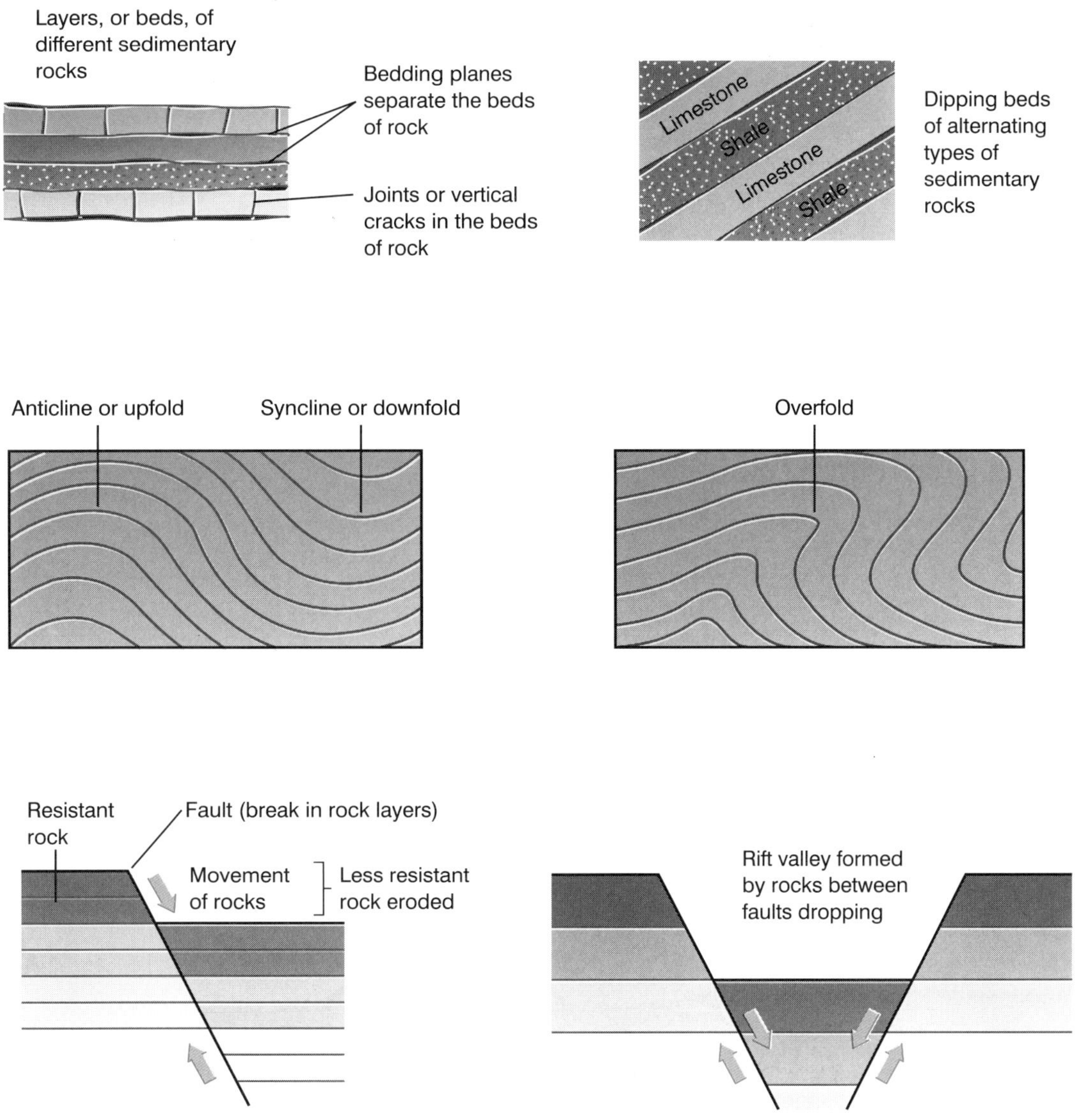

Large- and small-scale rock structures

The surface of the higher ground is often called the **dip slope** as it follows the line of the dip of the rock itself (Figure 5).

A scarp and dip slope form a **cuesta**. Much of the landscape of south and east England consists of scarp and dip slopes. In some areas, like the Weald and the Thames Basin, the landforms are the result of the erosion of an anticline and a syncline.

Figure 5

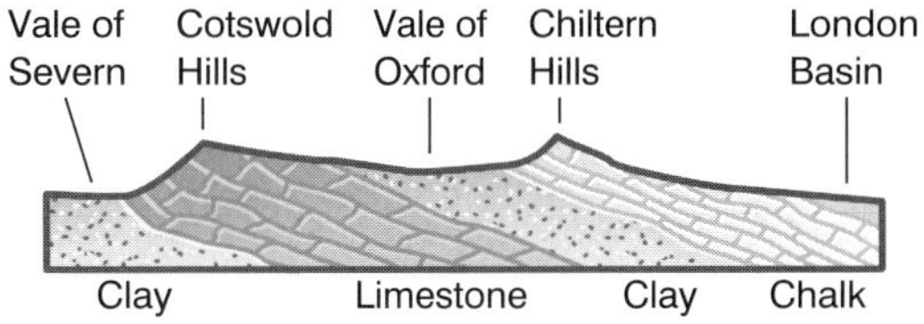

Scarp and dip landscapes

Test yourself

Look at Figure 6. It shows a landscape of different rocks and rock structures.

Label the diagram using words from this unit. It summarises the most important points.

Chalk scenery

Chalk **downs** cover many areas in south-east England.

Chalk is highly permeable and resistant compared with other rocks. This, with folding, has resulted in a scarp and vale landscape (Figure 7).

Its other landscape feature is the lack of surface drainage, that is, no rivers and streams over wide areas. This is also because chalk is highly permeable. There are rivers in the valleys where they cut into the permanent water table. Elsewhere there are dry valleys, showing where streams used to flow and still do after long periods of heavy rain.

Figure 6

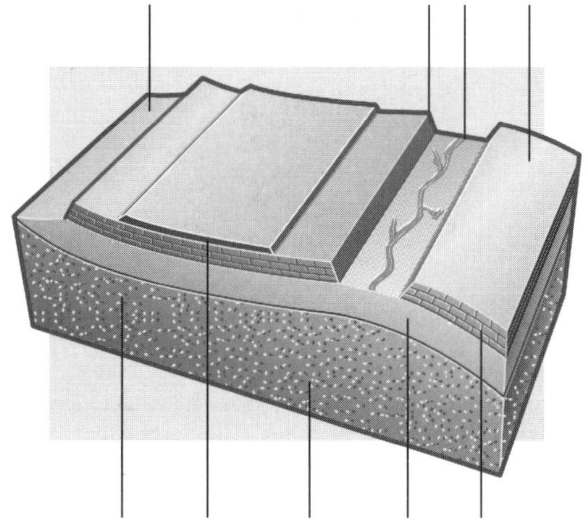

Figure 7

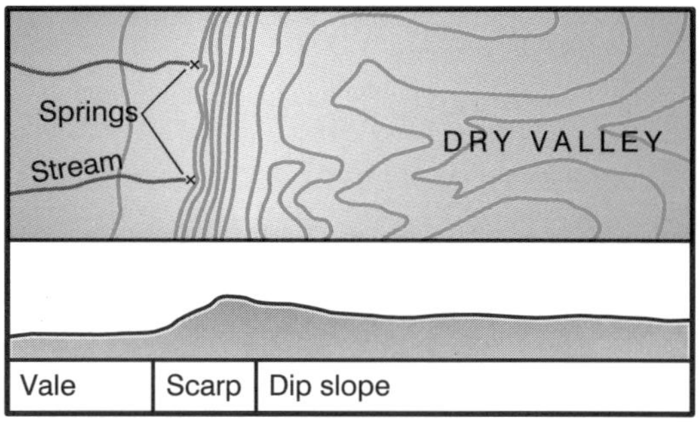

Chalk scenery

review

Make a Mind Map to summarise the information in this unit. Remember to include:

- The features of different sorts of rock
- The different structures of rocks
- The effects of rocks and rock structures on landforms and landscapes.

Weathering and landslides

Syllabus check

Remember to check your syllabus; you may not need everything in the unit.

Types of weathering

Weathering is the term used for the breakdown of rock. It is not just caused by the action of the weather.

Physical or mechanical weathering

This breaks up exposed rock. It is done by **freeze-thaw action** or **frost shattering**. Water in cracks freezes and expands as ice forms. The pressure forces the crack open. Repeated freezing and thawing eventually breaks the rock apart. The more natural joints there are, the quicker the process works.

Figure 8

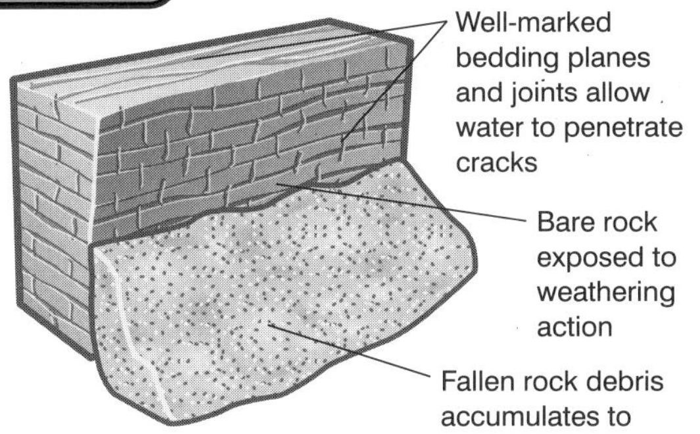

Scree formation

When it happens on vertical rock faces the broken rock debris piles up at the foot of the cliff, forming a **scree slope** (Figure 8). These are very common in mountainous regions.

Chemical weathering

Because rain water has absorbed carbon dioxide from the atmosphere it is a mild carbonic acid. Most rocks will ultimately break down in the presence of carbonic acid. Part of the rock is then taken away in solution by the ground water and part is left as an insoluble residue. This forms the basis of soil, unless it is transported away.

The most spectacular effects are seen in limestone (Figure 9). The rock is composed largely of calcium carbonate which is highly soluble in rain water. Only a small residue is left to form soil. In cities, chemical weathering is a very active process. Decaying stonework is a direct result of air pollution from industry and particularly from traffic.

Biological weathering

Roots of plants grow into cracks in the rocks forcing them apart, and small animals burrow into the ground and dig away partly broken rock.

Mass movement

This is the movement of material downslope and includes landslides.

Soil creep occurs when soil gradually moves down even gentle slopes. It is washed downslope by rain. Where soil is bare a lot of soil is washed away. **Soil flows**, **soil slides** and **mud flows** occur when the soil becomes waterlogged after periods of heavy rain. The soil structure breaks down with the extra water. The risk is greater with steeper slopes.

Landslides and **slumping** are more severe and include rock as well as soil. They are especially likely where a heavy rock lies above a weaker rock. Figure 10 shows soil creep, landslides and slumps.

Figure 9

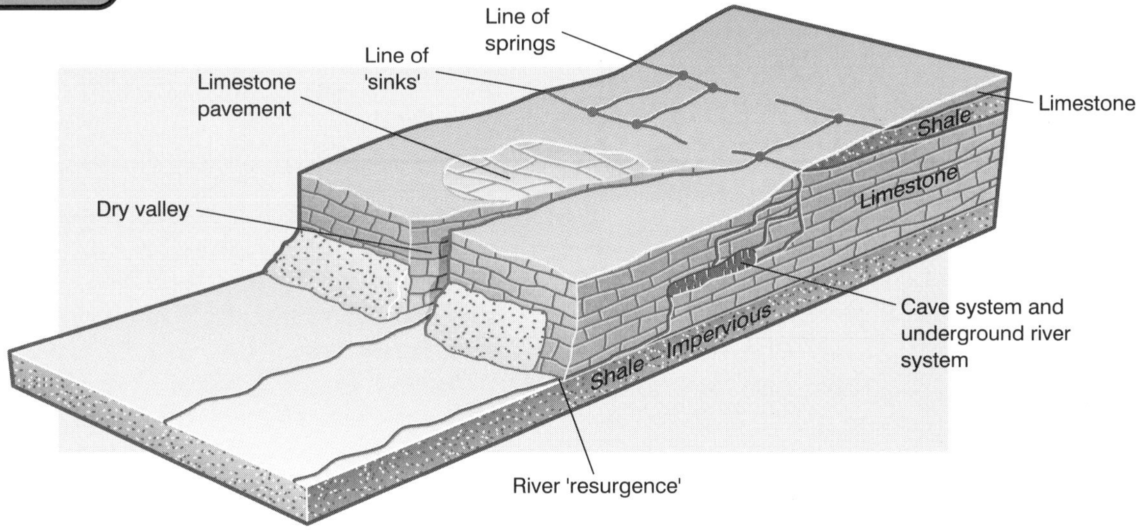

Limestone scenery

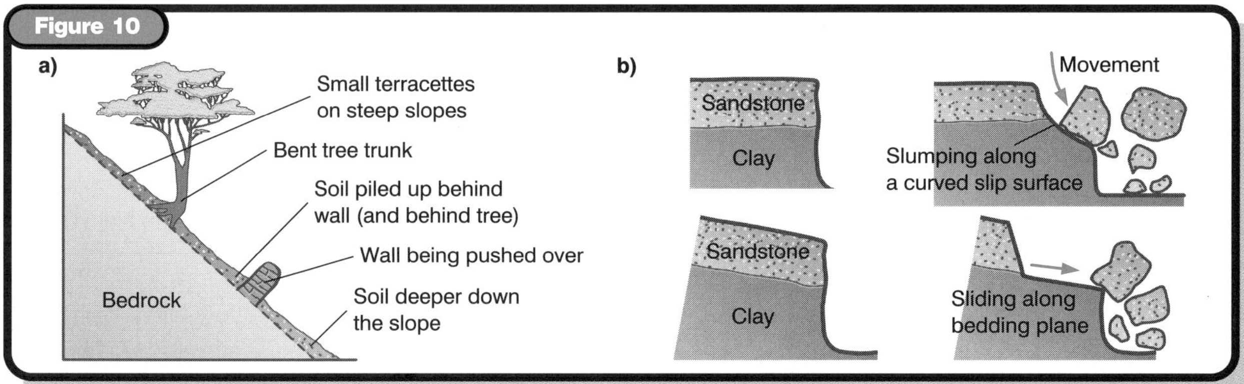

(a) Soil creep

(b) Landslides and slumps

Figure 11 a-c

Test yourself

The photographs in Figure 11 show some features covered in this unit. What processes are at work here and what features are formed?

Ice and the landscape

Task

Browse through this unit for only five minutes. Don't forget the summary at the end.

Now work through the unit carefully. Make sure you understand each part. Make summaries of each part. Make a large Mind Map. Use it to summarise what you learn as you go along.

Glaciers

Types of glacier

- ★ **Ice sheets**. These are huge. The only ones are in Antarctica and Greenland.
- ★ **Ice fields**. They form on high land and cover large areas, as in Iceland.
- ★ **Valley glaciers**. These are tongues of ice which move down into valleys from ice fields. Most major mountain ranges have examples.
- ★ **Corrie glaciers**. These form in hollows on the sides of mountains.

Figure 12

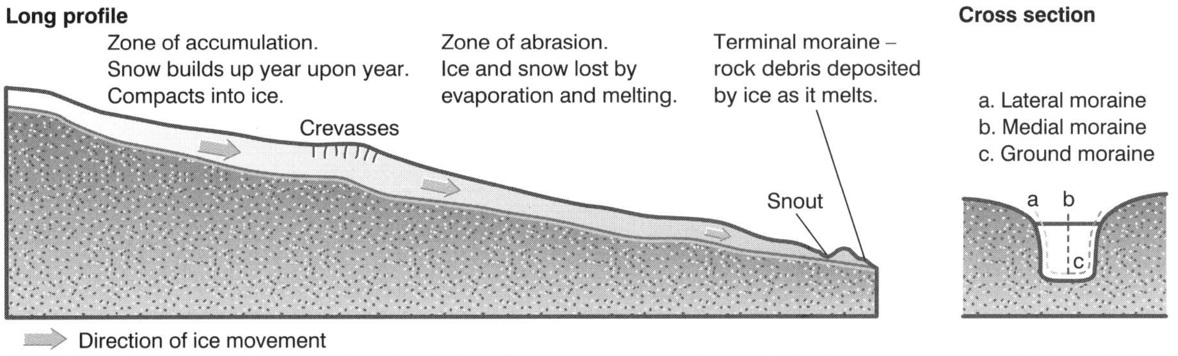

Glaciers: formation and features

Glacier features

Glaciers form when winter snowfall is greater than summer snow melt. The snow builds up and the weight compacts it into glacier ice. The effect of gravity sets it moving downslope, but movement is slow.

Test yourself

Look at Figure 13.

(a) Name the features marked by arrows.

(b) Explain how the terminal moraine is formed.

(c) When the glacier melts, what could build up behind the terminal moraine?

Figure 13

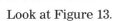

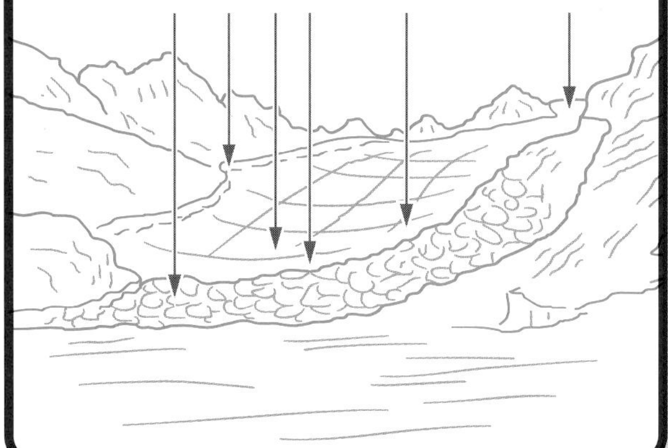

Glacial processes

Erosion

- **Plucking or quarrying**. The ice freezes around blocks of rock and and as it moves on it tears the blocks of rock away.
- **Abrasion**. The ice scrapes away loose soil and rock. The rocks in the ice cut into and scrape away the solid bedrock. The rock is left smoothly polished or with lines of scratches or **striations**.

Transport

- Ice carries the debris (eroded soil and rock) along with it as it moves, either within the ice or dragged along by the base of the glacier.
- **Melt water** also moves rock material. This happens on and in the ice as well as at the snout of the glacier.

Deposition

- Ice eventually comes to a standstill and then it dumps its load. The material it dumps is called **till**.
- Melt water from the glacier spreads gravel and sand over a wide area. This is called **outwash**.

Landscape features

Mountain areas

Valley glaciers have tremendous erosive power, because of the huge volume of ice. They change V-shaped river valleys into **U-shaped glaciated valleys** or **glacial troughs**. They make them:

- deeper • straighter • wider • steeper-sided.

They do this by cutting away at the sides and bottom of the valley.

Figure 14

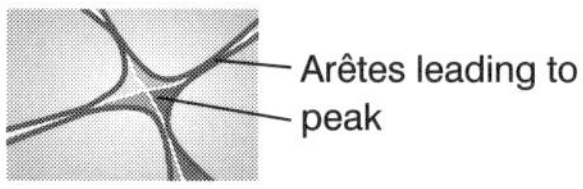

Pyramidal peaks are sharp mountain tops which have been cut away as corrie glaciers on all sides have eroded back.

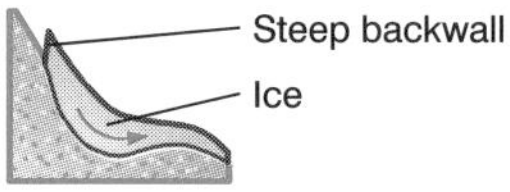

Corries are hollows scooped out by the rotational movement of the ice. After the ice melts the hollow often holds a small lake.

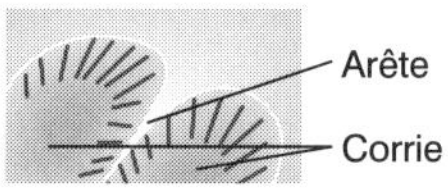

Arêtes are sharp ridges formed when the back and side walls of neighbouring corries are cut back to meet each other.

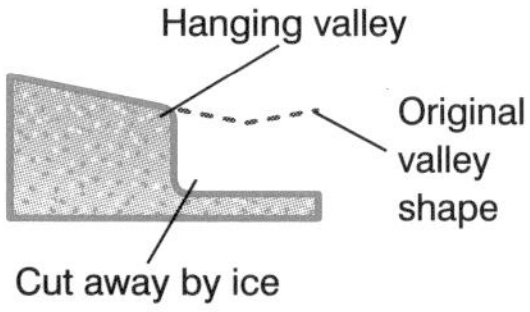

Hanging valleys are formed when valley glaciers cut away the sides of the valleys. They leave side valley 'hanging' with a steep or even vertical drop to the main valley floor.

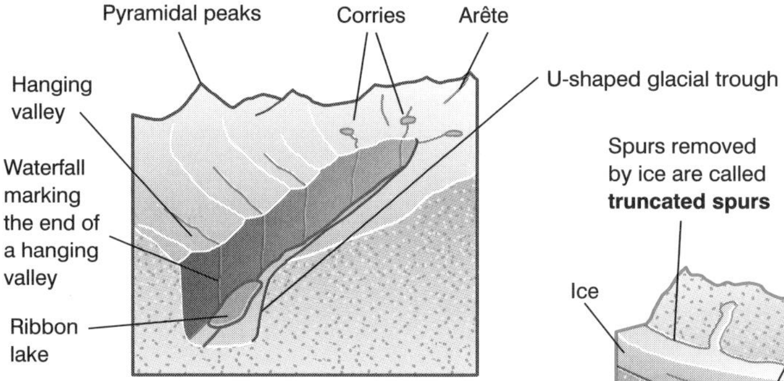

Ribbon lakes form in long narrow hollows in the valley. These are the result of the valley glacier overdeepening the valley in places where there are less resistant rocks or where extra ice enters the valley.

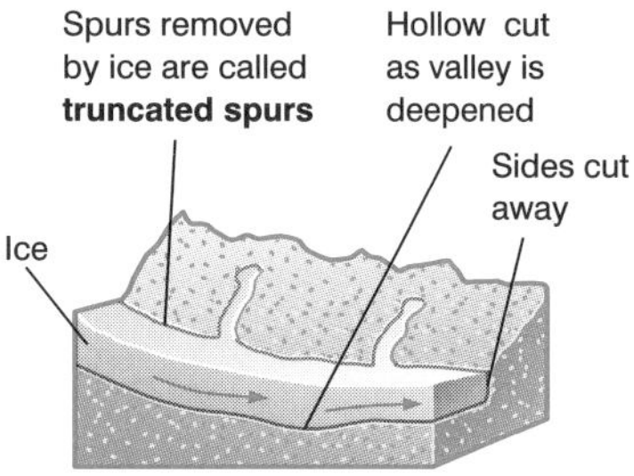

Glacial trough is formed as the valley glacier deepens the valley and cuts away at its sides, straightening it.

Glaciated mountain landscape

Test yourself

(a) Match the features in Figure 14 to the features labelled A to G on Figure 15.

(b) Explain how any two of the features were formed.

Figure 15

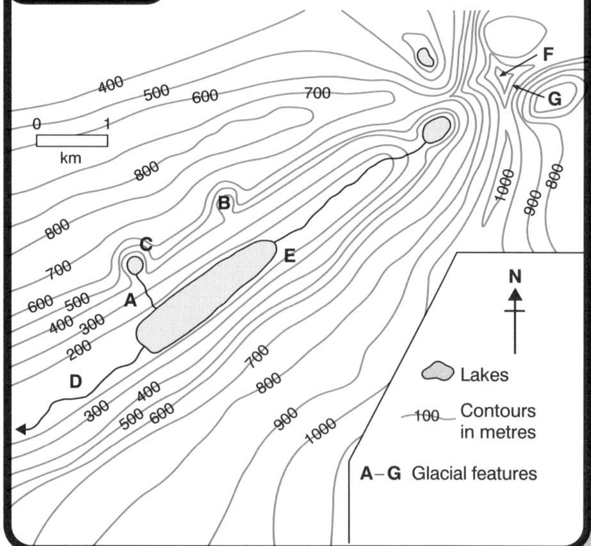

Exam tip

Think about what you need to remember:

1. The map contours, to recognise shapes of features.
2. The map symbols; they might give you an answer.
3. How ice erodes (the processes of erosion).
4. What the processes of erosion do in different places.

Figure 16

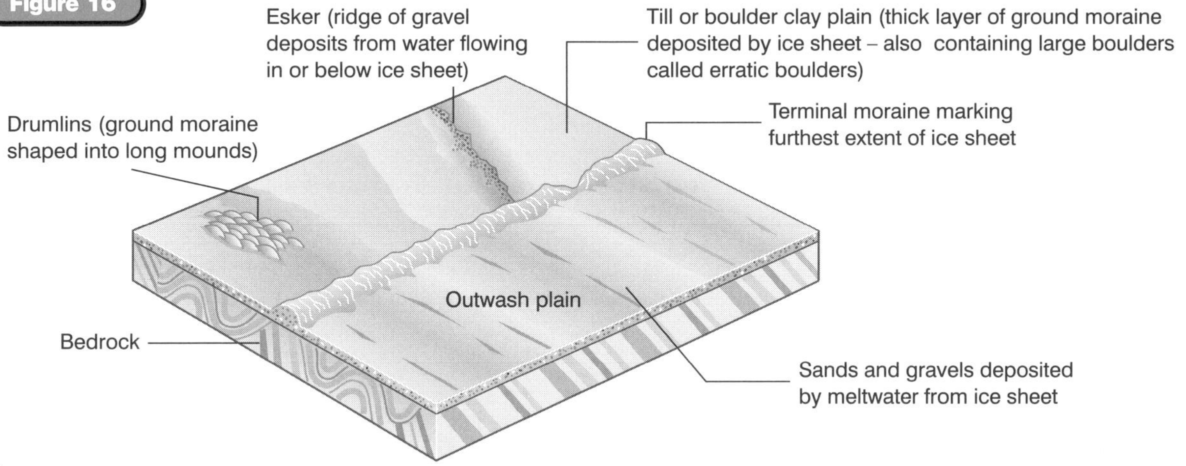

Glaciated lowland

Lowland areas

Sheet glaciers spread across lowland areas. Their furthest limits are marked by deposits of debris called **terminal moraines**. The terminal moraines are sometimes hundreds of miles long, for example from Denmark, through Germany, Poland and across Russia.

Beneath the ice a mixture of clay and rock was deposited which formed **till plains** (till is also called boulder clay). Sometimes this material was shaped into long, low mounds called **drumlins**.

Erratic boulders are rocks which have been carried by the ice from their source and dumped when the ice melted, perhaps hundreds of miles away.

review

1. Summarise all the work on a large Mind Map. You can use Figure 17 as a base. Take about 30 minutes. If you did this as you went along, check to see that you have included work you have done in school, especially examples (e.g. how glaciation has affected people). Make a new, neat copy if necessary.
2. Add glaciation to your general revision plan.
3. Don't forget to review your Mind Map in ten minutes' time, and tomorrow ... keep to your review plan.

Figure 17

Sample question 1

Foundation

a) Study Figure 1.

(i) What is the broad relationship between the distribution of earthquakes and plate boundaries? [1 mark]

(ii) Why does Japan have frequent earthquakes but the British Isles does not? [3 marks]

b) Study Figure 2.
State two ways in which the San Francisco area was affected by the earthquake. [2 marks]

c) Suggest two reasons why people remain in areas where there is a risk of earthquakes or other natural hazards. [2 marks]

d) Urban areas usually suffer greater damage from earthquakes than rural areas.

(i) Explain why this is the case.

(ii) Suggest two ways of reducing damage and casualties. [4 marks]

e) **(i)** For any natural hazard, except earthquakes, name a place where the hazard has caused problems.

(ii) Explain why the hazard occurs in that place.

(iii) Describe the effects of the hazard. [8 marks]

Figure 1

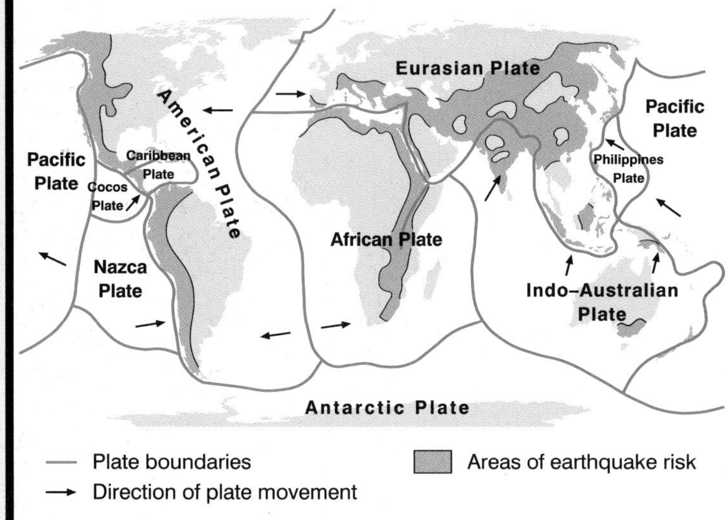

Figure 2

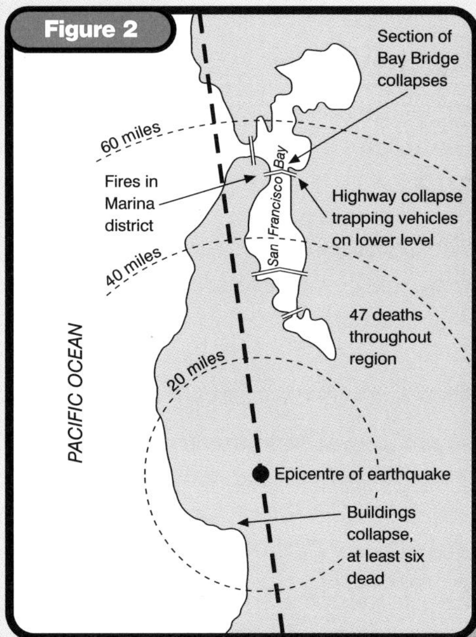

Suggested answer

a) **(i)** Earthquakes coincide with plate boundaries.

(ii) Japan is at plate boundaries where plates are moving rapidly towards one another, but the British Isles is not near a plate boundary.

b) Deaths; fire and collapse damage in places; water, gas and electricity cut off; bridge and highway collapse; transport disrupted, airports closed. Any two of these points.

c) Rich soils; population pressures; any one place is affected very infrequently; long occupation of the area; developed region where precautions can be taken. Any two points.

d) **(i)** Greater concentration of buildings and people so more scope for damage. Fires spread easily.

(ii) Building designs to withstand earthquake shocks; avoidance of most vulnerable places; training for emergencies; well-prepared emergency plans.

e) **(i)** For example, flooding of the Brahmaputra river in Bangladesh.

(ii) Low-lying area; river has a very large catchment; heavy monsoon rainfall in the catchment; deforestation within the catchment causing more rapid run-off; silting of the river as a result of more rapid erosion in the mountains.

(iii) Flooding of rural areas and urban areas; damage to crops or complete loss of crops; destruction of homes and other buildings including industrial buildings; dislocation of transport; disruption of trade.

2 Landforms 2

preview
What you need to know

- Drainage basin systems and features
- River processes
- River landscapes and landforms
- River basin mapwork
- Features formed by erosion, transport and deposition along a coast
- How coastal landforms are produced
- The influence of geology
- The effect of human interference with coastal systems
- Issues involved in coastal management
- Hydrological cycle
- Factors affecting river basin hydrology
- The effects of changes in the river basin
- Floods
- River basin management

River processes and landforms

Syllabus check

Does your syllabus specify that you must do:

a special study of one landform; or study two contrasting river basins; or study one named river basin?

River systems

A river system consists of:

- a river basin or drainage basin
- water inputs (rainfall and ground water)
- rock waste from weathering and mass movement
- river network. (Figure 1)

Figure 1

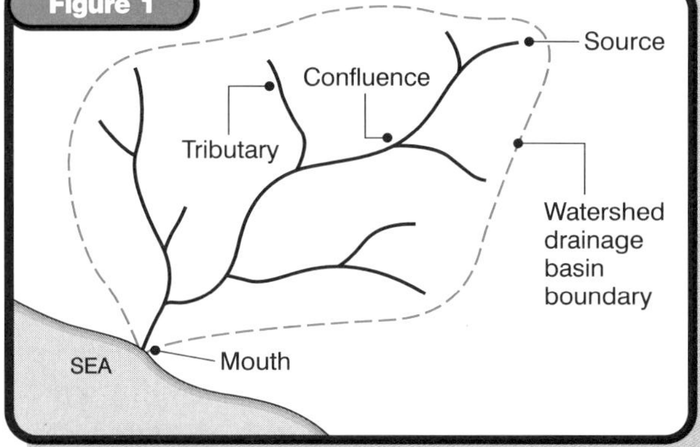

Drainage basin features

River landscapes

A river landscape is made up of:

1 A river valley, which changes along its length (Figure 2);

2 Landforms which are the result of river processes (Figures 3 and 4).

Figure 2

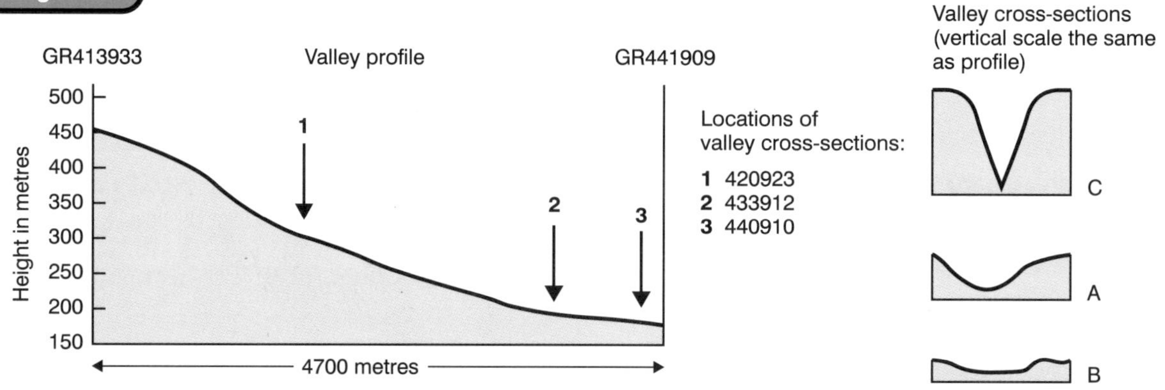

River valley profile and cross-sections (*see* OS map extract on page 82)

Figure 3

EROSION		
Corrasion or abrasion	The river load (boulders and pebbles) wears away the river bed, particularly by pot-holing. Pebbles are swirled around in cracks, widening and depositing them into deep, circular holes.	
Attrition	Larger pieces of bed load are broken into smaller pieces, and rounded and smoothed by contact with each other and the river bed.	
Hydraulic action	Rock is torn away from the river bed if the force of water is great enough.	Water forces out blocks of rock from river bed
Solution or corrosion	Soluble rocks and minerals are dissolved by chemical processes.	

TRANSPORT		
Rolling	Material too large to be picked up by the water flow is rolled along by the water's force.	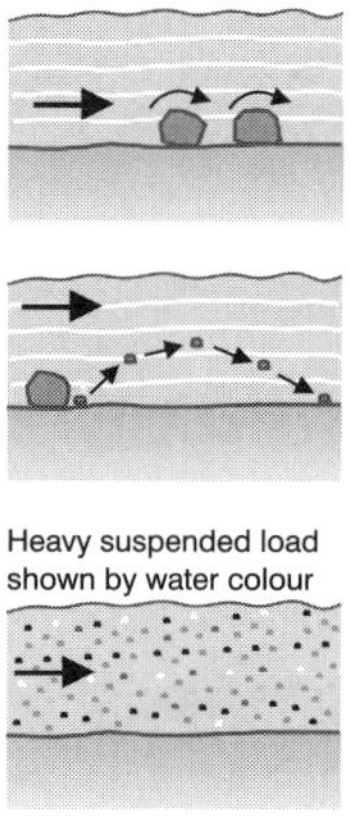
Saltation	Particles are dislodged or bounced off the bed and carried along suspended in the water for a short distance before falling back to the river bed.	
Suspension	This is material carried along suspended in the water itself. Finer material, like silt, can be carried at slower river speeds than coarser material, like sand.	Heavy suspended load shown by water colour
Solution	The dissolved load is the result of chemical processes.	

DEPOSITION	
This occurs when river velocity falls. Within the river bed pebble, sand and silt bars and banks are formed and re-formed over time.	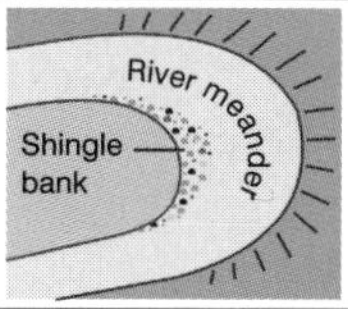

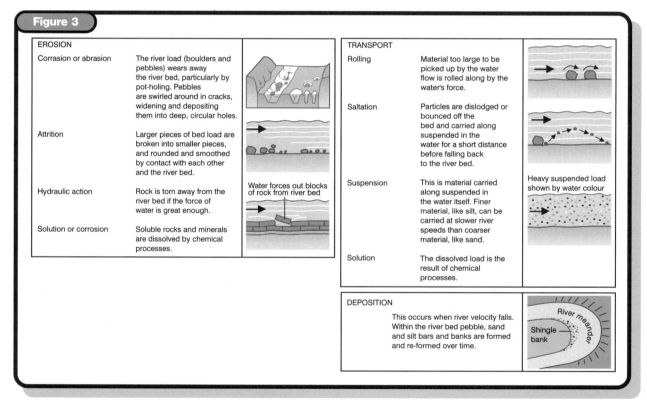

River processes

Test yourself

Study the Ordnance Survey map extract (page 82).

1 Find and locate (give the Grid Reference) one example of each of the following: source, confluence, mouth, waterfall, gorge, meander, flood plain.

2 Match up cross-sections A, B and C (Figure 2) with the correct location along the valley of the River Callow.

3 Choose one of the cross-sections. Describe the shape of the valley and explain what river processes have formed it.

Figure 4

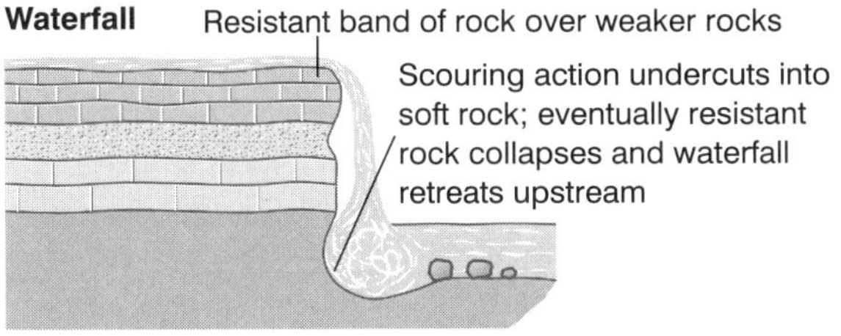

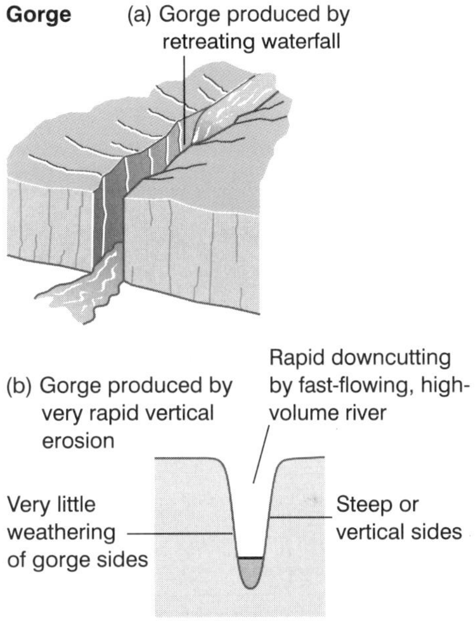

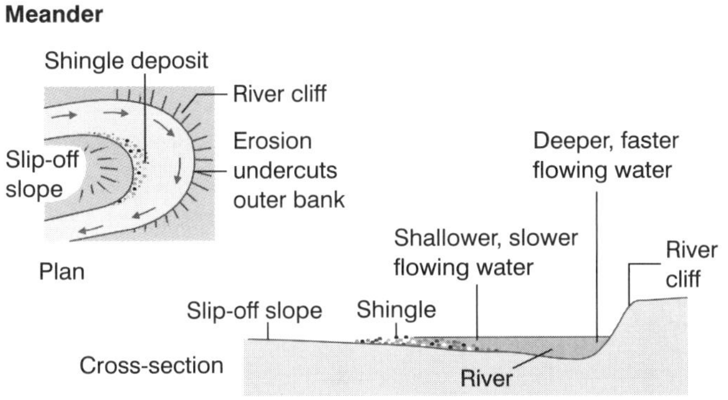

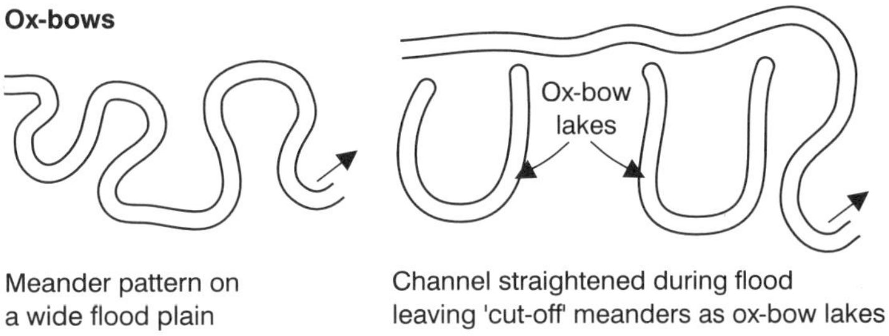

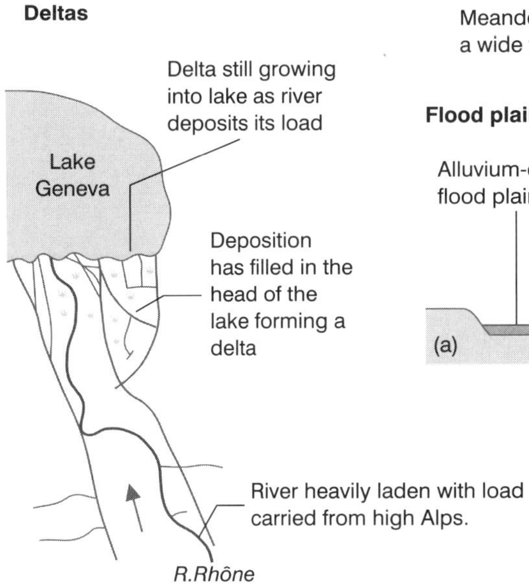

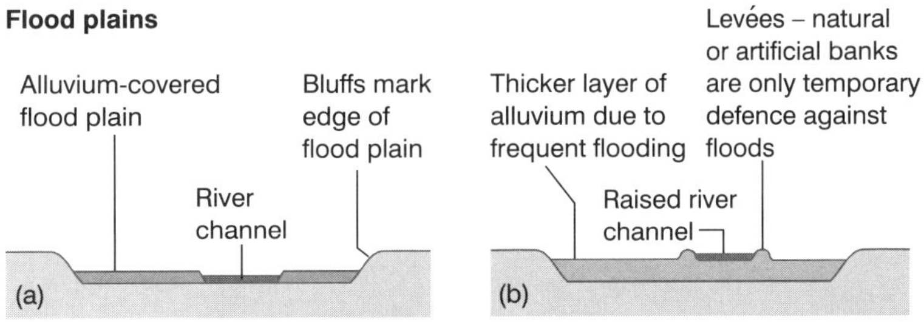

River landforms

review

Make a Mind Map of river processes and landforms.

Each word or picture you include will remind you of much more.

2

Coastal scenery

Coastal system

Figure 5 shows most coastal landforms and the processes at work along coasts. The labelling includes many important terms.

Task 1

The basic coastal processes are the same as with other landforming agents.

What are they? Fill in their names opposite. Look back over pages 12 to 19 and 21–3 if necessary and use Figure 5.

(a) ______________________________

(i) ______________ ______________.
As waves break against the rocks they exert a tremendous force. They compress air in cracks in the rocks; the cracks are expanded breaking the rock apart.

(ii) ______________ or ______________.
Rocks broken away from the cliff are thrown at the cliff base by waves. They gradually cut away at the rock.

(iii) ______________ occurs as the broken rocks themselves break apart as a result of wave action. The rocks are also rounded and smoothed to make pebbles and ultimately sand.

Figure 5

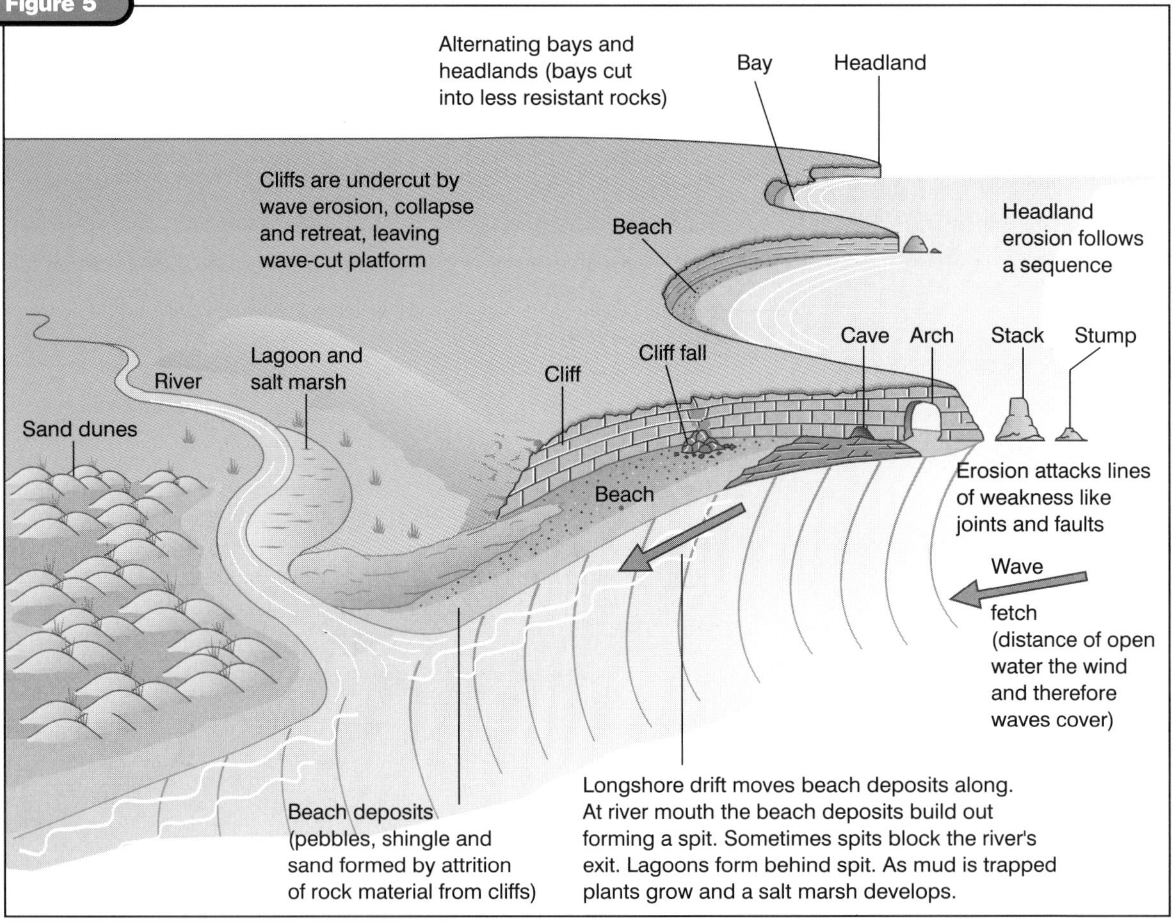
Alternating bays and headlands (bays cut into less resistant rocks)
Bay
Headland
Cliffs are undercut by wave erosion, collapse and retreat, leaving wave-cut platform
Beach
Headland erosion follows a sequence
Cave
Arch
Stack
Stump
Cliff fall
Cliff
Lagoon and salt marsh
River
Sand dunes
Beach
Erosion attacks lines of weakness like joints and faults
Wave
fetch (distance of open water the wind and therefore waves cover)
Beach deposits (pebbles, shingle and sand formed by attrition of rock material from cliffs)
Longshore drift moves beach deposits along. At river mouth the beach deposits build out forming a spit. Sometimes spits block the river's exit. Lagoons form behind spit. As mud is trapped plants grow and a salt marsh develops.

Coastal landforms

(b) _________________ carried out by waves moving material backwards and forwards and particularly by longshore drift moving eroded material along the shoreline.

(c) _________________ , which is a result of movement of material.

Task 2

(a) Look at Figure 5 very carefully and make a list of landforms produced by erosion.

(b) Look at Figure 5 again and make a list of landforms produced by deposition.

(c) Pick one landform from each list. Explain how each is formed.

Exam tips

1. Make a note of key words to act as a framework.
2. Use the key words in the correct order; that will ensure that your answer follows a logical pattern.
3. Use diagrams as well as or instead of writing, but label them fully, especially noting explanations.
4. Make sure you do what the question says. If it tells you to use a drawing, you will lose marks without one. If it asks for an example, the same applies.

Managing coasts

Management of coasts is often a major issue.

Locally, cliff erosion may threaten houses, or longshore drift may take away beaches, or it may block the entrance to harbours. At a regional or national scale, large areas of low-lying land may be threatened by inundation (or flooding).

Figure 6 shows the types of issues or problems and methods that have been used to deal with them.

review

Make a review Mind Map.

Add to it the names of case studies to illustrate different landforms and issues.

Figure 6

Issues	Solutions	Results
Coastal erosion – cliff erosion endangering built-up areas, farmland, recreational land.	Engineering work – sea walls, groynes, breakwaters.	Problems transferred elsewhere along the coast.
Flood protection – low-lying land and settlements always at risk of flooding, especially on land reclaimed from the sea.	Sea walls and embankments; drainage canals and flood gates.	Continued risk.
Conservation – pressures on landscape and wildlife from many conflicting activities, e.g. recreation, military training, changes in agriculture.	Designate areas for protection, such as National Parks, nature reserves.	Continued pressure; conflicts between groups.

Coastal management issues

Water and hydrological systems

Hydrological cycle

The **hydrological cycle** operates from world scale down to small river basin scale. The same key words are used throughout (Figures 7 and 8).

Storm hydrographs

A **storm hydrograph** shows the water flow in a river from the start of a period of rain. It is often used for graphing river flow following a single period of heavy rain.

Storm hydrographs show how rivers rise and fall at different rates. Rivers rise quickly if water reaches them quickly; they rise slowly if water takes a longer and slower route.

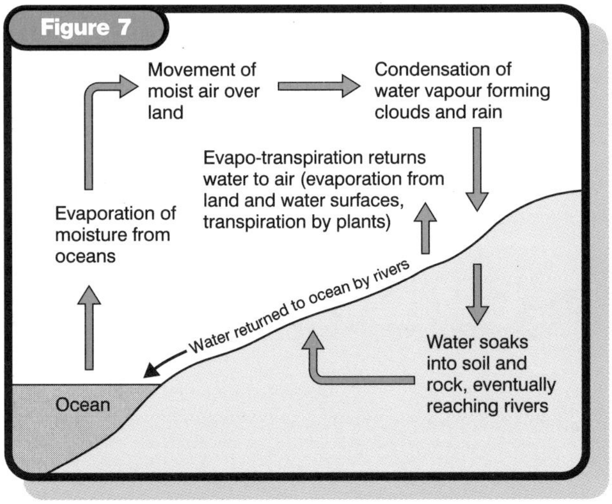

General hydrological cycle

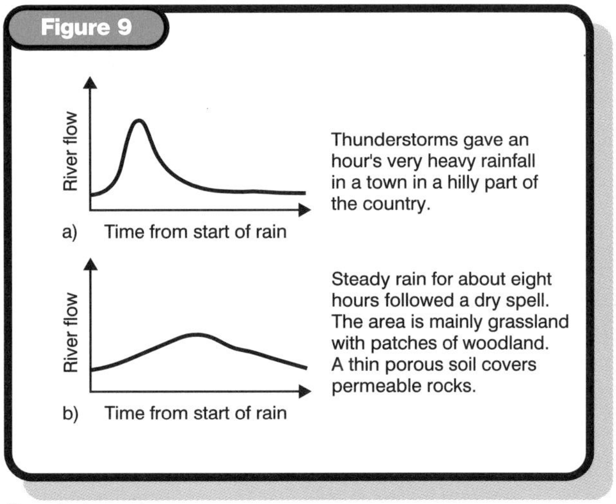

Storm hydrographs

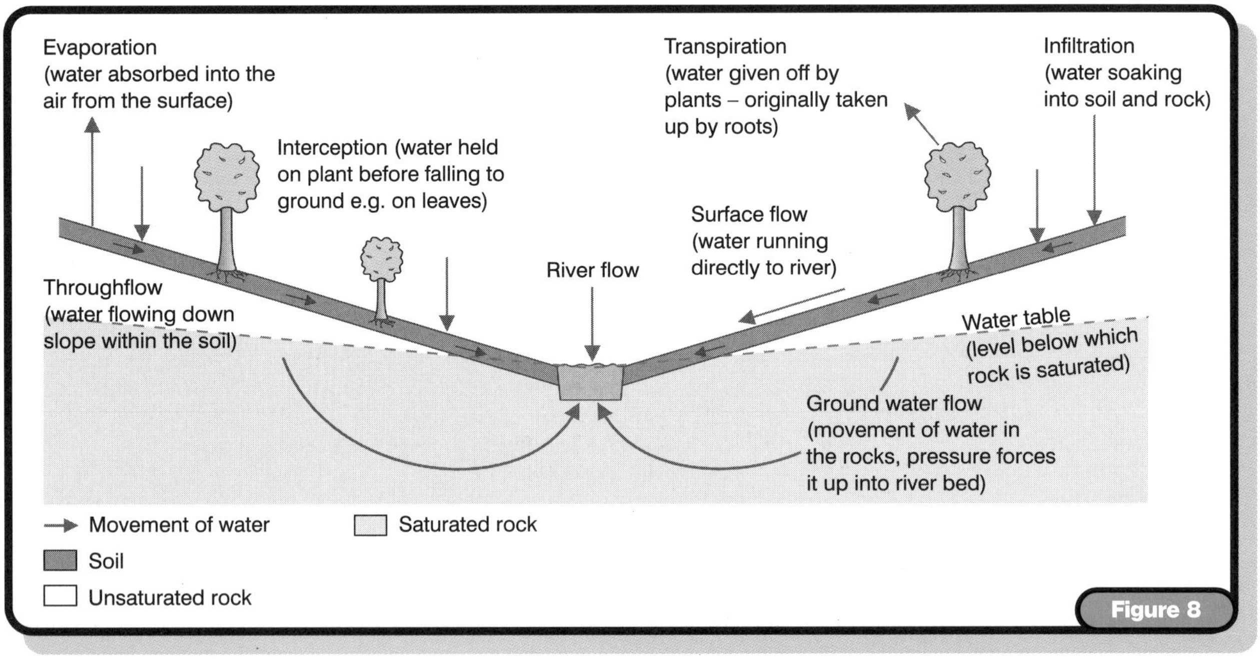

River basin hydrological cycle

Figure 10

Feature	Hydrological effect	Picture
Drainage density	The more streams there are, the quicker water can reach a stream and the quicker water levels will rise.	
Relief	High land produces relief rain; heavier rainfall than lowland areas. Water runs off steeper slopes more quickly and is less likely to infiltrate, so there is more surface flow.	
Geology	Permeable rocks absorb water unless they are already saturated; impermeable rocks ensure that water stays on the surface.	
Soils	Deep, porous soils will absorb more water than shallow, heavy soils.	
Vegetation	Denser vegetation increases interception, so water reaches the ground more slowly and is therefore more likely to soak in.	
Temperature	High temperatures increase water loss by evaporation and transpiration so less water reaches rivers.	
Previous weather	If there has been a long wet period the soil and rock could well be saturated. All rainfall would then run off as surface flow and river levels would rise quickly.	
Land use changes	Removal of vegetation, e.g. forest removal, reduces interception and infiltration and speeds up run-off. Changing crop types or leaving farmland bare has similar effects.	
Building	Large-scale building makes an impervious surface of buildings and roads, with drains to take water away to the rivers quickly. With heavy rains, river levels rise quickly.	
Improving drainage	Channels to take water away from marsh areas, for example, removes a 'sponge' that holds water back for a while and helps reduce flood risk as well as ensuring a steady flow of water in dry periods.	

Draw a picture, diagram or map in each box to help you remember the point.

What affects water movement?

Task

Look at Figure 9. Study the labelling and match it to the right parts of Figure 10. Tick them off on Figure 10 as you do them.

Exam tips

Questions often involve variations of the factors listed in Figure 10. Some of the options are:

- using OS map extracts where you compare map information and perhaps other information to explain river flow;
- diagrams or written information which describe different river basins and your task is to explain river flow differences;
- information about the changes in one river basin and the effects of the changes on river flow.

In all cases you can use the same ideas and terms (from Figures 7, 8 and 10) to explain differences or changes (as in Figure 9).

Hazards in river basins

Changes in the river basin affect water flow and very often cause **flood hazard**. For example, the clearing of forest to make way for housing on the slopes of a small tropical drainage basin in Brunei speeded up the flow of water. This caused flooding at lower levels.

Flooding has widespread effects.

1 Large-scale deaths, from direct flooding or resulting famine.

2 Loss of agricultural production.

3 Use of development funds for emergency relief.

4 Use of development funds for food imports.

5 Poverty amongst farmers as a result of losses causes migration to the cities.

Figure 11

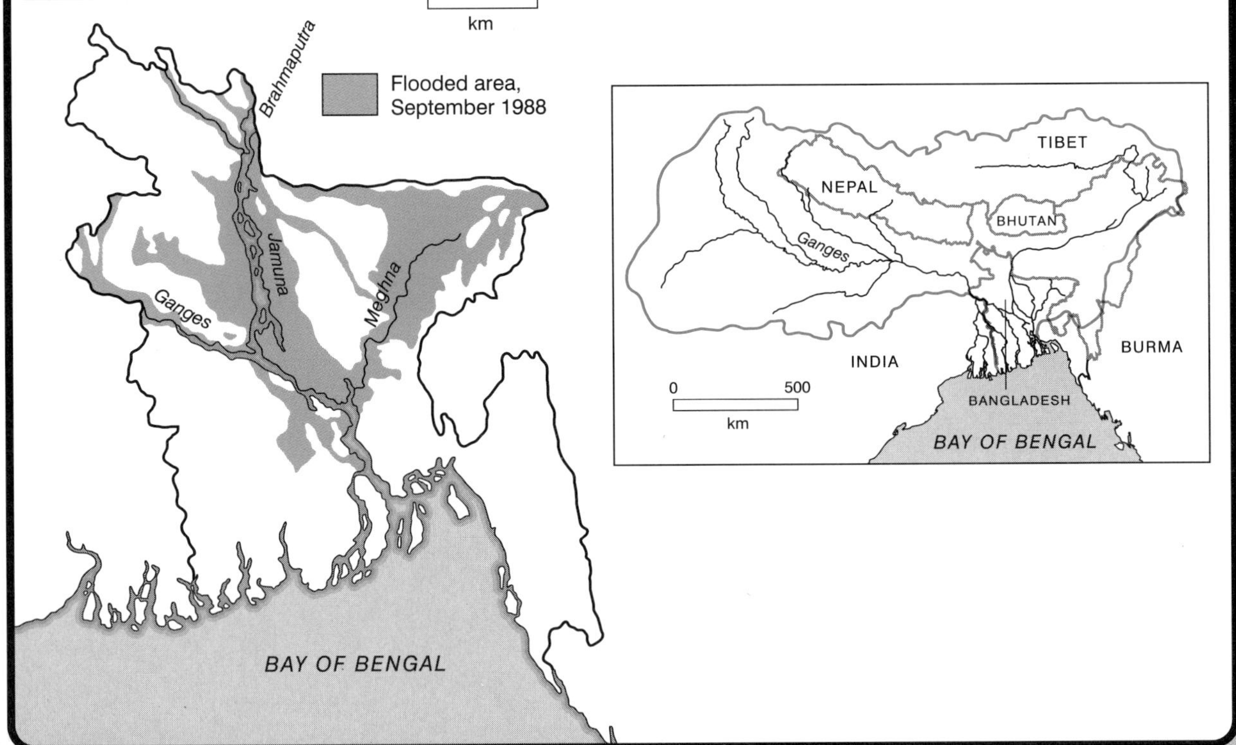

The Ganges–Brahmaputra river catchment (*see* Case study on page 29)

Case study

The Ganges—Brahmaputra river catchment

At a larger scale the Ganges and Brahmaputra rivers illustrate the effects of flood hazards within one large river basin (*see* Figure 11). The flood hazard is especially great in Bangladesh. Several features put Bangladesh at particular risk.

1. 80% of the country is made up of flood plains of the two major rivers and other smaller ones.
2. The rivers have an enormous catchment of 1 million square kilometres.
3. Only 7.5% of the catchment lies within Bangladesh so the country has little control over management of the whole river basin.
4. The catchment has a tropical monsoon climate with most rain coming between May and September. In the Himalayas and the Assam and Tripura Hills annual rainfall is extremely heavy, reaching 5000 mm in places.
5. Rain water movement is boosted by snowmelt from the high mountains.
6. 80% of the country's 110 million people are rural. They live in the flood plain areas.

A very large proportion of the country therefore faces flood risks.

Flood prevention schemes have been produced, with major works planned for all areas. Lack of funds is a major handicap.

The measures to deal with flood hazards involve changes to the rivers and their channels (Figure 12).

Bangladesh has less than 10% of the catchment of its rivers. As a result **river basin management** over the whole catchment is not possible. To cope with all the risks, including those resulting from human action, whole catchment planning is necessary.

Figure 12

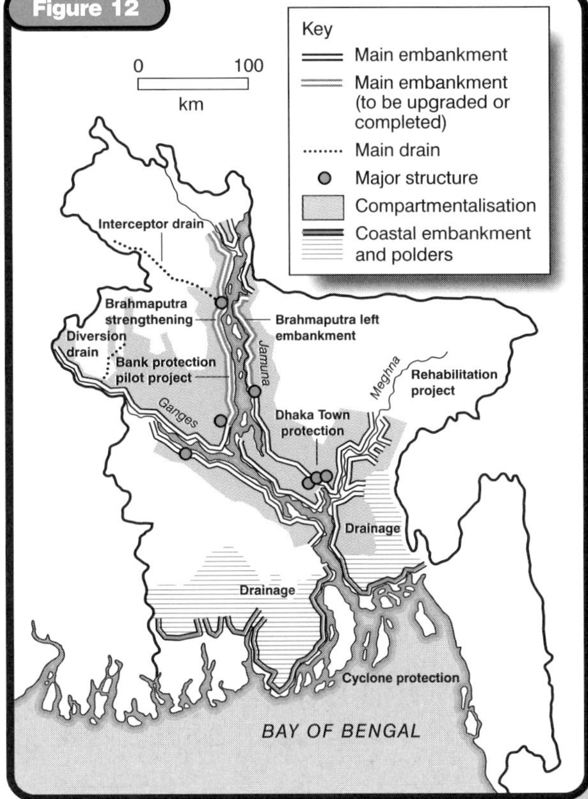

Flood prevention schemes in Bangladesh

review

Use this Mind Map as a base for summarising what you have revised in this unit.

Figure 13

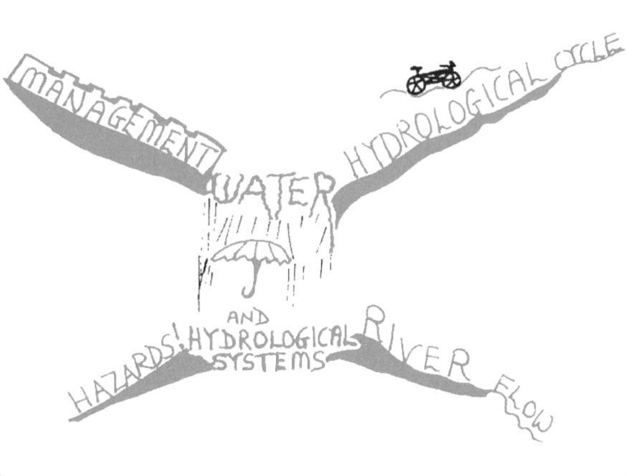

Weather and Climate

3

preview

What you need to know

- The elements of weather and climate and their measurement
- Climate graphs
- Importance of climate and weather
- Weather patterns and sequences
- Forecasting
- Air masses
- Depressions
- Winter and summer anticyclones
- How temperatures vary
- The factors that affect temperature differences
- Patterns of rainfall
- Types of rainfall
- Main types of world climates
- Climates of one or more region
- Local factors affecting weather and climate, and their effects
- Major weather hazards and their effects

Importance of weather and climate

Weather is what happens in the atmosphere (e.g. temperature, pressure, precipitation) at a particular time.

Climate tells us what conditions are like over a period of time.

Task 1

(a) What are all the elements of weather? Complete Figure 1 by writing in missing names or drawing missing pictures.

(b) How are they measured? Add the instruments or method to the diagram. Remember that not all need instruments.

What's important about climate and weather?

Climate and weather affect peoples' lives as well as affecting other aspects of the environment. For example:

- **weather hazards** cause problems, like drought, strong winds, fog, ice;
- climate is a **resource** for activities, like farming and tourism;
- **global warming** and **climate change** may have major worldwide effects.

Figure 1

Element		Measurement
Temperature		
Precipitation – rain, snow, sleat, hail		Rain gauge
Air pressure		
Wind speed		Anemometer Beaufort scale
		Wind vane
Visibility		Eye
Cloud cover and type		Eye
Humidity		Hygrometer
Sunshine hours		Sunshine gauge

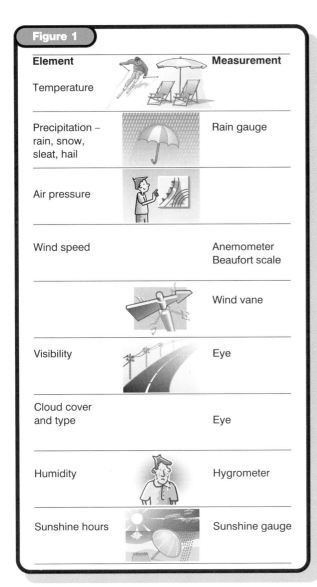

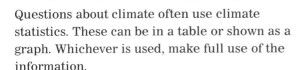

Elements of the weather

Climate graphs

Exam tip

Questions about climate often use climate statistics. These can be in a table or shown as a graph. Whichever is used, make full use of the information.

On pages 39 and 40 we look at different climate regions. Make sure you can recognise them from climate statistics or graphs.

Using a climate graph or climate statistics — questions to ask

Temperature

What is the maximum mean monthly temperature?

When does it occur?

What is the minimum mean monthly temperature?

When does it occur?

What is the temperature range? (The difference in degrees between the maximum and minimum.)

Is this extreme or temperate?

Is the place in the northern hemisphere, the southern hemisphere or in the tropics?

Rainfall

What is the mean annual total rainfall?

Is there rain all the year?

Is there rain all year with a maximum in one or more seasons?

Is there a definite dry season and wet season?

Is the wet season in summer or winter?

What the answers to these questions will tell you

1 Which climatic zone the place is in.

2 What problems the climate might cause.

3 What benefits the climate might bring.

Where in the world is it?

Climate statistics tell you that a place is in:

- an equatorial region because the temperatures do not vary much throughout the year;
- in mountains in an equatorial region if the temperatures are the same but lower all through the year;
- in the northern hemisphere because the highest temperatures are in June, July and August;
- in the southern hemisphere because highest temperatures are in December, January and February.

Figure 2

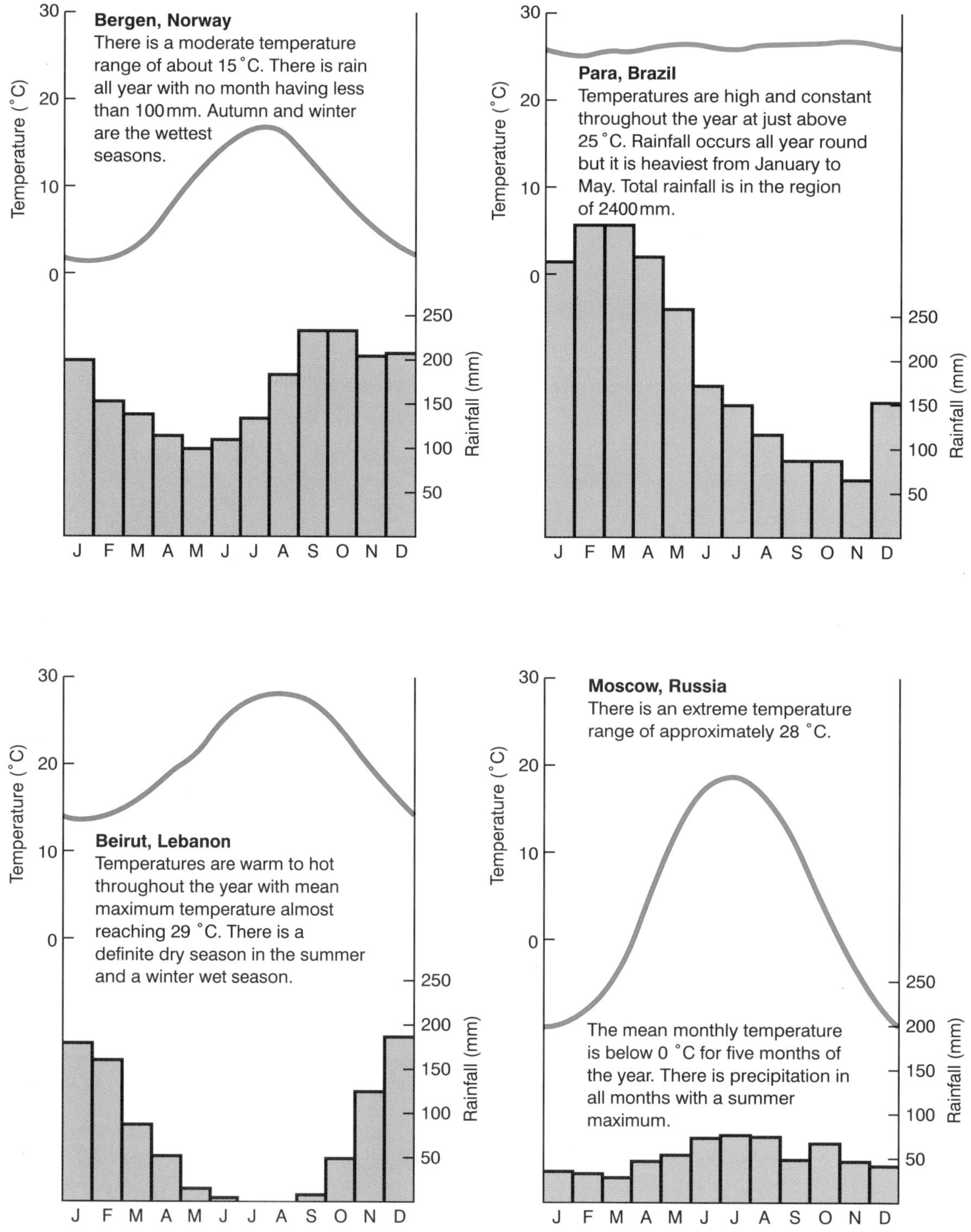

30
20
10
0
Temperature (°C)
Bergen, Norway
There is a moderate temperature range of about 15 °C. There is rain all year with no month having less than 100 mm. Autumn and winter are the wettest seasons.
250
200
150
100
50
Rainfall (mm)
J F M A M J J A S O N D
Para, Brazil
Temperatures are high and constant throughout the year at just above 25 °C. Rainfall occurs all year round but it is heaviest from January to May. Total rainfall is in the region of 2400 mm.
Beirut, Lebanon
Temperatures are warm to hot throughout the year with mean maximum temperature almost reaching 29 °C. There is a definite dry season in the summer and a winter wet season.
Moscow, Russia
There is an extreme temperature range of approximately 28 °C.
The mean monthly temperature is below 0 °C for five months of the year. There is precipitation in all months with a summer maximum.

Climate graphs

Task 2

Look at the climate graphs (Figure 2). Use the questions on page 31 to analyse each graph. Write the answers in the spaces on the graphs.

review

Make your own Mind Map to summarise the content of this short unit. You can use Figure 3 as a base.

Figure 3

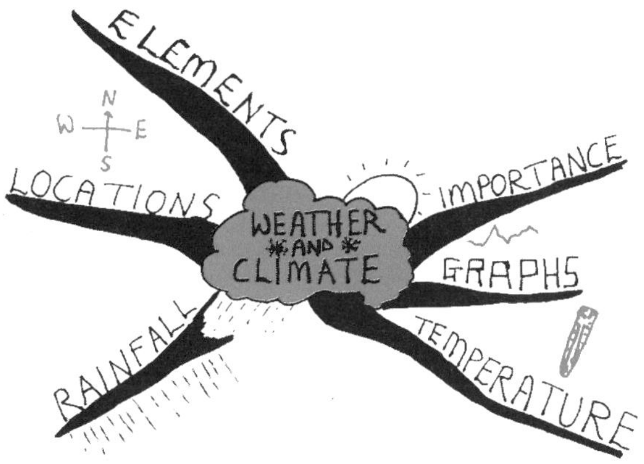

Syllabus check

Whatever your syllabus covers on weather and climate this unit will be useful. *But check exactly what else you have to do.* Your syllabus might specify case studies so make sure you incorporate them from your school work in your revision summaries. They could include the different climates of western Europe, the effects of drought in West Africa, hurricane damage in the USA or local fog problems.

Weather types and systems

Test yourself

What do you know already?

Give a short answer to each of these questions.

How do air masses affect our weather?

What sort of weather goes with (a) winter anticyclones and (b) summer anticyclones?

What sorts of weather go with depressions?

Weather systems

Air pressure is measured in millibars. It is shown on a weather map by lines called **isobars**. They join places with the same air pressure.

Figure 4

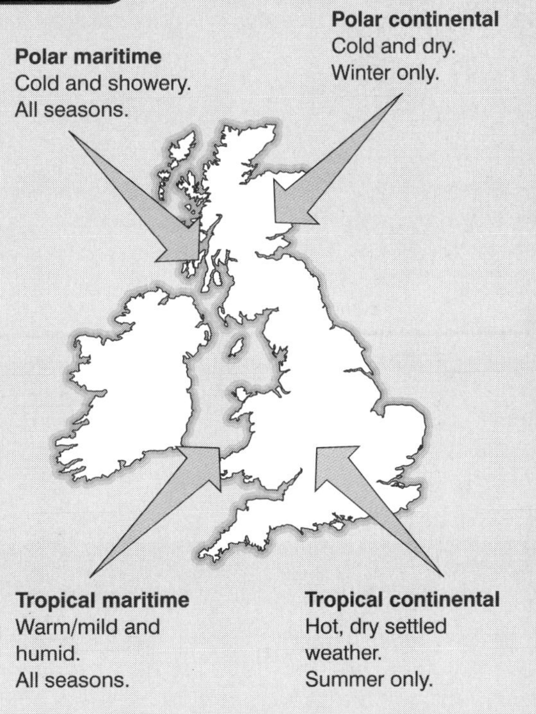

Air masses

Figure 5

(a) Low pressure

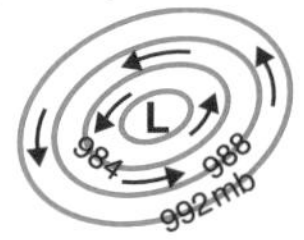

Surface winds blow anti-clockwise. Isobars are generally closer together so winds are stronger.

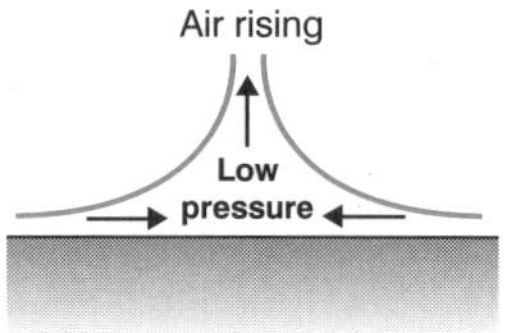

Rising air is unstable and produces cloud and rain.

(b) High pressure

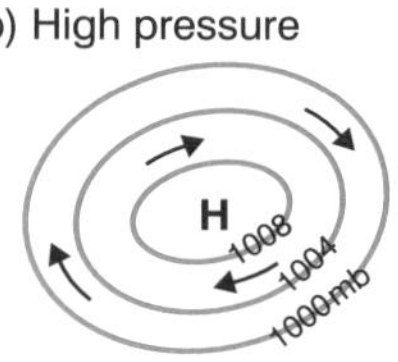

Surface winds blow clockwise. Isobars generally further apart so winds are gentle.

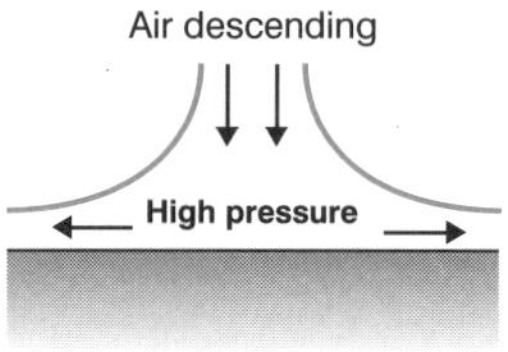

Descending air gives stable conditions and more settled weather.

High and low pressure systems

Figure 6

Summer

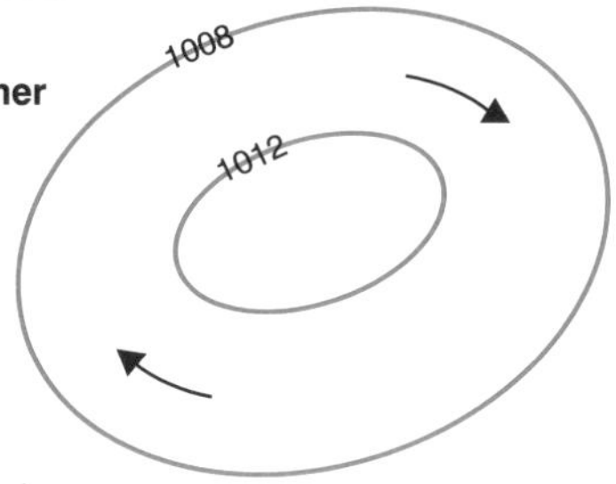

Clear skies and long days give long hours of sunshine. High temperatures. In densely populated areas, pollution builds up at and near the surface.

Winter

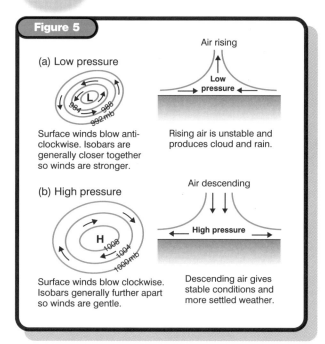

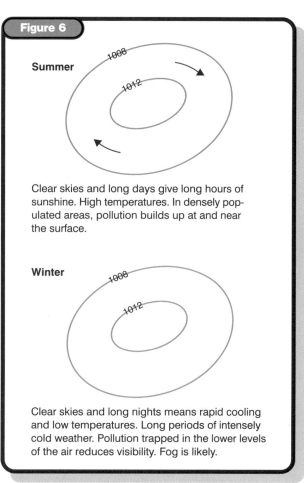

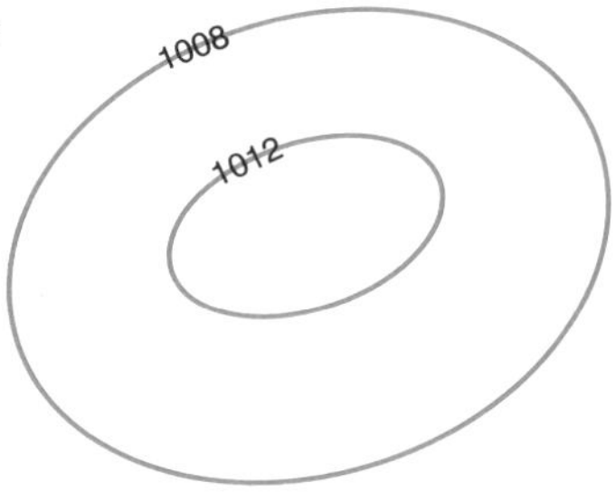

Clear skies and long nights means rapid cooling and low temperatures. Long periods of intensely cold weather. Pollution trapped in the lower levels of the air reduces visibility. Fog is likely.

Anticyclones in summer and winter

Anticyclones

Anticyclones stay in place for days, weeks or even months. So the weather stays much the same, too. The kind of weather depends on the season.

Depressions

Depressions come from the west and bring changeable weather. This is because they form on the boundary between **tropical** and **polar air**. The boundary is called the **polar front**. Within a depression this boundary marks the line between warm, moist, tropical air and colder, less moist polar air.

The way a depression develops means that the tropical air makes a wedge cutting into the polar air (Figure 7). As a depression passes over a place on the ground there is a particular pattern of weather. The cross-section in Figure 7 shows the typical **weather sequence**.

Depressions follow one another. As a result, the weather sequence is also broken by the **ridges of high pressure** between the depressions. These ridges bring a short period of more settled, often sunny weather between the more changeable weather of the depressions.

Task

Look at Figure 8. It shows all the weather systems already mentioned.

(a) Identify the following. Write the letters from the weather chart by the correct words below:

anticyclone

depression

warm front

cold front

ridge of high pressure

warm sector

cold sector

(b) Describe the weather shown by each set of weather station symbols. They show the weather at G, A and D on the map.
Write the correct letter beside each weather station diagram.

(c) What is the weather like in the area covered by the ridge of high pressure?

(d) What is the weather like in the middle of the anticyclone?

Forecasting

Weather forecasting uses the knowledge you applied to the last task.

Anticyclones are stable. This means that in the short term the weather will stay roughly the same.

Depressions are unstable and moving. This means that each depression will produce a sequence of weather changes.

review

Make your own review Mind Map.

Figure 7

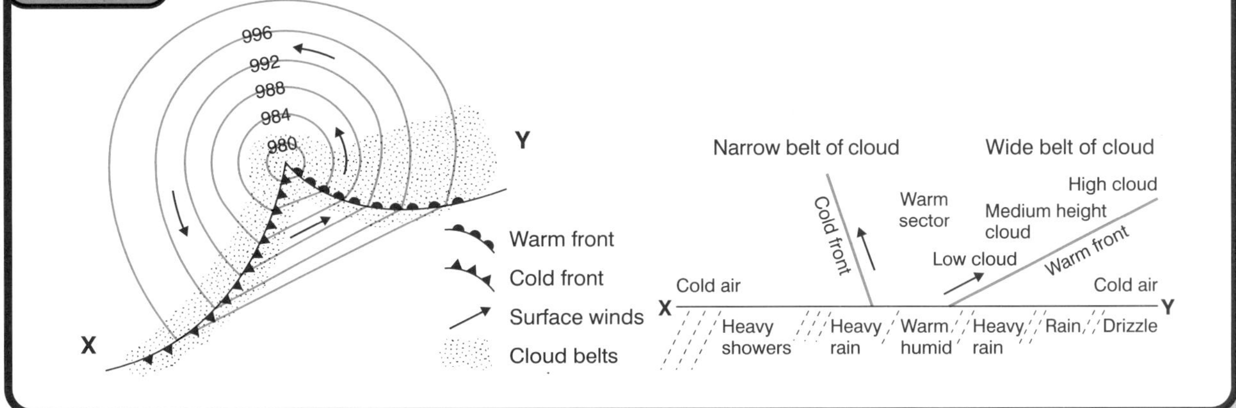

Depressions and their weather

Figure 8

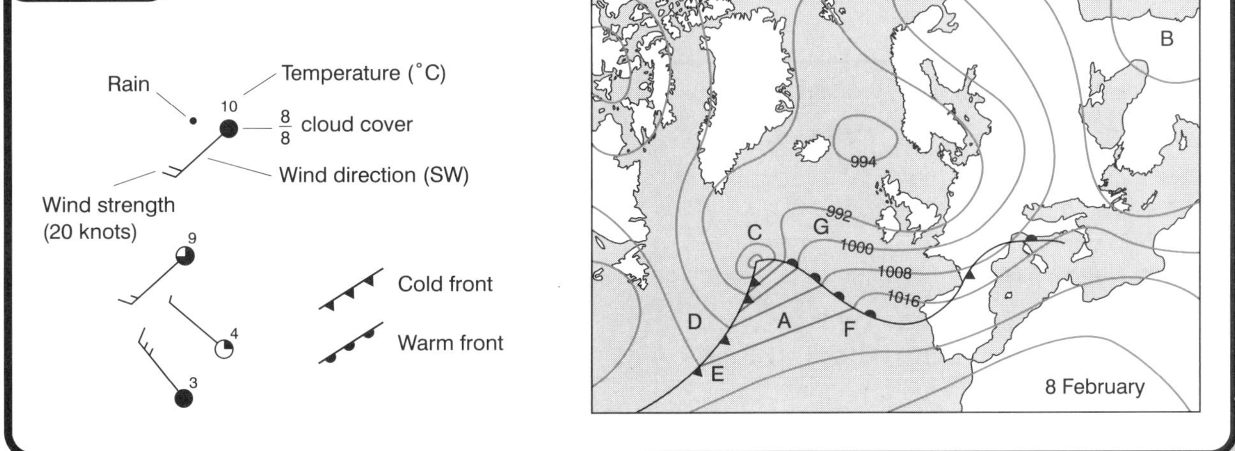

Weather chart

Temperature patterns

Figure 9 shows summer and winter temperatures in the British Isles. The lines joining places with the same temperatures are called **isotherms**. Their arrangement brings out the pattern of temperatures. The summer pattern is described for you. Pencil in a list of points about the winter pattern.

Factors affecting temperature

Temperatures vary from place to place due to a number of factors.

Figure 9

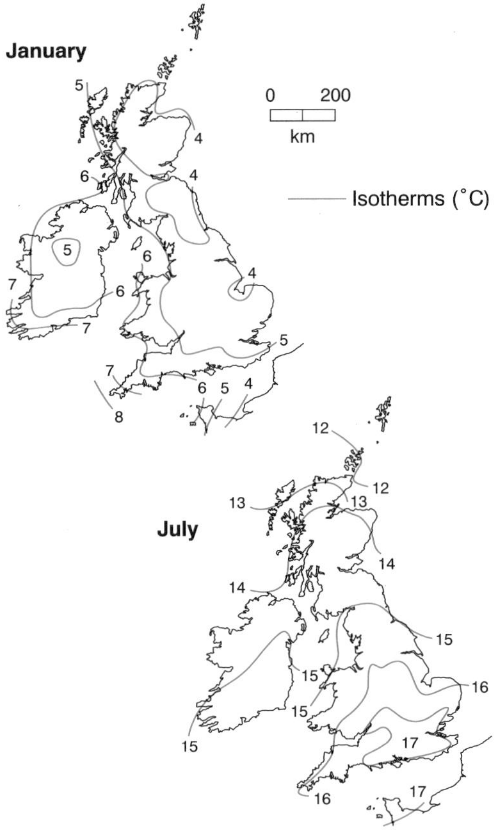

Temperatures decrease northwards. Warmer inland than on the coasts. Highest temperatures in south-east.

Temperature patterns in the British Isles

Latitude or distance from the equator

This explains why, in general, temperatures decrease northwards or southwards from the equator because the sun is lower in the sky away from the equator, so heating is less intense.

Seasons

The length of daylight varies with the seasons once you are away from the tropics, so in winter:

- the shorter daylight means less heat is received from the sun;
- the lower sun in the sky means less intense heat.

For summer reverse these points.

Land and sea

Water, especially the sea, acts like a huge storage radiator. It absorbs heat during the summer and releases it slowly during the winter. Compared with the land it is cool in summer and warm in winter. The result is that places near the sea are warmer in winter and cooler in summer than places inland.

Ocean currents

The warm and cold currents in the oceans have a huge effect on temperatures. The warm currents bring warm water from the tropics to middle and high latitudes. The warm water in turn warms the air bringing much warmer conditions in winter than would otherwise be expected. This makes the land areas affected much warmer. Cold currents bring colder conditions.

Altitude

Temperature decreases with height. The result can be that places quite close together in distance can have very different climates because of their altitude difference.

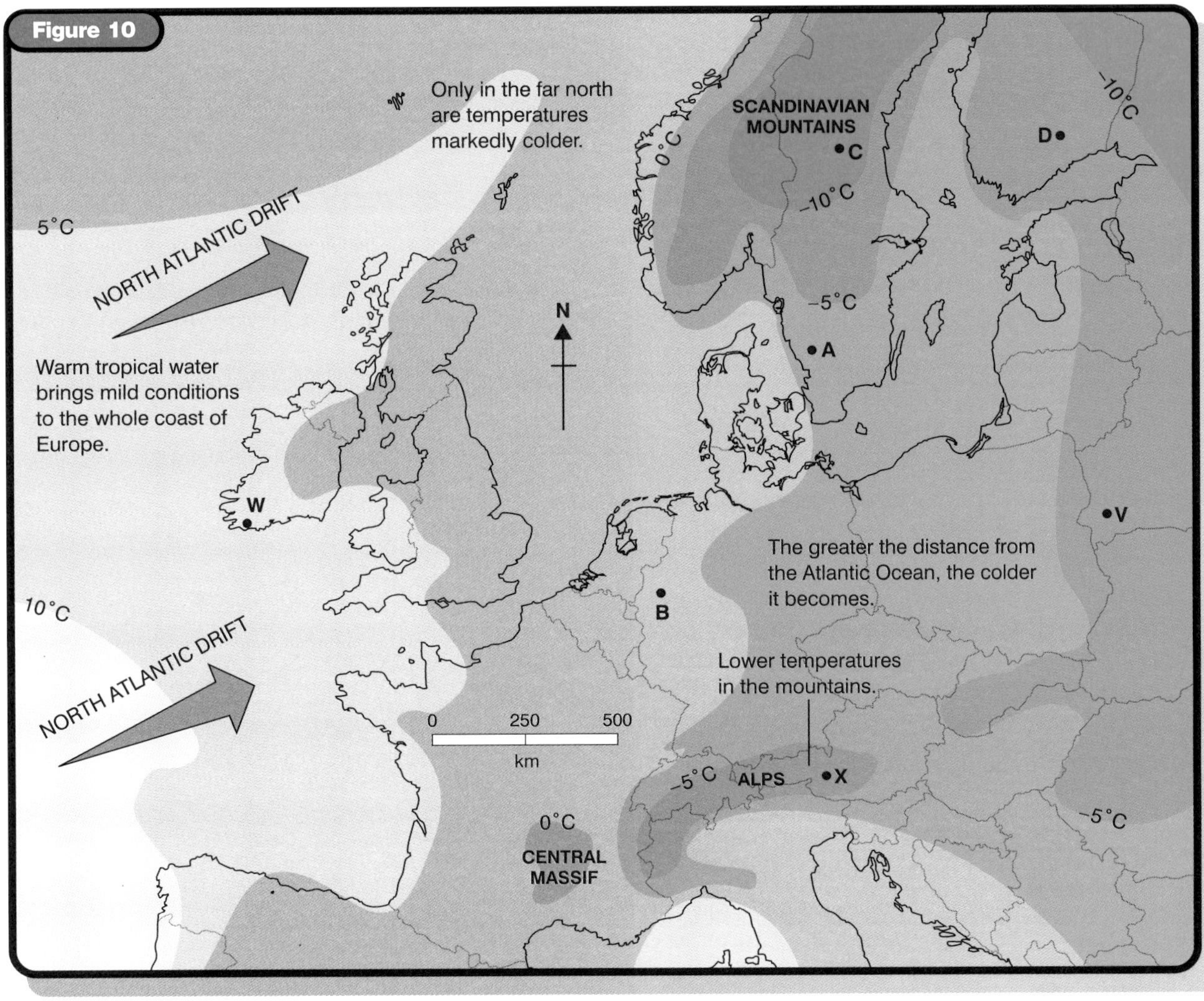

Winter temperatures in Europe

Test yourself

If you have studied this unit carefully, you'll be able to answer the following questions about Figure 10 which shows mean winter temperatures in Europe. Other information is given to tie in with the five factors affecting temperature, to help you.

1 Match these temperatures to locations A, B, C and D.
–8°C, –10°C, 1°C, –3°C.

2 Why is there a permanent snowfield at X?

3 Why is the west coast completely free of ice?

4 Account for the temperature difference between W and V.

review

Draw a Mind Map showing the factors affecting temperatures. Add to it:

(a) what effect each one has;

(b) an example.

Rainfall patterns and types

Scan this unit quickly. Do you need to look back at the first unit in this chapter?

Rainfall patterns

Seasonal

Describing and explaining the geographical pattern of rainfall is often part of a question. You may have to do it based on a particular case study (check your syllabus) or by applying your knowledge to a new example.

Types of rainfall

★ **Frontal rain**. Most British rainfall is associated with depressions (pages 34–5), with the rain coming in bands along the lines of the fronts. The bands of clouds you see on satellite pictures on weather forecasts bring the rain.

★ **Relief rain**. In hilly or mountainous areas air is forced to rise. This forces cooling of the air, condensation of water vapour and the formation of cloud and then rain.

★ **Convection rain**. Rainfall in equatorial regions is of this type. So is the rain associated with thunderstorms in Britain. It occurs when heating of the land in turn heats the air in contact with it. The air expands and rises, and at high altitude cooling produces heavy condensation which results in heavy rainfall.

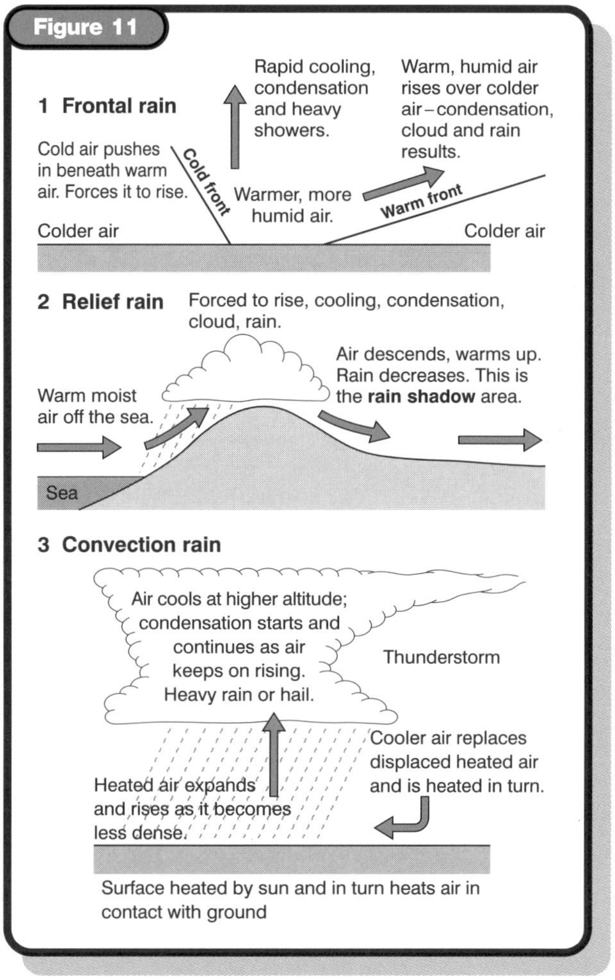
Figure 11
1 Frontal rain
Rapid cooling, condensation and heavy showers.
Warm, humid air rises over colder air – condensation, cloud and rain results.
Cold air pushes in beneath warm air. Forces it to rise.
Cold front
Warmer, more humid air.
Warm front
Colder air
Colder air
2 Relief rain
Forced to rise, cooling, condensation, cloud, rain.
Air descends, warms up. Rain decreases. This is the rain shadow area.
Warm moist air off the sea.
Sea
3 Convection rain
Air cools at higher altitude; condensation starts and continues as air keeps on rising. Heavy rain or hail.
Thunderstorm
Cooler air replaces displaced heated air and is heated in turn.
Heated air expands and rises as it becomes less dense.
Surface heated by sun and in turn heats air in contact with ground

Types of rainfall

Exam tips

Exam questions often provide resources (e.g. a map of British rainfall and a relief map). Questions you can answer directly from the resources give the first few marks. More marks depend on your using your knowledge and understanding.

For example, 'Describe and explain the distribution of rainfall of the British Isles' means do more than just use the map.

1 The questioner will want to know about the relationship between high land and rainfall; that's relief rain.

2 The questioner will also want to know that the frontal rain brought by depressions coming from the west is increased as the depressions cross the mountainous regions.

3 Remember to mention the areas of lighter rainfall to the east. These are in the rain shadow.

Test yourself

Complete the crossword.

review

Make a review Mind Map of this unit. Add case study details if your syllabus specifies a particular area of the world.

Figure 12

Across

1 Common type of rainfall in equatorial regions (10)
4 A belt of heavy showers often marks the passing of a ______ front (4)
6 Rainfall comes at a particular time of year (8)
7 It is on the leeward side of the mountains (4,6)
8 Fronts are marked by belts of _________ (5)

Down

2 Moisture is released by _________ (12)
3 They come from the west and bring most of Britain's rainfall (9)
5 Mountains, even in the middle of the deserts, cause this sort of rain (6)

Climatic regions

Syllabus check

Whatever your syllabus says it is useful to know something about world climates generally. This is because it is important to agriculture, economic development, climate and weather hazards, climate change and global warming.

You already know a great deal about different climates. You have studied them in Key Stage 3 as well as during your GCSE course. So this unit just summarises main points.

Task

(a) Review the information on Figures 13 and 14.

Note certain points:

1 Where are different climates within each continent? Only on the east coast, only on the west coast, or in the interior?

Figure 13

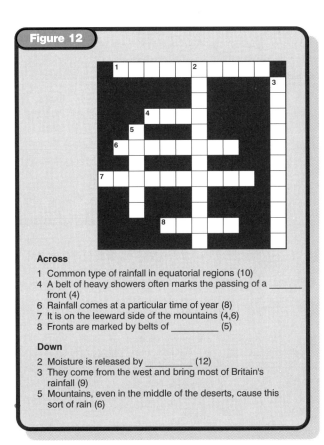

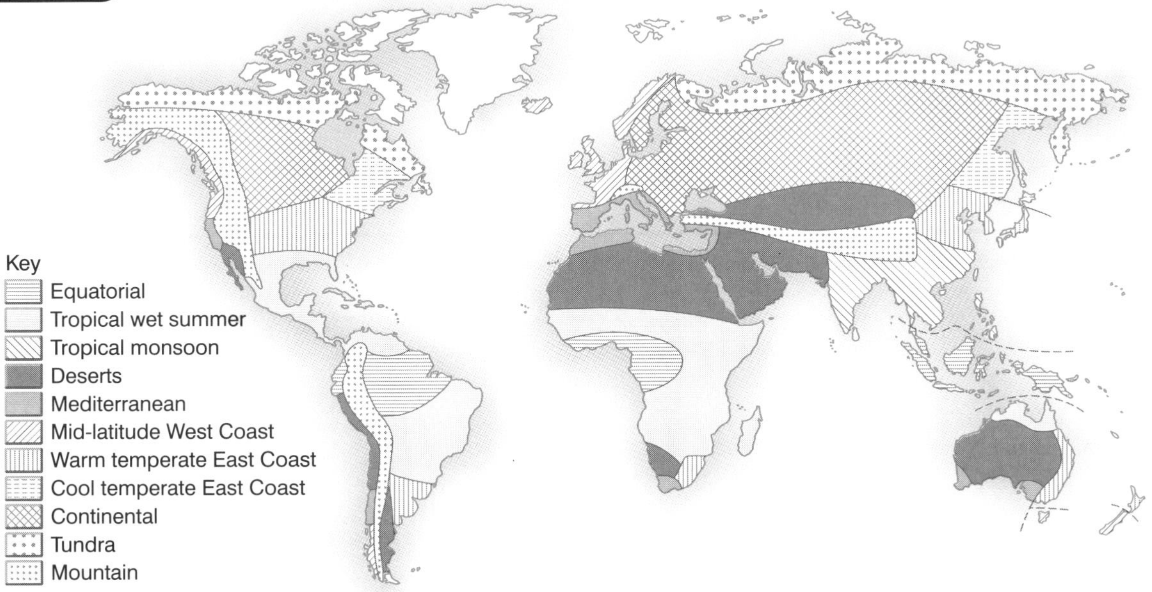

World climates

Figure 14

Climatic type	*Example*	*Description*
Tropical		
Equatorial	Para, Brazil (1°S)	Rain all year (2437 mm), ranging from maximum of 357 mm in February to minimum of 66 mm in November. Temperatures high, only varying between 25 °C and 26.7 °C
Tropical wet summer	Kano, Nigeria (12°N)	Total rainfall of 861 mm, rising gradually from 68 mm in May to a maximum of 310 mm in August before decreasing rapidly. Temperatures range from 21.7 °C in January to 30.6 °C in May
Tropical monsoon	Bombay, India (19°N)	Total rainfall of 1800 mm, almost all during June to September. Temperatures are high, ranging from 23.9 °C in January to 29.4 °C in May. Rainy season starts suddenly
Hot desert	Aswan, Egypt (24°N)	No rainfall (unusual as most desert places have some). Temperatures vary from 15.6 °C in January to 33.3 °C in July
Temperate		
Mediterranean	Algiers, Algeria (37°N)	Total rainfall of 762 mm, most falling November to January. Summers dry and hot (25.6 °C) and winter warm (12.2 °C)
Mid-latitude West Coast	Brest, France (48°N)	Rain all year (861 mm), heaviest in winter. Maximum temperature 17.8 °C, minimum 7.2 °C, small range of 10.6 °C
Warm temperate East Coast	Raleigh, N.Carolina, USA (36°N)	Rain all year but summer maximum. Heavy rainfall of 1142 mm. Mild winters (5 °C in January) and hot, humid summers (26.1 °C)
Cool temperate East Coast	Vladivostock, USSR (43°N)	Rain falls mainly May to October, totalling 606 mm. Extreme temperature range (–13.9 °C in January and 20.6 °C in July)
Continental	Prince Albert, Saskatchewan, Canada (53°N)	Rain all year (snow in winter) with summer maximum. Total 404 mm. Extreme temperature range from –20 °C in January to 17.2 °C in July
Cold		
Tundra	Thule, Greenland (76°N)	Negligible rainfall (88 mm). Minimum temperature –29.4 °C, maximum temperature 4.4 °C. Only three months above 0 °C

World climates

2 Compare areas north and south of the equator. Are the same climates in the same latitudes and same general locations you noted in 1?

3 Where does it rain all year?

4 Where is there seasonal rain? Separate areas with winter rain from areas with summer rain.

5 Where are the deserts?

(b) Add labelling to the climate graphs on page 32, including the name of the climate (check back to remind yourself of the points to notice).

(c) What kinds of places throughout the world would also have conditions similar to cold regions?

Local weather and climate

Fog

Fog often covers very large areas. However, it affects us directly so we think of it more as a local event.

Fog and mist are made up of water droplets formed by condensation of water vapour. For this to arise the air has to be cooled. This happens in two ways, giving two types of fog:

- **radiation** fog
- **advection** fog.

Hill fog is sometimes classed as a third type but it is really low cloud.

Places where fogs occur regularly can be dangerous. Along roads accidents are frequent at places where fog accumulates. These are often at the foot of a slope.

Frost

Frost occurs when temperatures fall to freezing point or below. Obviously this will happen if a very cold, stable air mass covers the country.

Test yourself

What sort of air mass is most likely to bring freezing conditions? (Look at the unit on Weather systems on page 34 to help you.)

However, frosts occur at other times. When there are calm, clear conditions between early autumn and late spring frost is possible. Anticyclones provide the right conditions.

Ground frost and air frost

Weather forecasters often talk about these. What is the difference? Air frost occurs when the temperature of the air (normally measured by thermometers in a Stevenson Screen 1.25 metres above the ground) falls below 0 °C. Ground frost occurs when the temperature at ground level is at or falls below 0 °C.

Ground thermometers measure the surface temperatures. Ground temperatures are more extreme than air temperatures, that is, there is a greater difference between the maximum and minimum. The result is that the air temperature may be 1 °C or 2 °C, but the ground temperature may be at or below 0 °C.

Ground frost in the spring is particularly damaging to crops. At any time, it produces dangerous icy surfaces.

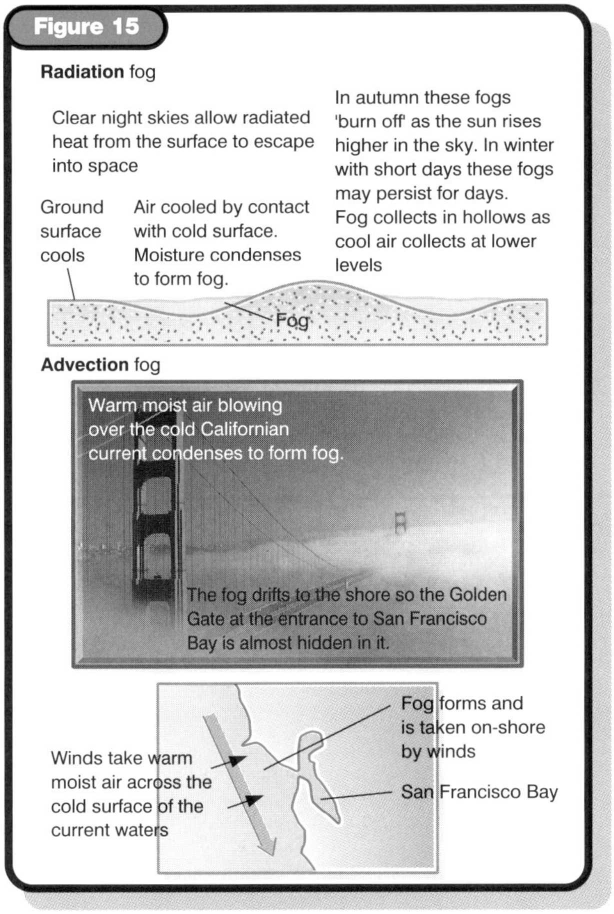

Fog

Land and sea breezes

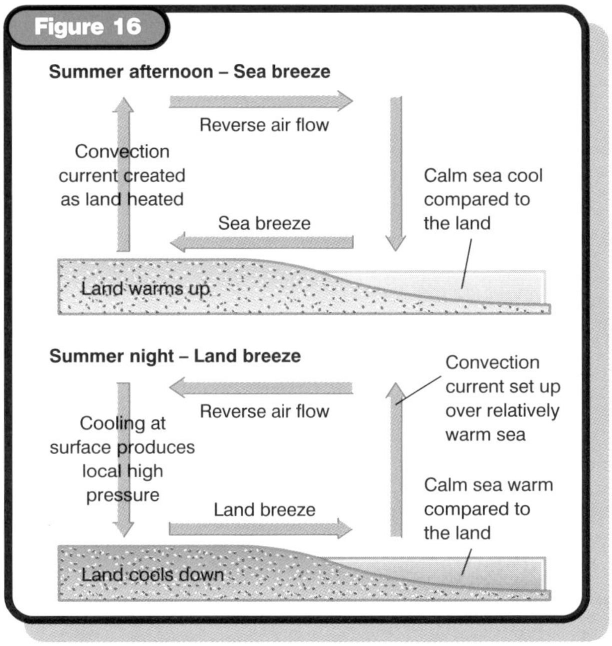

Land and sea breezes

Urban climate

Heat

Individual buildings lose heat. So cities produce a great deal of heat, with traffic adding to the heat from homes, factories and offices. There is a definite difference between the temperatures of cities and the surrounding rural areas in winter and summer. It is most obvious under calm conditions. Cities make what is called an '**urban heat island**'.

Rainfall

In thundery conditions the higher temperatures in a city may trigger thunderstorms.

Wind

The arrangement of streets and individual buildings affects wind direction and strength. Winds can be funnelled along streets and blow in quite a different direction from the general winds at that time. When the wind is channelled along narrow streets it becomes stronger. Places where several narrow streets meet can be particularly windy places. New building developments often have particular problems of this sort.

Project ideas

Local climate and weather gives you lots of opportunities for projects:

Temperature differences measured at different locations between the centre and edge of a city.

Temperature differences between built-up areas and open spaces within a city.

Temperature patterns around a large building set in open space, like your school.

At the small scale, you can investigate temperature patterns in a garden.

Investigating windy places in a city centre or at a local shopping area, or even around your school buildings.

review

1. Review the unit one section at a time. Five minutes for each should be enough.
2. After each section summarise its main points in a Mind Map.
3. Check the section to see if you have missed anything important.

Weather hazards

Task

Make a list of weather hazards at two scales:

(a) Local, the kind of weather hazard you could experience in your home area;

(b) Worldwide, the kinds of major weather hazards which affect different regions of the world.

What are the effects?

Figure 17

Did you miss any of these?

Avalanche
Blizzard
Drought
Flood
Fog
Frost
Gale
Hail
Hurricane
Ice
Lightning
Tornado
Blizzard

Checklist

Here is a list of effects. Add them to your list of hazards.

epidemics of disease
loss of life
loss of crops
failure of water supplies
transport disrupted
destruction of buildings

Warning systems help to reduce problems. Think about what action could be taken if there was a warning of each hazard. Possible actions are:

barriers
evacuation
staying indoors
staying indoors in a secure place
protection (sand bags, boarding)

Which hazards do these apply to?

Add others if you can.

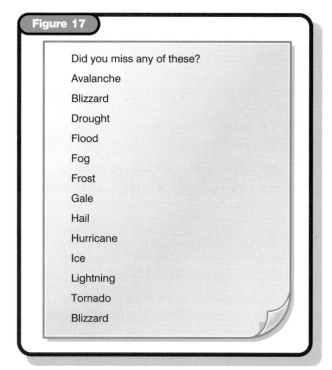

Hurricane hazard

Hurricanes are areas of intense low pressure. They form over warm tropical seas. The ocean's heat is the source of energy which sets the weather system going. This is why hurricanes slowly die out over land and why they do not affect areas nearer the poles.

Task

Use Figure 18.

(a) Make a list of the features of hurricanes.

(b) Make a list of the areas which suffered damage as a result of the hurricane.

(c) Make a list of types of damage suffered.

(d) Make a list of how the damage was caused.

(e) How did the US coastal areas avoid large numbers of casualties?

review

(a) Spend five minutes reviewing the first part of the unit.

Reorganise the material into one table with four columns. The first three are hazards, damage and action. The fourth is examples; add one example to each as you come across them in the news.

(b) Reorganise your lists about hurricanes in a Mind Map.

Figure 18

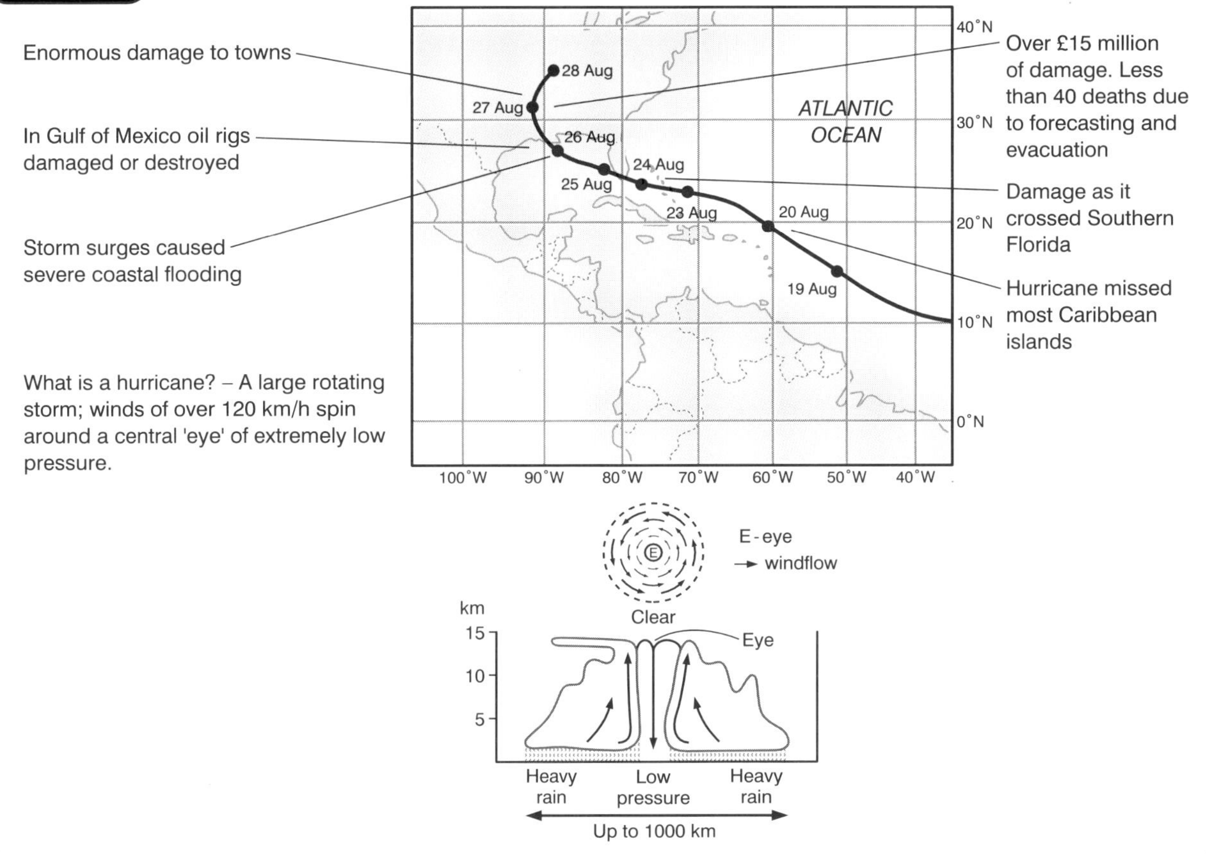
Enormous damage to towns
In Gulf of Mexico oil rigs damaged or destroyed
Storm surges caused severe coastal flooding
What is a hurricane? – A large rotating storm; winds of over 120 km/h spin around a central 'eye' of extremely low pressure.
28 Aug
27 Aug
26 Aug
25 Aug
24 Aug
23 Aug
20 Aug
19 Aug
ATLANTIC OCEAN
40°N
30°N
20°N
10°N
0°N
100°W
90°W
80°W
70°W
60°W
50°W
40°W
Over £15 million of damage. Less than 40 deaths due to forecasting and evacuation
Damage as it crossed Southern Florida
Hurricane missed most Caribbean islands
E
E - eye
windflow
km
15
10
5
Clear
Eye
Heavy rain
Low pressure
Heavy rain
Up to 1000 km

Physical Geography

Vegetation and Soils

4

preview

What you need to know

- What is an ecosystem?
- Types and features of soil
- Inter-relationship between soil, vegetation and climate
- Changes to systems (natural and human)
- Global pattern
- Case studies
- Inter-relationship between parts of the ecosystem
- The effects of people on ecosystems, including case studies

Ecosystems

What is an ecosystem?

An **ecosystem** is made up of living things and their physical environment. Remember – an ecosystem depends on the **inter-relationships** between its different parts.

Remember that a local-scale ecosystem is also part of the global system.

Global questions and answers

Q How is climate important globally?

A The temperatures and amount of rainfall determine what kinds of plants can grow.

Q What do we mean by vegetation?

A Vegetation types depend on their structure, for example, whether they are dense forest or grasslands or a mixture of scattered trees and grassland.

Q Where does soil come in?

A The kind of soil depends on the climate and the vegetation.

Ecosystem changes

Changes happen to an ecosystem as part of the natural process of development and as a result of human activity.

Plant successions

When an area clear of vegetation is colonised by plants, it is the first stage in a **succession**. As time passes new plants replace the original plants. Ultimately a stage is reached when the **plant community** stops changing. This is called the climax, or **climatic climax**.

At the climax stage the ecosystem is tied in closely to the local climatic conditions. To reach this stage takes a long period of time, often well

Figure 1

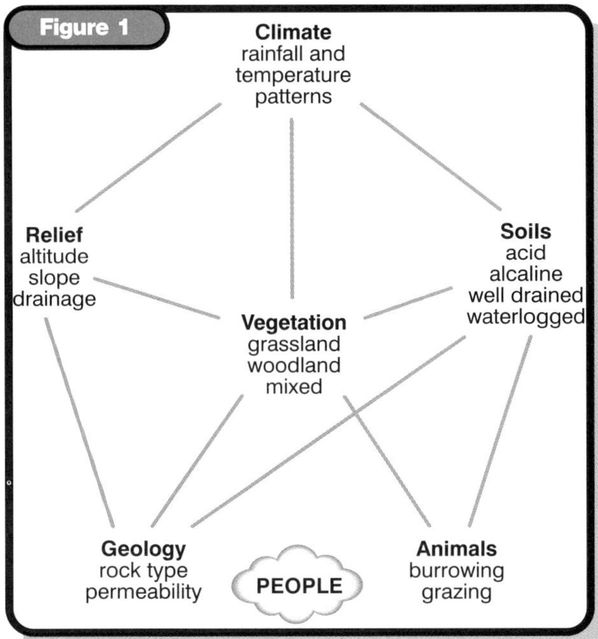

Ecosystem inter-relationships

over 1000 years, but we can see the stages of colonisation in some places. Volcanic areas give some good examples and in the wet tropics the stages develop very quickly.

Soils

What is soil made from?

- mineral particles (weathered rock)
- organic material (rotted plant and animal remains)
- water
- air

How do soils differ?

Soil texture is one way of identifying soils. This looks at the mineral content of the soil.

Clay soils are mostly made of clay particles.

Sandy soils have mostly sand grains.

Loam soils have a mixture.

What types of soil are there?

Soil types are based on their profiles.
A **soil profile** is a cross-section from the surface down to the bedrock.

Two examples are podsols and chernozems.

Figure 2

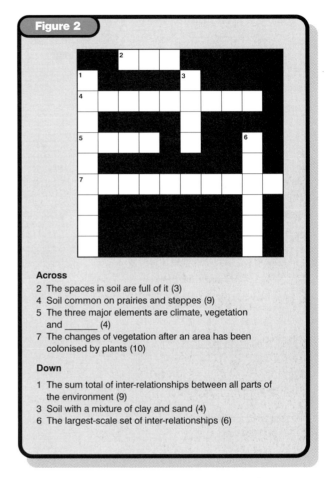

Across

2 The spaces in soil are full of it (3)
4 Soil common on prairies and steppes (9)
5 The three major elements are climate, vegetation and _______ (4)
7 The changes of vegetation after an area has been colonised by plants (10)

Down

1 The sum total of inter-relationships between all parts of the environment (9)
3 Soil with a mixture of clay and sand (4)
6 The largest-scale set of inter-relationships (6)

Test yourself

Complete the crossword.

review

Check that you now know:

- What an ecosystem is
- What makes up soil, the texture of soil and what a soil profile is
- How ecosystems change under natural conditions
- What plant succession means
- How the physical aspects of ecosystems are inter-related at global and local scales.

Vegetation types and climates

Scan this unit for two minutes, then go directly to the review task (Task 2).

Figure 3 shows world patterns of vegetation zones or ecosystems. Compare it with world climatic zones on page 39. On the world scale, climate is an important factor.

Remember

In the tropics there is plenty of warmth for plants. What matters is how much rain there is and when it falls.

In middle and high latitudes most areas have rainfall, so heat matters more. Whether plants grow or not depends on the length of the warm season and how warm it is.

Figure 4 gives you a basic description of each vegetation zone.

Task 1

(a) Reorganise Figure 4's sub-sections into these groups:

- hot all year
- definite cold season
- cold all, or almost all, year.

(b) Now take each new group and divide it up according to rainfall:

- rain all year
- rain in hot season
- rain in cool season
- no rain.

(c) Now work out how to show them all on one diagram.

Task 2

Check your syllabus for case study regions.

Make a list of the features of each of the case studies.

Figure 3

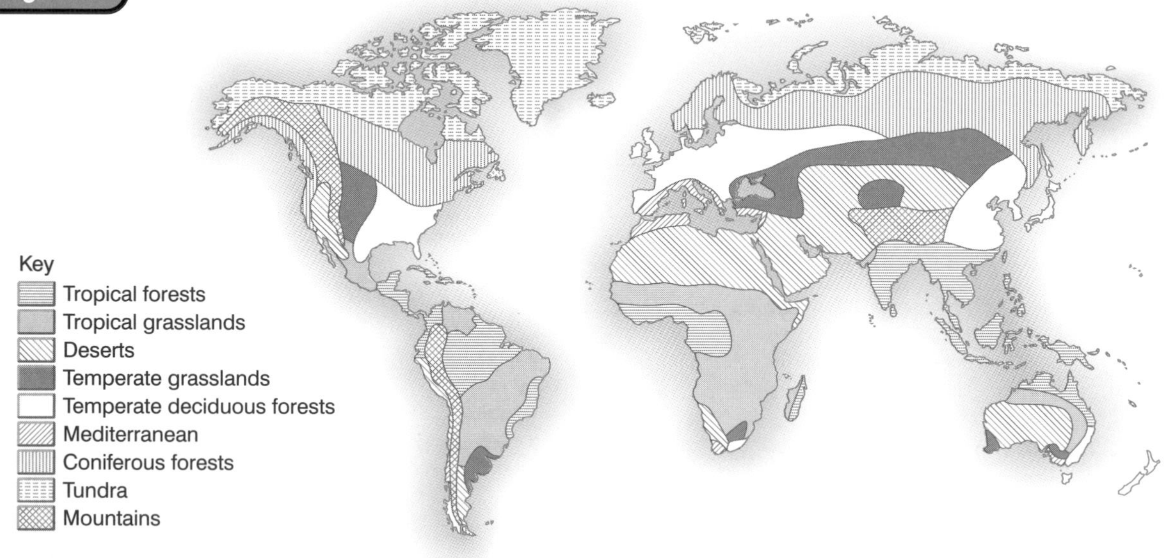

World vegetation zones

Figure 4

Tropical forests The tropical rain forests of the Amazon, Zaire Basin and West Africa and South East Asia, together with the monsoon forests, are notable for the enormous variety of species. The trees form layers at different heights and shade out most light from the ground.

Tropical grasslands These are located between the tropical forests and the deserts and are also called **savanna**. The type of grass varies according to rainfall as does the number of trees. Towards the boundary with the tropical forest are more trees, whereas towards the desert even grass becomes sparse. Trees are adapted to withstand drought.

Deserts On the fringes of the deserts are highly specialised plants which can withstand drought. Within deserts, the only significant vegetation is at oases and along rivers.

Temperate grasslands Called **steppe**, **prairie** and **pampas**, these are now the world's major wheat-producing areas, as well as being used for grazing. The low rainfall, high summer evaporation rates and cold winters restrict tree growth.

Temperate deciduous forest Mostly cleared for cultivation, especially in Europe. They occur where there is more rainfall and less extreme temperature conditions. There is a much more restricted range of species than in tropical forests.

Mediterranean forest Very little real forest remains, having been cleared by burning and grazing. Trees are adapted to overcome the summer drought as is the scrub vegetation which now covers much of the land not used for cultivation.

Coniferous forest The Taiga or northern coniferous forest has conifers adapted to withstand the cold winters. There is a very limited range of species; often there are large stands of one species.

Tundra Extreme cold and short growing season eliminate all but the hardiest plants. The landscape is treeless with a very limited range of common plants. Alpine regions have similar but more varied plants.

World vegetation zones

Figure 5

(a) Coniferous forests (Taiga)

North (South in southern hemisphere)	Tundra	Taiga	*South* (North in southern hemisphere)
	Arctic wastes, too cold	Conifers Spruce, pine, fir, larch Well adapted to low winter temperatures and short growing season. Needle leaves with thick cuticle reduce transpiration. Pointed tree tops shed snow. Temperatures down to –40 °C	Deciduous forest or steppe Deciduous trees more successful under warmer conditions. Steppe where it is drier.

(b) Tropical grasslands (Savanna)

South (or North) — Tropical rain forest — Savanna — Desert — *North* (or South)

Savanna
Very varied grasslands depending on availability of water – as rain or in the ground.
Influences are: climate
grazing animals
fire
human activity
Savanna changes from forest to desert

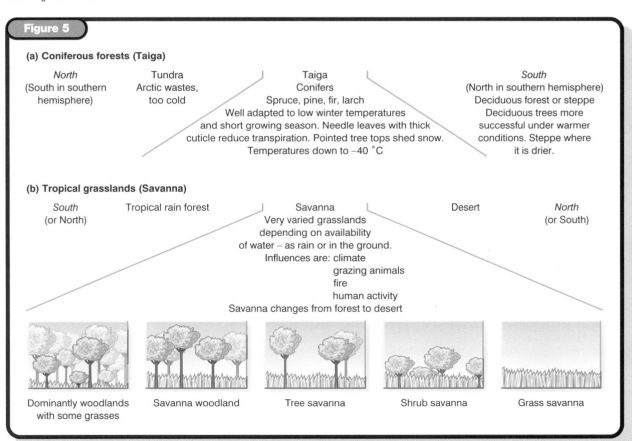

Dominantly woodlands with some grasses — Savanna woodland — Tree savanna — Shrub savanna — Grass savanna

Case studies

Local-scale patterns

Syllabus check

There are major differences between syllabuses on this topic.

Project idea

Local-scale relationships between the different parts of an ecosystem can be studied as an individual project. Depending on where you live you could study peatland, woodland, ponds or coasts. Most studies would have to include the effect of people on ecosystems.

Sand dunes form one local-scale ecosystem. The same elements make up the ecosystem at this local scale as at the world scale.

Project sand dunes

Decide what aspect of sand dunes to examine.

Think of as many questions as you can about sand dune ecosystems. For example:

- Does the wind, temperature and humidity vary between different parts of the dunes?
- Are there different bands of vegetation?
- Can you show that as plants colonise areas they change those areas?
- Do soils differ across the line of dunes?
- What effects are people having?
- Have there been any measures taken to manage or conserve the dunes?

Use the same approach whichever type of local ecosystem you study.

Figure 6

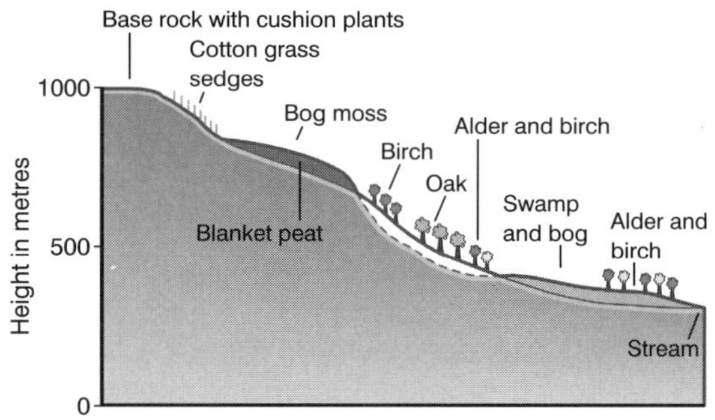

A hillside in western Scotland

Task

A hillside in western Scotland shows the relationships between different parts of the ecosystem.

Study Figure 6 and use the list of words below to complete the following sentences. Some words need to be used more than once.

(a) Peat and bog are found where water accumulates. This is where the ____________ is gentle.

(b) ____________ is better where the slopes are steeper.

(c) The ____________ changes with increasing altitude.

(d) The thickness of the ____________ varies with the slope and altitude.

(e) The ____________ is thinnest on the highest and steepest land.

(f) Vegetation varies with ____________

(g) The local ____________ changes with altitude.

(h) Temperature differences between the high and low ground affect the pattern of ____________

List of words:

altitude	slope	soil
drainage	vegetation	climate

Sample question 2 (Higher)

a) The United Kingdom's weather is often affected by depressions, or low pressure systems. The weather map in Figure 1 shows one such system.

(i) State:
the location with clear skies;
the wind direction at location B;
the temperature at location C;
the wind speed at location C. [2 marks]

(ii) Compare and contrast the weather at locations A and D. [4 marks]

(iii) Give the weather forecast for location C for the next 24 hours. [4 marks]

Figure 1

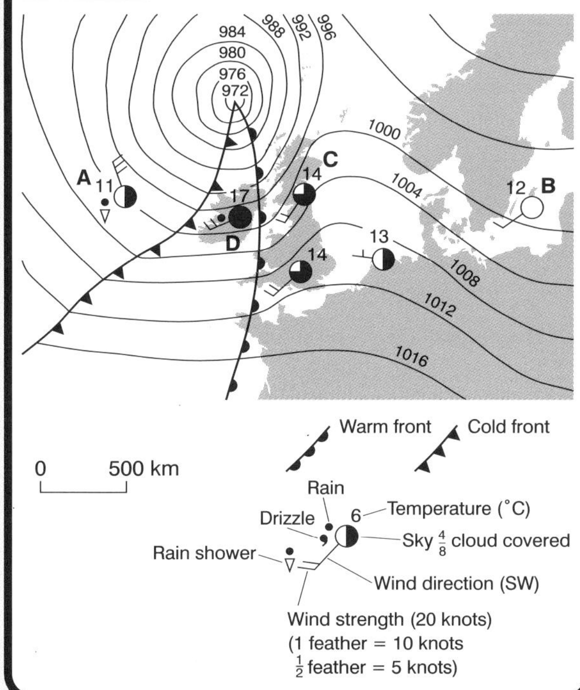

b) The east and south-east of England has been particularly badly affected by water shortages in recent years. Suggest ways by which the problems could be reduced. Refer to examples in your answer. [5 marks]

c) For any weather system you have studied (other than a depression in the United Kingdom):

(i) explain its effect on people and their activities;

(ii) describe measures taken to solve, prevent or reduce any problems caused by the weather system. [8 marks]

Suggested answer

a) **(i)** B; south-west; 14 °C; 10 knots.

(ii) Completely overcast at D but sky half clear at A; steady rain at D but heavy showers at A; considerable temperature difference with A at 11 °C and D at 17 °C; wind WSW, 15 knots at D but NNW at A at 30 knots.

(iii) Temperatures will rise as the warm front approaches and passes over; at the same time cloud cover will increase and it will rain; wind direction will turn more westerly. Later as the cold front crosses temperatures will fall markedly, winds will increase in strength and turn more northerly. Cloud cover will decrease but there will be heavy showers.

b) Transfer water from water surplus areas by pipeline and by river systems. For example, piping water from Wales to the headwaters of the Thames. Make lowland storage reservoirs throughout the region, like the proposal near Abingdon. Emphasise need to conserve water by reducing consumption and reducing water loss through leaks.

c) Name a weather system. For example, a high pressure system stationary over the country for several months.

(i) Describe the effects: drought; high temperatures; pollution problems; ill-health as a result, particularly for some groups like elderly and asthmatic; agricultural problems affecting growing crops, animals and fodder for animals in following winter; water supplies to urban populations; effect on industries which use large amounts of water.

(ii) Measures taken: short-term include rationing water, banning some uses, bringing tankers of water from areas still with surplus, reducing road vehicle pollution where possible; longer-term measures include improvements to water storage and supply, general reduction in vehicle pollution and other forms of pollution; advanced warning systems for pollution emergencies.

Population preview

5

What you need to know

- Distribution of world population
- Factors influencing distribution
- The patterns at different scales
- World population growth
- Demographic transition model
- Birth rates, death rates and natural increase
- Age structure and population pyramids
- Ageing populations
- How population change occurs
- The importance of migrations
- Push and pull factors
- Internal migrations
- Urbanisation
- Inequality
- Indicators of inequality
- Inequality at different scales

Distribution and density

Look through the unit quickly (two to three minutes). Then work through it carefully, one section at a time. At the end of each section make a summary.

Distribution

Population is distributed unevenly throughout the world. The same is true about each continent, each country, each region within a country and even within a city.

Distribution factors

The **pattern of distribution** is affected by a large number of factors (Figure 1). These can be divided into two basic groups.

★ **Positive or attractive factors** make it possible for the area to support greater numbers of people.

★ **Negative or repelling factors** make the area a difficult place in which to settle and live.

Figure 1

Physical factors	Human factors
relief	location of major cities
climate	levels of poverty and wealth
soils	systems of farming
natural vegetation	development and location of industry
resources	migration
	historical factors
	planning policies

Factors affecting population distribution

Figure 2

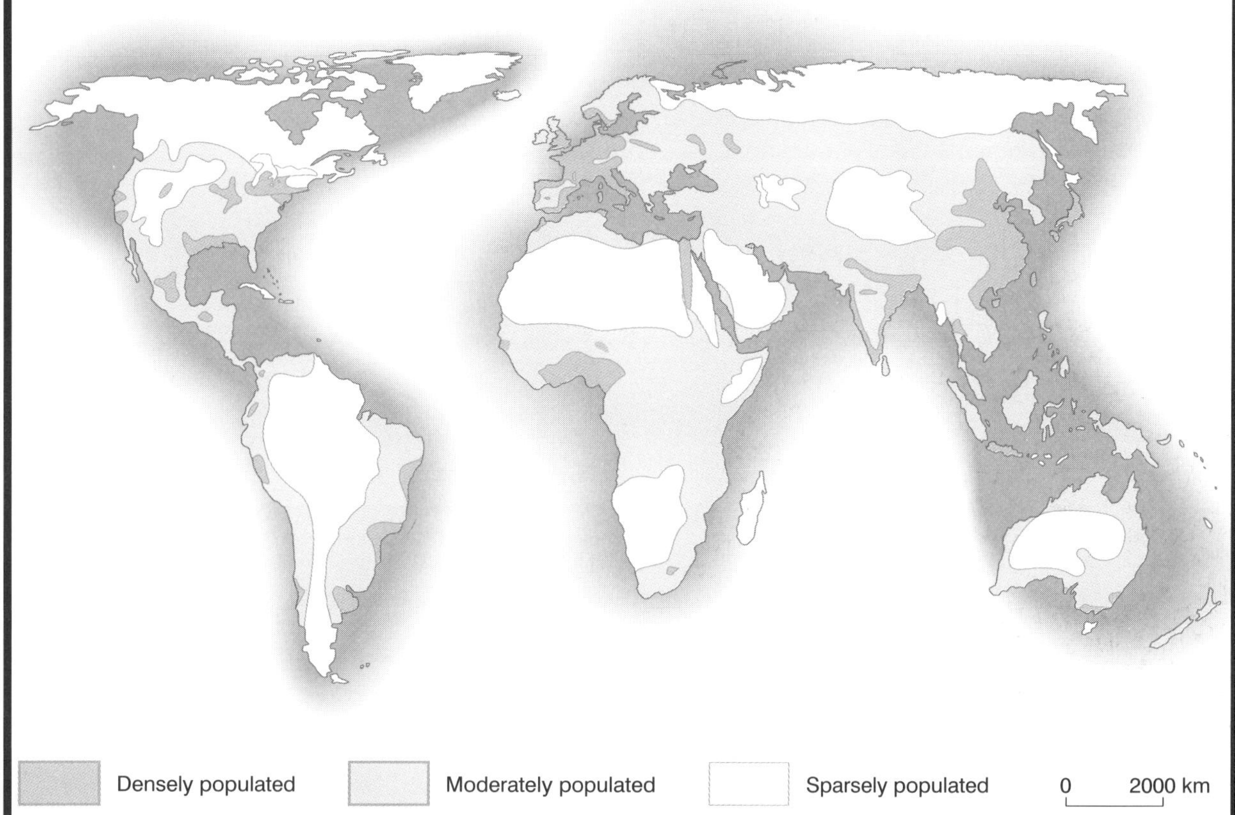

World population distribution

You can see the positive and the negative areas on the world map (Figure 2). The densely populated areas actually have over 70% of the world's population. The major concentrations of population are:

1 South and east Asia

2 Europe

3 North-east USA

4 Lower Nile valley in Egypt

5 West Africa

6 Coastal regions of South America

There are also other smaller concentrations on the map.

Close your eyes and try to visualise millions of people on the areas of the map where they are actually clustered.

Densely populated areas

The **densely populated areas** can support large numbers of people for two basic sets of reasons:

- favourable climate and soils for highly productive agriculture;
- resources from which well-developed manufacturing could grow.

Exceptions are specific countries which have mostly made use of their locations and based their support on trade (e.g. The Netherlands).

Sparsely populated areas

The **sparsely populated areas** are clearly hostile environments. They are:

1 Cold areas of high latitudes and high altitudes.

2 Hot deserts and the temperate deserts.

3 Denser and less accessible tropical rain forests.

In these regions even natural resources, like mineral deposits support only small numbers of people who leave when the resources become exhausted.

Many densely populated regions have major natural hazards, like earthquakes, volcanoes and tropical storms. Large numbers of people live in these regions simply because they have so many other advantages especially for agriculture. The hazards normally do not hit the same places very often.

National-scale population distribution

Figure 3

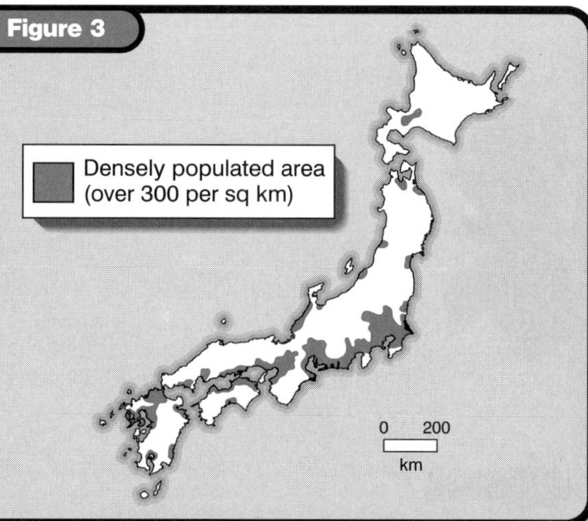

Population distribution in Japan

Case study

Japan

Japan is a good case study of a national-scale population distribution. It shows the application of many of the factors in Figure 1 very clearly.

Japan has more than 120 million people and it is one of the most densely populated countries in the world. However, the population is distributed very unevenly. About 75% of the country is either very sparsely populated or uninhabited. As a result the settled areas have extremely high population densities, usually over 1000 people per square kilometre.

Population distribution

1. The population distribution is largely coastal.
2. The major concentration is in what is called the Pacific Belt. This stretches from Tokyo westwards along the south coast of the island of Honshu as far as the northern end of Kyushu island.
3. Other coastal areas are less densely populated.
4. The north of Honshu and Hokkaido are also less densely populated.

Reasons for the distribution pattern

1. More favourable climatic conditions in the Pacific Belt, with large areas of lowland especially rich alluvial land.
2. Much of the rest of the country is mountainous with a harsher climate, particularly in the north.
3. The Pacific Belt was the original major centre of settlement in Japan. It also had the advantages of rich fishing grounds and the use of the sea for communications.
4. This region is the main concentration of urban, industrial and commercial development. This is the core area of Japan.

Task

(a) Look back at Figure 1. Which of the factors in the lists apply to Japan? Match them to the reasons given for Japan's population distribution.

(b) Summarise the case study in a diagram. Draw a very simplified sketch map of Japan. Use labelled arrows to describe the population distribution and more labelled arrows to explain it.

review

Check that you now can:

- Describe and explain the world and continental patterns
- Use a case study to show how population density varies at a country level and explain the pattern
- Apply your knowledge to different resource material.

Make a Mind Map to summarise all the content of this unit. Add examples of your own, if possible.

Growth and structure

Use your time effectively!

Skim through the unit quickly.

Note the main section headings.

Remember the diagrams and tables.

Jot down the key words or phrases from each section.

Then work through the unit again carefully.

Make a summary Mind Map of the unit when you have finished.

World population growth

Until about 1750 the world's population had been growing steadily but slowly. In 1750 it was about 800 million. By 1900 it was 1700 million and by 1950, 2500 million. It took only to 1990 to reach 5300 million. By the year 2000 it is expected to be about 6000 million.

Figure 4 shows populations, growth rates and other vital rates which affect population change. Study the differences carefully.

Vital rates

- ★ **Birth rates** are written per thousand (‰), so a birth rate of 26‰ for Asia means that there are 26 births for every 1000 people in the population.
- ★ **Death rates** are the same, so Asia's rate is 9‰.
- ★ **Natural increase** is written as a percentage, so for Asia it is 1.8%. It is actually the difference between birth and death rates but expressed as a percentage.
- ★ **Infant mortality** measures the death rate of children under the age of five. It is used as a good measure of general health levels.

Task 1

(a) Which regions have a high natural increase (or growth rates) and which ones have low growth rates?

Figure 4

Region	Population (millions)	Birth rate (‰)	Death rate (‰)	Natural increase (%)	Infant mortality (‰)
World	5420	26	9	1.7	68
Africa	654	43	14	3.0	99
Asia	3207	26	9	1.8	68
Europe	511	12	10	0.2	11
Former USSR	284	17	10	0.7	39
Oceania	28	20	8	1.2	33
North America	283	16	8	0.8	9
Latin America	453	28	7	2.1	54

Population change by major world region

Figure 5

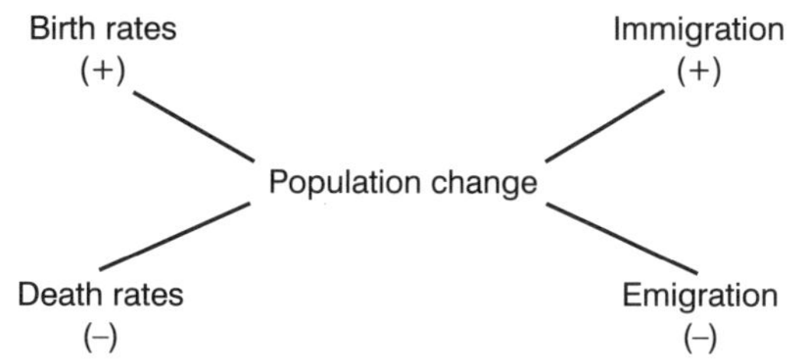

Population change model

Figure 6

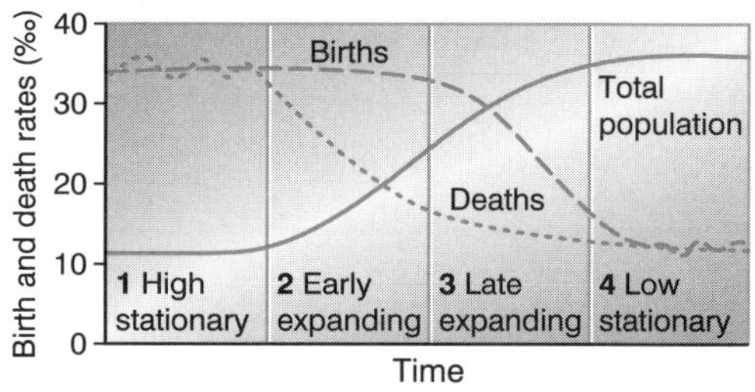

Demographic transition model

(b) What does natural increase mean? 3% will double the population in 24 years, 2% in 35 years and 1% in 70 years.

Remember

Natural increase is only one part of change. Migration also affects the size of population (Figure 5).

The demographic transition model

Changes in the rate of growth of a country's population depend on changes in birth rates and death rates. In the industrialised countries of the world changes followed the pattern shown in Figure 6. There are four stages.

Stage 1. The population grew slowly. Birth rates and death rates were high.

Stage 2. The industrial revolution and economic growth brought a fall in death rates. The rate of natural increase grew and grew giving rapid population growth.

Stage 3. Eventually the birth rate began to fall and the death rate began to level out so the rate of growth gradually decreased. The population kept on growing but more and more slowly.

Stage 4. Birth rates and death rates reached similar, but low levels, giving slow or no growth.

The original fall in death rates accompanied better diet, improvements in public health and control of diseases. The fall in birth rate was the result of a combination of:

- the realisation that infant mortality had fallen (infant mortality was the main cause of the high death rates);
- a shift of public opinion in favour of smaller family sizes.

Britain took more than 200 years to go from Stage 1 to Stage 4. Many less developed countries show signs of making this transition much more quickly.

Population structure

Population structure is about the proportions in different age groups. The groups are usually given in five-year bands. They can be shown by **population pyramids** (Figure 7). These graphs normally show each age group, divided into males and females, as a percentage of the total.

Uganda has the pyramid structure typical of a less developed country. Its wide base shows a high birth rate. The rapid narrowing of the pyramid in the next few age groups indicates high infant mortality. As infant mortality rates fall, the large groups will work their way up the age range. The big difference between 10–14 and 15–19 suggests that childhood deaths have already come down.

The UK's population pyramid has a different shape. There is very little difference between age groups, so it is almost rectangular. The narrowing at the top shows that there are relatively few deaths until old age.

Figure 7

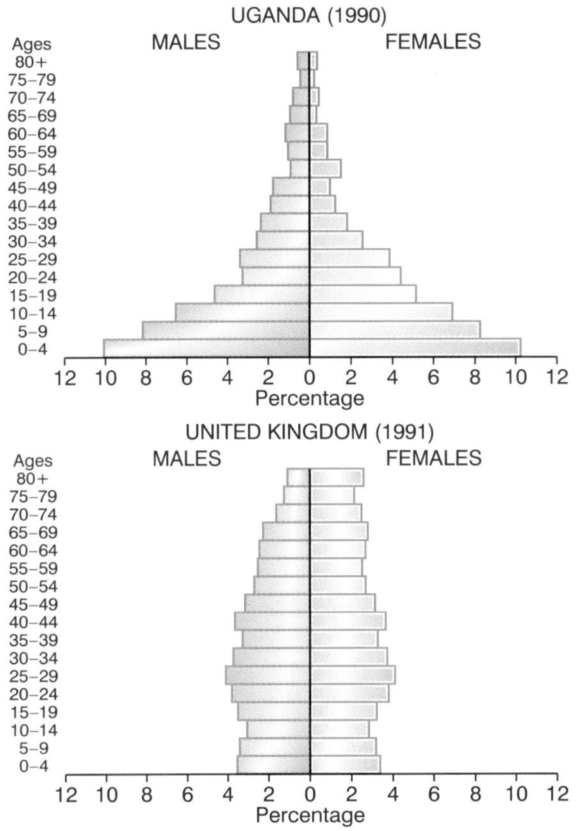

Population pyramids – Uganda and UK

Differences between the two population structures are:

- Uganda has a large proportion of its population in the under 15 group (49%).
- The UK has a much smaller proportion of under 15s (19%).
- Amongst the over 65s, Uganda has a small over 65 group with just 2% of the total population.
- But the UK has 16% over 65.

The effects of different population structures

The proportions in different age groups is important.

The very young population of Uganda places demands on services. Food production, provision of schools and health facilities are immediate needs. In the future there will be a greater demand for jobs.

In the UK the large proportion in the older age groups puts greater pressure on health and care services, and special accommodation for the elderly.

The two groups, old and young, are the **dependent population**. Remember that the British dependent population is really larger than just under 15s and over 65s because:

- everyone up to 16 is in full-time education, and also a large proportion of the 16 to 21 group is in full-time further education;
- most people over 60 are retired.

A large dependent population has only a small working population to provide the wealth needed to support it.

Ageing populations

In less developed countries over 65s make up 4% of the population but they are increasing rapidly. In the more developed world the figure is 12% and still growing.

review

Check that you now know how to interpret and use:

- Facts about population size, growth and structure
- Ideas about the significance of changes
- Examples to apply in examinations.

Make a review Mind Map of this unit; it will take some time working through.

Add examples as reminders of key points.

5

Migration and change

Population change occurs partly due to immigration and emigration (*see* Figure 5).

Migrations

In recent history the biggest migrations have been:

1 The forced migration of millions of slaves from Africa to North and South America.

2 The European colonisation of North America, South America, Australia and New Zealand.

Many other migrations have occurred, including:

1 Movements of millions of people in Europe at the end of the Second World War.

2 Workers from southern Europe and North Africa to the main industrial regions of Europe.

3 Highly qualified people moving between jobs in different parts of the more developed world.

4 Movements of refugees to escape conflicts.

Migration occurs for many reasons. Figure 8 summarises them under two headings: push factors (the reasons why people leave) and pull factors (the reasons they go to particular places).

Migration is not only international. Internal migration within countries involves large numbers.

Figure 8

Push factors	Pull factors
Poverty	Freedom
Political persecution	Higher living standards
Religious persecution	Employment prospects
Natural disaster	Available land
Poor prospects	

Push and pull factors

Figure 9

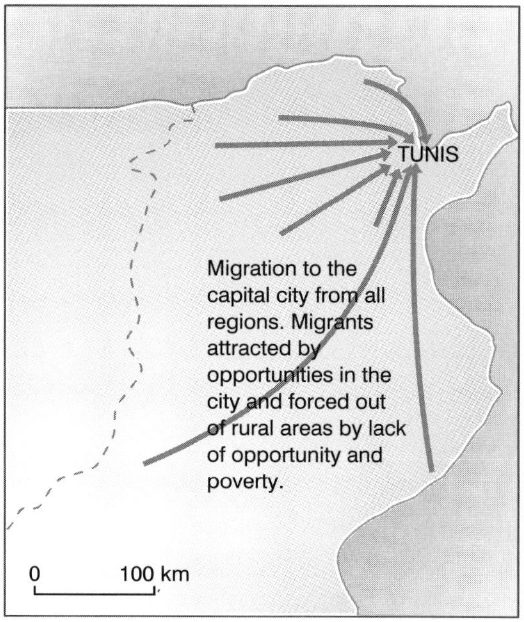

TUNIS
Migration to the capital city from all regions. Migrants attracted by opportunities in the city and forced out of rural areas by lack of opportunity and poverty.
0
100 km

Migrations within countries: Tunisia

Some of the kinds of migration which are important within countries are:

- rural to urban movement
- movement to more prosperous regions
- movements out of large cities in more developed countries.

Urbanisation

The term **urbanisation** is defined in two ways:

- the percentage of the population living in urban areas;
- the study of the actual growth of towns and cities.

This section concerns the first definition of the word.

Rural to urban migration is very important to the growing percentage of the world's population living in cities.

The more developed countries are already highly urbanised.

In less developed countries it is a process which is going on rapidly. Figure 10 illustrates this.

Figure 10

Percentage living in urban areas

	1960	1980	1990
Canada	70	76	78
Zaire	14	30	40
World	33	41	43
More developed	60	70	73
Less developed	21	25	37

Urbanisation levels

Why do people migrate from the countryide to the cities? Figure 11 is another push–pull list.

Migration to the cities changes the population structure. Migrants are more likely to be younger than older adults. As a result they are more likely to be raising families. Even though birth rates are actually lower in the cities, the way the population structure is weighted more than makes up for this. So the cities grow by migration and by natural growth.

Overall, it is big cities which are growing most dramatically. 'Million cities' grew in number from only 24 in 1920 to 200 in 1980. In 1920 most were in more developed countries, but by 1980 most were in less developed countries. Notice that on the world population map on page 72 most of the largest cities in the world shown are also in less developed countries.

Figure 11

Push	Pull
Lack of land	Work opportunities
Land degradation	Higher incomes
Unequal land distribution	Bright lights
Droughts	Joining other people from their village
Storms	Freer lifestyles
Water shortage	Better health care
Lack of opportunities	Better education for children

Push–pull and the cities

review

Check that you now know:

- How population change occurs
- The importance of migrations through history
- Push and pull factors
- Factors affecting internal migrations
- What is urbanisation?

Make sure that you summarise these and review them regularly.

Inequalities

Inequality is to do with wealth and quality of life. There are many different measures used to deal with inequality. Wealth is often used by itself.

GNP

Gross National Product (GNP) per person is usually used to measure inequality. It is the total value of all the goods and services produced by a country divided by the population. For example, the GNP per person of the USA is 67 times that of India.

There are problems with using GNP:

- it does not include cash deals which are not recorded (the black economy);
- it does not take account of the difference in the cost of living between countries;
- it does not allow for other differences, like heating costs in cold countries, which raise their GNP;
- GNP is an average figure, it does not tell you how the wealth is distributed so 5% of the population could have 90% of the wealth.

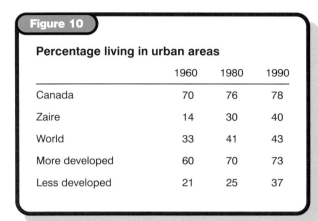

Figure 12

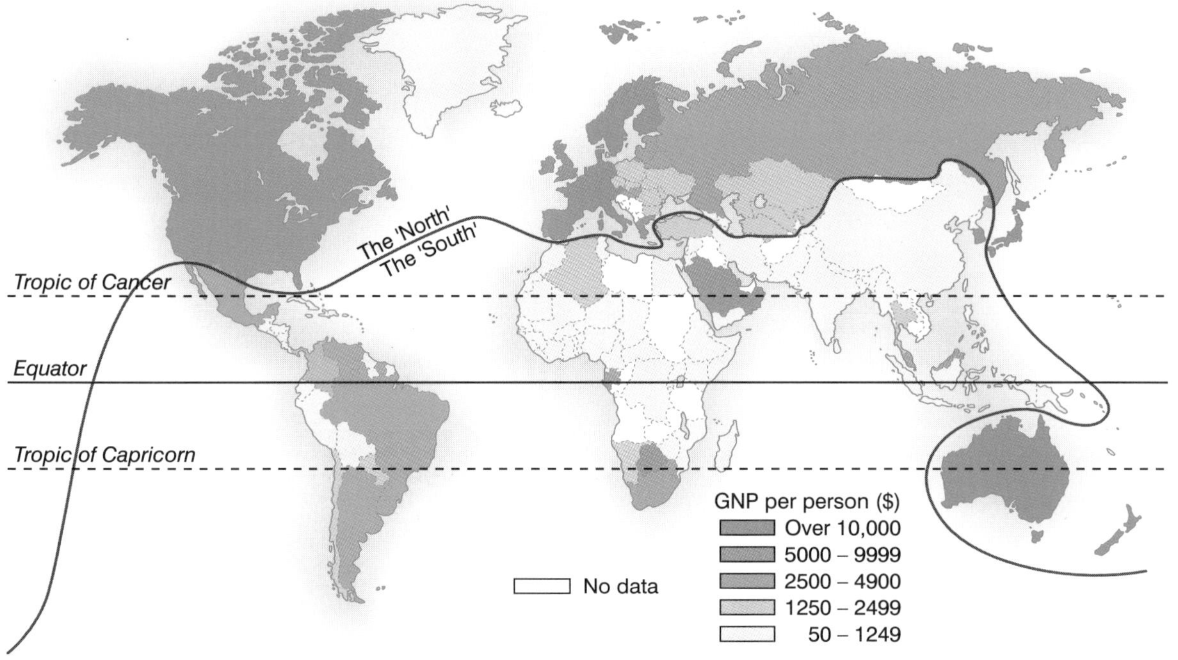

World inequalities (GNP per person)

Figure 13

Wealthier countries	Poorer countries
North	South
More economically developed	Less economically developed
More developed	Less developed (and least developed)
Developed	Third World
	Developing

World inequalities – different names

Indicators of development

Apart from GNP there is a wide range of indicators which are used to examine inequality (Figure 15). They are often called **indicators of development**. Taken together you get a more reliable picture than by just using GNP.

Infant mortality by itself makes a good indicator. Another index called the Human Development Index uses it with levels of education and health. It also uses incomes but only up to a certain point.

Less developed countries or the South (Figure 12) include a great variety of income levels. This is why there is a distinction made between the middle income and the low-income countries (the latter are also called the least developed countries).

There is also a small group of **newly industrialised countries**, which should not be counted as less developed any more. It includes Hong Kong, Singapore, Taiwan and South Korea.

Figure 14

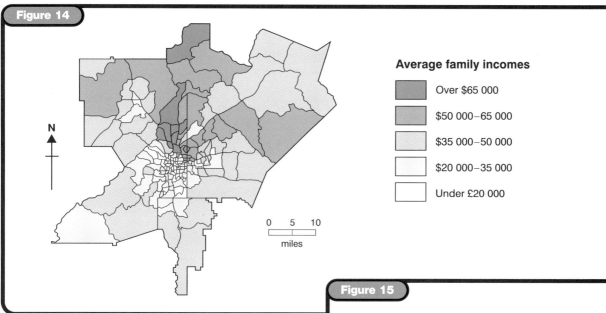

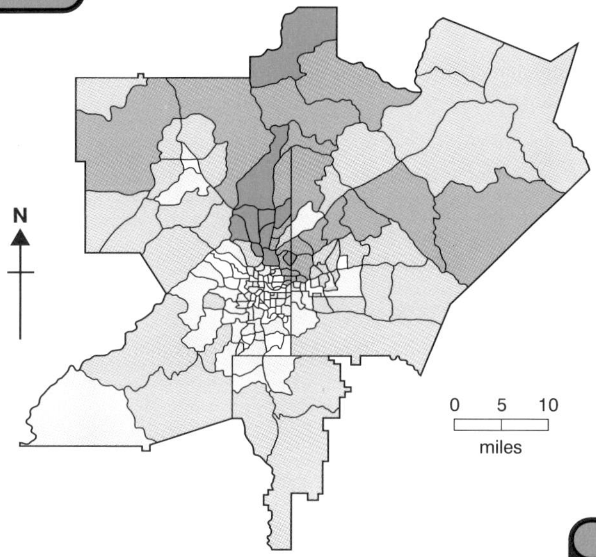

City-scale inequalities – Atlanta, USA

Task

Look at Figure 14.

1 What measure is used to indicate inequalities?
2 Identify and mark the areas of highest and lowest incomes.
3 Is the measure used better than GNP? Why?
4 What other measures could be used in the cases of Figure 14?
5 Look at Figure 15. It shows a very wide range of indicators of development. Think about what the figures mean. By the side of each number write the letter H or L, according to whether it means a high or low level of development.

review

This unit looked at measures for judging inequality. Inequalities affect the quality of life.

Think about the minimum that all people should expect. What are the best measures for checking that the standards you set are reached? Summarise your conclusions in a table or a Mind Map.

Figure 15

Indicator	UK	Indonesia	Ethiopia
Populations growth (%)	0.4	1.7	3.0
Birth rate (‰)	13.4	27.4	43.7
Death rate (‰)	8.8	11.2	23.6
Infant mortality (‰)	9.0	84.0	153.0
Life expectancy (years M/F)	72/78	55/57	39/43
Doctors per million	1615	95	11
Calories per day	3257	2513	–
Urbanisation (%)	89	31	12
GNP per person ($)	14 570	490	120
% working in agriculture	2.1	50	75
Illiteracy rate (%)	–	18	76
Attendance at secondary school (%)	100	46	15
Energy consumption (kilos per head/coal equivalent)	5107	274	28
Telephones per 100 people	49	0.9	0.2
% under 15 years	19	35	45

Indicators of development

Settlement

6

preview

What you need to know

- Types of settlements
- Sites of settlements
- Locations of settlements
- The pattern and hierarchy of settlements
- Changes in urban areas
- Changes in rural areas

Types and patterns

Settlements are places where people live. They range in size from the single farm to the megacity. Settlement size can be measured by population or by area of land.

Classifying or describing settlements

There are different ways of describing settlements.

★ **Rural or urban**. This divides cities and towns from villages, hamlets and single dwellings.

★ **Functions**. For example, towns may be called industrial towns, university towns, dormitory towns or holiday resorts.

★ **Location**. Features such as route centre or lowest bridging point on a major river.

★ **Nucleated and dispersed**. These describe patterns of rural settlement. Nucleated means the settlements are made up of clusters of buildings. Dispersed means a scatter of single dwellings, usually isolated farms.

Types of settlement

The names used for settlements vary. In some countries a place with only a few hundred people may be called a city. The set of names below is useful in geography:

Farmstead separate farm or other building

Hamlet small cluster of houses and farms; few or no services

Village larger cluster, but with a range of services

Town urban settlement, provides a wide range of services for the surrounding area and has some industry

City larger urban settlement with a very wide range of services and more industry: it serves a region covering a large population and including many smaller towns

Metropolis this may be the capital city with the greatest range and number of services and other functions (Larger countries may have several places which can be classed as a metropolis)

Conurbation a large urban area formed by the growth of a major city, swamping surrounding smaller settlements

Megalopolis where major cities, perhaps including the metropolis, grow so that they merge into one super city.

Settlement sites, locations and patterns

Sites and **locations** help to explain why a settlement developed in a particular place. For modern large cities the original site might no longer be important at all. In fact, it might even cause problems. For example, a site that could be defended easily in the Middle Ages nowadays is likely to cause traffic bottlenecks.

Rural settlements

Original **sites** needed water supply but also needed to avoid flooding. Other resources needed would have been arable land, grazing land and woodland. Nearly all villages were established well before the Norman Conquest. So you have to look in the past to find the reasons for their sites.

Task 1

Look at the Ordnance Survey map extract on page 82.

Find and locate (that means give the grid reference and/or a description) an example of each of these:

nucleated settlement; dispersed settlement; village at the foot of a hill; a settlement on the edge of a wet area.

Patterns can be divided into nucleated and dispersed. Figure 1 gives some labelled examples of different rural settlement sites and patterns.

The pattern can also be described according to its **density** and the **spacing** of settlements. The greater the density the closer together the settlements area.

Figure 1

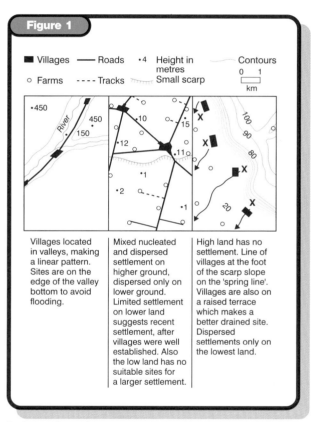

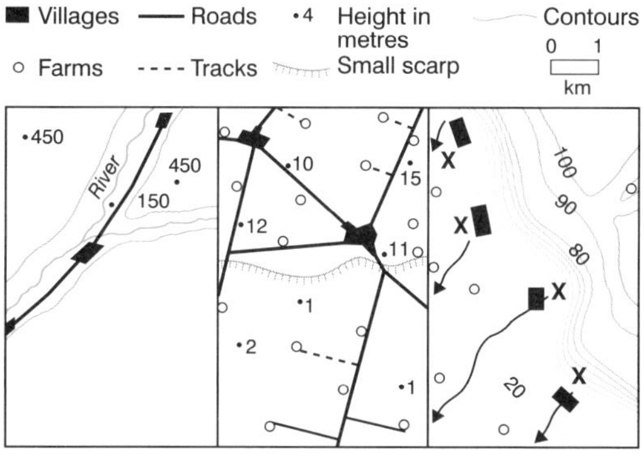

Villages located in valleys, making a linear pattern. Sites are on the edge of the valley bottom to avoid flooding.	Mixed nucleated and dispersed settlement on higher ground, dispersed only on lower ground. Limited settlement on lower land suggests recent settlement, after villages were well established. Also the low land has no suitable sites for a larger settlement.	High land has no settlement. Line of villages at the foot of the scarp slope on the 'spring line'. Villages are also on a raised terrace which makes a better drained site. Dispersed settlements only on the lowest land.

Settlement sites and patterns

Urban settlements

Location means the position of the settlement in relation to the surrounding area and settlements. Figure 2 gives examples. The locations gave those settlements advantages because they became more **central** and more **accessible**. These places grew into towns and cities.

Task 2

How did its location help Church Stretton on the OS map extract (page 82) to grow? Look at Figure 2.

Figure 2

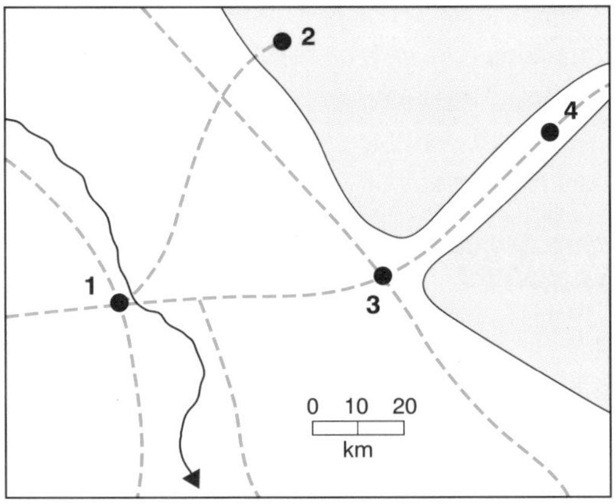

1 City at bridging point on a major river. Focus of routes centring on the crossing point. Major regional centre status developed from its location as a route centre.

2 Town developed only because mineral resources were found there. Its location makes it isolated.

3 Major town where routeways along the foot of the mountains meets routes from the city and through the high land.

4 Small town which is a local centre on the main route through the mountains.

Settlement locations

Figure 3

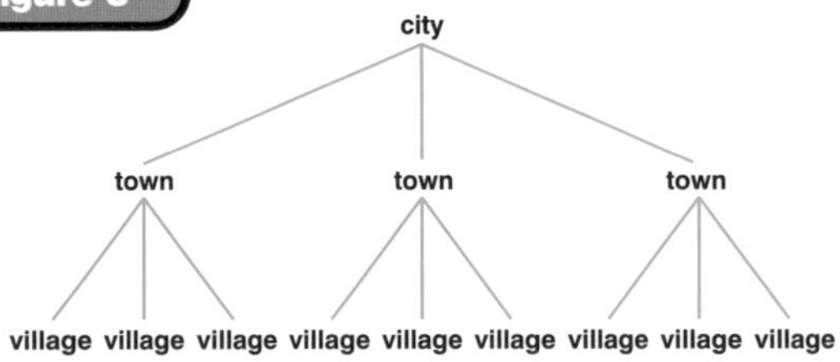

Why is it possible today for a very specialised business, which needs to draw people from a very large area, to be found in a village?

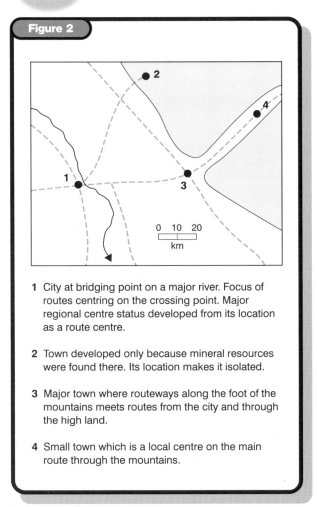

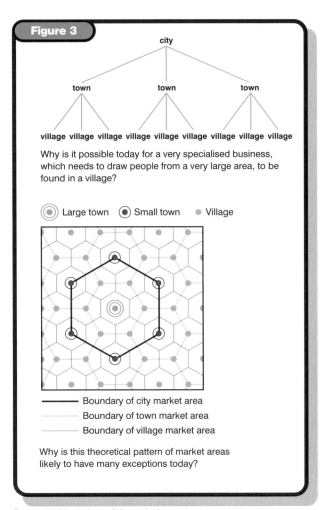

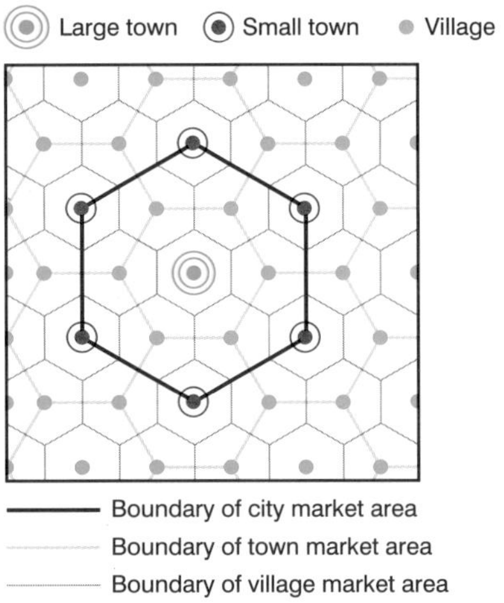

Why is this theoretical pattern of market areas likely to have many exceptions today?

Settlement hierarchy and theoretical pattern

Settlement hierarchies

The whole system of settlements ranging from the largest and most imporant down to the smallest is called the **settlement hierarchy**.

The importance of a settlement is linked to its size and, in particular, its **range of functions**. Functions usually refers to services but also includes industry and transport.

The most important settlement is at the top with a wide range of functions. It serves the whole region; this is where regional offices of government and major banks and insurance companies are located; it is where the regional university is located and the major hospitals, as well as the largest shopping centres.

At the bottom of the hierarchy are the villages. There are many of them. They are small with a very tiny range of functions, serving only the immediate district.

The towns come above villages but they have a very much greater range of functions than the villages. A village might have 6 to 10 functions but a small town would have 60 to 100.

The following ideas are important to understanding settlement hierarchies.

★ **Order of services or goods**. Low-order services or goods are ones people are not prepared to travel far to obtain; they are also called convenience goods (e.g. food). Where a comparison is involved or where it is a specialist service it is called a high-order service or comparison goods and services.

★ **Sphere of influence**. This is the area from which people travel to use the services of a particular settlement.

★ **Threshold**. This is the number of customers needed to make a business viable. If the sphere of influence of a place is not great enough there will be too few customers or clients for some kinds of business.

Figure 4

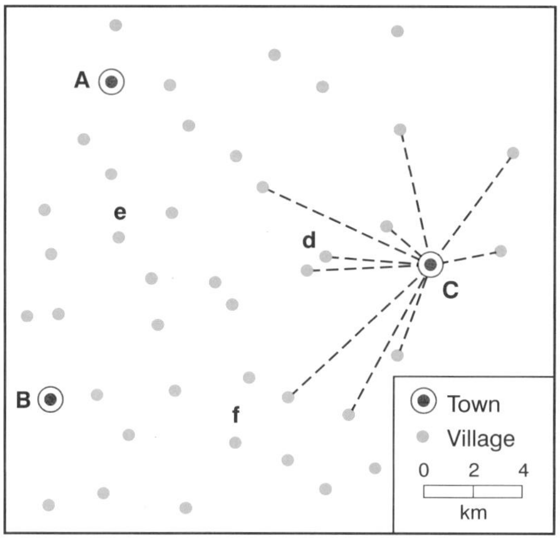

Sphere of influence mapped from survey results of question asking where people shopped last

Towns and villages identified by plotting functions on a scattergram.

<table>
<tr><th>Settlement \ Function</th><th>Bank</th><th>Supermarket</th><th>Dentist</th><th>Post Office</th><th>General store</th><th>Greengrocer</th><th></th></tr>
<tr><td>A</td><td>|</td><td>|</td><td>|</td><td>|</td><td>|</td><td>|</td><td rowspan="3">Higher order places</td></tr>
<tr><td>B</td><td>|</td><td>|</td><td>|</td><td>|</td><td>|</td><td>|</td></tr>
<tr><td>C</td><td>|</td><td>|</td><td>|</td><td>|</td><td>|</td><td>|</td></tr>
<tr><td>d</td><td>—</td><td>—</td><td>—</td><td>|</td><td>|</td><td>—</td><td rowspan="3">Lower order places</td></tr>
<tr><td>e</td><td>—</td><td>—</td><td>—</td><td>—</td><td>—</td><td>—</td></tr>
<tr><td>f</td><td>—</td><td>—</td><td>—</td><td>|</td><td>|</td><td>|</td></tr>
</table>

| = function is present
— = function is absent

Settlement hierarchy

review

Check that you now know:

- Types of settlements
- Sites of settlements
- Locations of settlements
- The pattern and hierarchy of settlements.

Organise summaries of the material under the four headings. Remember to review regularly. Remember to have examples to quote, so make proper use of your class work.

Changes and trends

In the United Kingdom, and in many other developed countries, urban and rural areas have changed. We are looking at these aspects of change together because they affect each other so much.

Changes in urban areas

1. The large cities and conurbations have lost people.
2. The gains have been in the medium-sized and small towns and cities.
3. Villages which are fairly close to major urban areas have gained people as well.
4. The size of the **commuter zone** is important. With the growth of car ownership more and more people have felt free to move further from their place of work. This has brought many villages within reach of cities.

Changes in rural areas

Jobs

1. There are far fewer jobs in farming and related activities.
2. Alternative work is almost always in towns.
3. In more isolated areas there are still the job losses from farming but no option of travelling to a town to work.
4. Newcomers very often oppose developments that would bring new jobs into the locality.

Housing

1 Many houses formerly tied to farmworkers' jobs have been sold to outsiders who commute to nearby towns and cities.

2 With new housing developments, prices are far too high for local people on low incomes.

Services

1 Newcomers tend to work and shop outside the village so services close down.

2 Fewer young families mean that village schools close.

3 Public transport becomes worse or disappears altogether.

4 Villages become more and more isolated for people without their own transport.

Urban–rural fringe

On the boundaries between urban and rural areas are other changes. The land may look rural at first sight but many land uses are actually urban, providing leisure facilities for the city people, and new sites for large shopping developments.

Exam tip

Many questions on these topics are concerned with people's views and attitudes to changes. You have to put yourself in other people's place and give their views and their reasons. You only give your own opinion and reasons if that is what is wanted. Read the question carefully!

review

Make a Mind Map summarising the following:

- The changes in urban areas that affect the countryside
- The changes affecting rural settlements
- The changes in urban–rural fringe areas

Figure 5

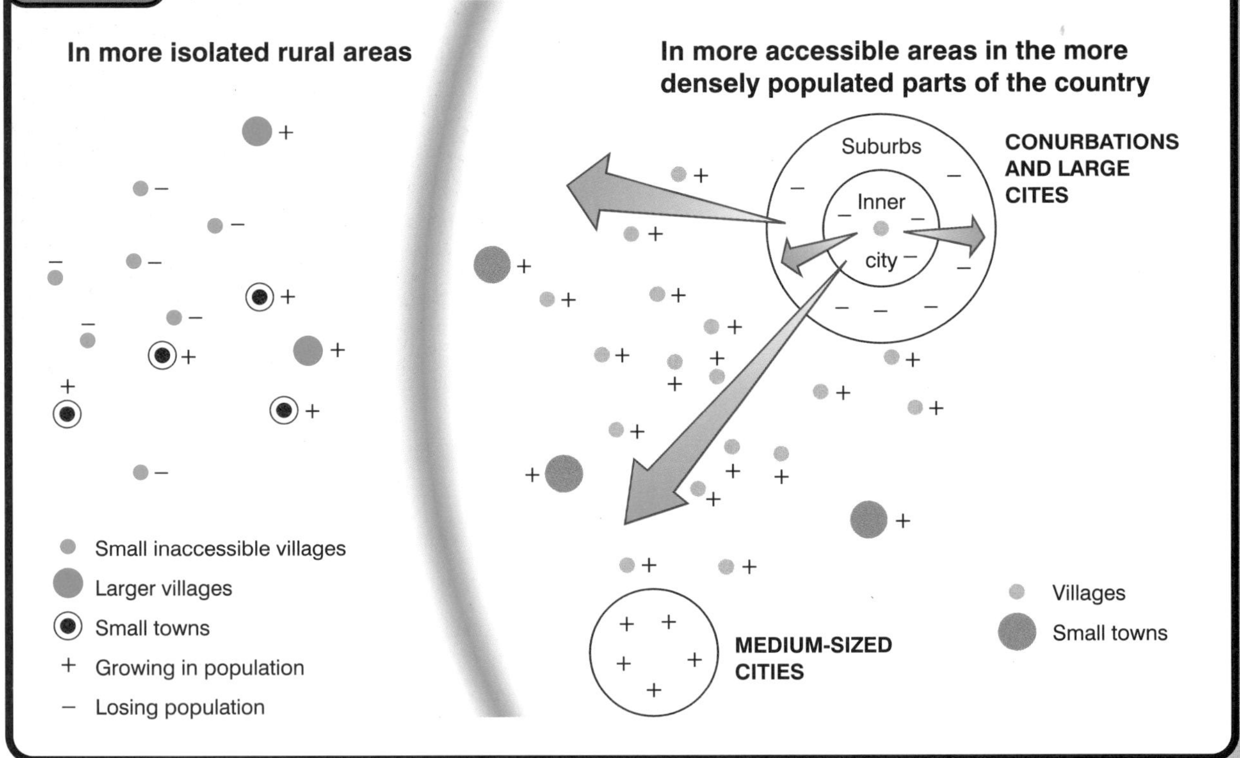

Population changes

7

Towns and Cities

preview

What you need to know

- Growth patterns
- Conurbations
- Local urban growth
- What are functional zones?
- Features of each functional zone
- Patterns of services in cities
- Inner city decline and regeneration
- Changing population patterns
- Inequalities in housing
- Environmental quality
- Planning
- Rates of growth in LDCs
- Shanty towns
- Housing programmes

Urban growth

Growth patterns

Towns and cities have generally grown in a series of concentric rings. Each new stage of growth forms a ring around the earlier one. They are also called **age–growth zones**.

Each zone or stage of growth shows differences in road patterns, building styles and density of buildings and population.

The map (Figure 1) shows the common growth pattern of most British towns and cities.

Age zones

1 City centre

The present city centre or **Central Business District** is usually on the site of the original settlement. But the buildings will be mostly modern.

2 Inner city

The first major phase of growth came in Victorian times, during the 19th century. This was also the first phase of industrial growth. These parts of cities had a mixture of tightly packed **terraced housing** and industry.

This zone was changed dramatically between the 1950s and 1970s by **urban redevelopment** (also called **urban renewal** or **comprehensive redevelopment**). Large areas were cleared and replaced mostly by high-rise tower blocks. The redevelopment did not normally rehouse everyone who had been displaced. This **overspill** population was rehoused on the city edges or in new or expanded towns elsewhere. Industry largely moved from this zone partly due to problems of space and congestion, leaving derelict land. In many such places new housing has been built.

3 Inner suburbs

Most of this zone was built between 1920 and 1939. It has mainly **low-density housing**. These were the **suburbs** and had more spacious street layouts and the houses were largely detached or semi-detached. The growth was made possible by the spread of cheap public transport, like trams, trolley-buses, electric trains and buses. Within the suburbs there were also industrial estates where new industry was concentrated in particular areas.

4 Outer suburbs

Since 1945 towns and cities have continued to grow with a mixture of large private and council-owned estates. Industrial areas also developed on the city edges. Retail and business parks have grown in these locations recently. Greater car ownership and greater emphasis on road transport generally has meant more road development, especially by-passes and ring roads.

5 Commuter ring

Outside the cities themselves are **commuter villages** and towns. Their importance has also increased with greater car ownership.

Green Belts were established around many of the country's largest cities to prevent uncontrolled growth. Under this planning policy building in such areas is controlled. However, throughout the country large areas of Green Belt countryside have been built on during the last 20 to 40 years as the demand for housing has increased faster than its supply.

Test yourself

Study Figure 2. It is a simplified model based on the descriptions on page 65 and this page. You can apply it to any British city. It will not match exactly but the main features will be there.

Part of the labelling has been done. Work through the material and add more details. Be concise but include all the key words. Compare the model with the map of Leicester (Figure 1).

Conurbations

What's a **conurbation**? Look back at page 61 if you can't remember!

Figure 1

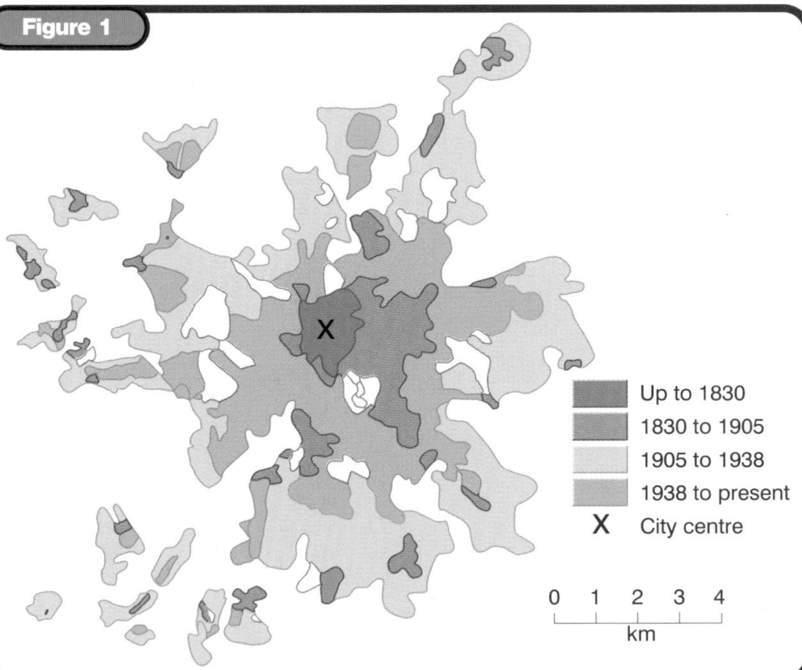

The growth of Leicester

Figure 2

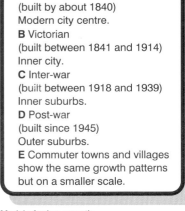

A Pre-Victorian (built by about 1840) Modern city centre.
B Victorian (built between 1841 and 1914) Inner city.
C Inter-war (built between 1918 and 1939) Inner suburbs.
D Post-war (built since 1945) Outer suburbs.
E Commuter towns and villages show the same growth patterns but on a smaller scale.

Model of urban growth

Case study

The Ruhr conurbation in Germany

In many questions you must use a case study in your answer. The Ruhr is useful because you can also use it to answer questions on industry (see page 104).

The Ruhr conurbation, with over 6 million people, was the result of the growing together of more than 20 cities. Dortmund, Bochum, Essen and Duisberg are some of them (*see* Figure 3).

The **growth of the conurbation** was based on heavy industries which developed on a coalfield. These industries and the way the conurbation grew have left two sets of problems:

1 Decline of heavy industries, like coal, steel and heavy chemicals.

2 The unplanned, crowded environment with old problems of land, air and water pollution affecting different parts of the region.

The **industrial problems** have resulted in changes:

- Coal mining has been reorganised with fewer mines and workers.
- Steel making has been concentrated in a few districts, especially along the River Rhine in the west, due to ease of import of raw materials.
- The central area of the conurbation around Bochum and Essen concentrate on steel-using industries, as well as other growth industries, like plastics and consumer products.

The **environmental problems** are being dealt with through changes brought about by the Ruhr Planning Authority. It has:

- Promoted schemes to improve the landscape and general physical environment;
- Developed new towns, housing schemes and leisure parks.

Figure 3

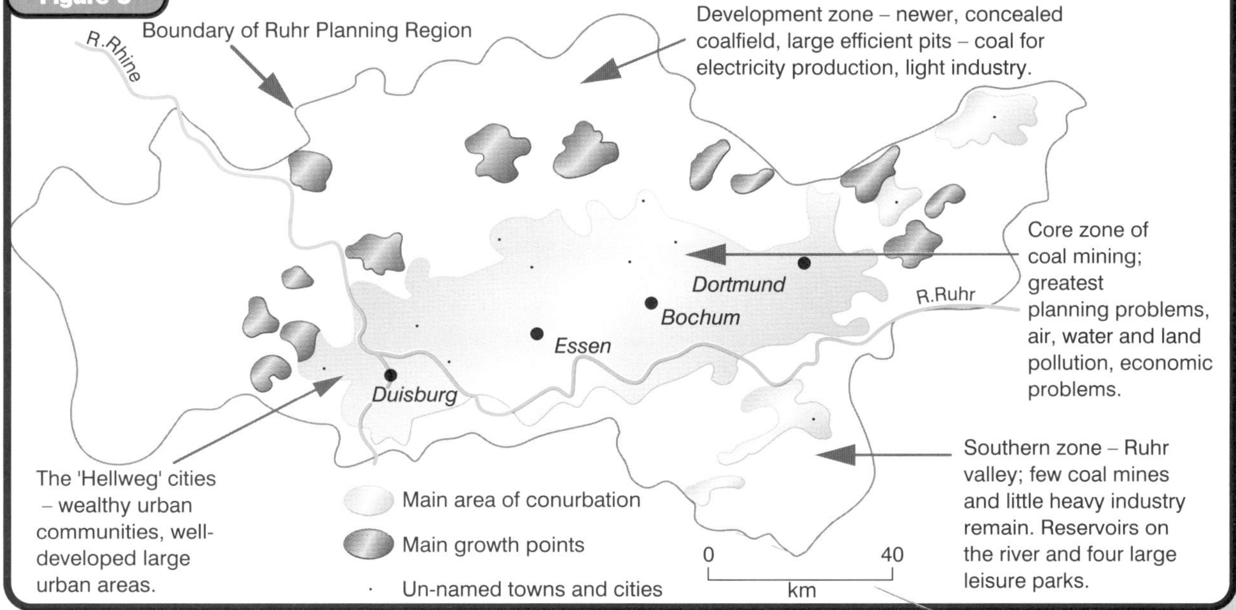
R.Rhine
Boundary of Ruhr Planning Region
Development zone – newer, concealed coalfield, large efficient pits – coal for electricity production, light industry.
Dortmund
Bochum
Essen
Duisburg
R.Ruhr
Core zone of coal mining; greatest planning problems, air, water and land pollution, economic problems.
Southern zone – Ruhr valley; few coal mines and little heavy industry remain. Reservoirs on the river and four large leisure parks.
The 'Hellweg' cities – wealthy urban communities, well-developed large urban areas.
Main area of conurbation
Main growth points
Un-named towns and cities
0
40
km

The Ruhr conurbation

Project idea

Find an example of urban growth in your own locality. Make a sketch map to show the area and the developments. Label it with the information you need to use it as a case study in an examination.

Develop this into a full project by examining:

- the original land use
- the effects of the changes
- the views of local people.

Urban land uses and patterns

Functional zones

Functional zones are areas which have mainly one use or function. Figure 4 shows the typical pattern in a city.

The functional zones are:

★ **Central Business District** or the city centre. The functions found here are shops, offices, public buildings and entertainment businesses. In all but the smallest CBDs the businesses concentrate in specialised zones so one area may be mainly offices while all the major shops are in another area.

★ **Residential areas**. The different types and ages of housing areas were described in the last unit. They contain other functions besides just housing. District and local shopping centres are spread throughout as are schools and other community services.

★ **Industry**. Industrial patterns have changed but industry usually occupies large areas devoted to just that function. Modern industrial areas are often in industrial parks on the city edge.

★ **Services**. The hierarchy of district and local shopping centres has been mentioned. However, large retail parks and superstore developments are also common. They are found on the edge of the city and on many large areas of former open space or reclaimed land elsewhere.

There is a **hierarchy** of shopping centres with the CBD at the top and the local centres or even single shops at the bottom. The **spheres of influence** of the CBD cover the whole city plus a large area beyond. The district centres cover parts of the city while local centres draw customers from the immediate area only.

The new retail parks and superstore developments do not fit into the hierarchy very well. Even where they are built as part of a new housing development they attract customers from a wide area of the city.

Figure 4

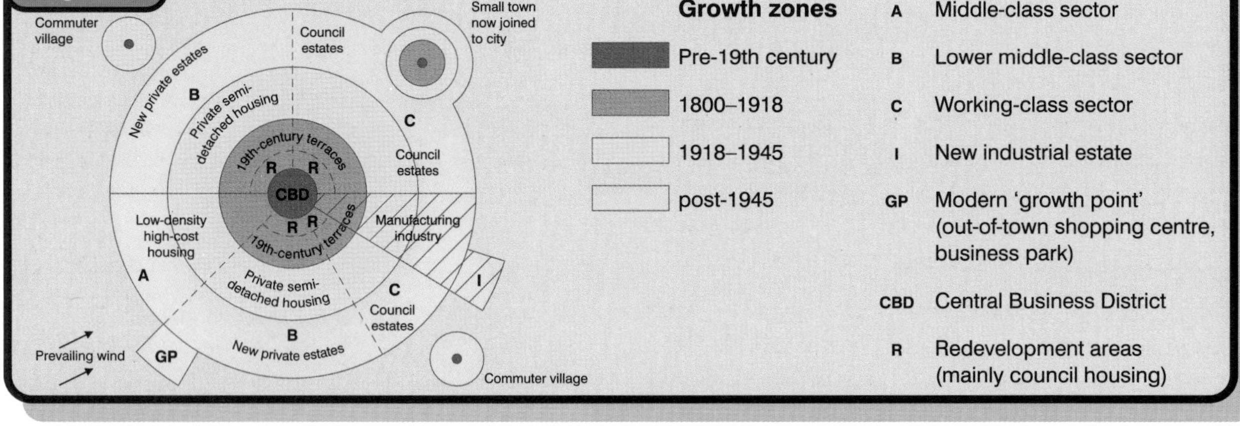

Model of functional zones

Figure 5

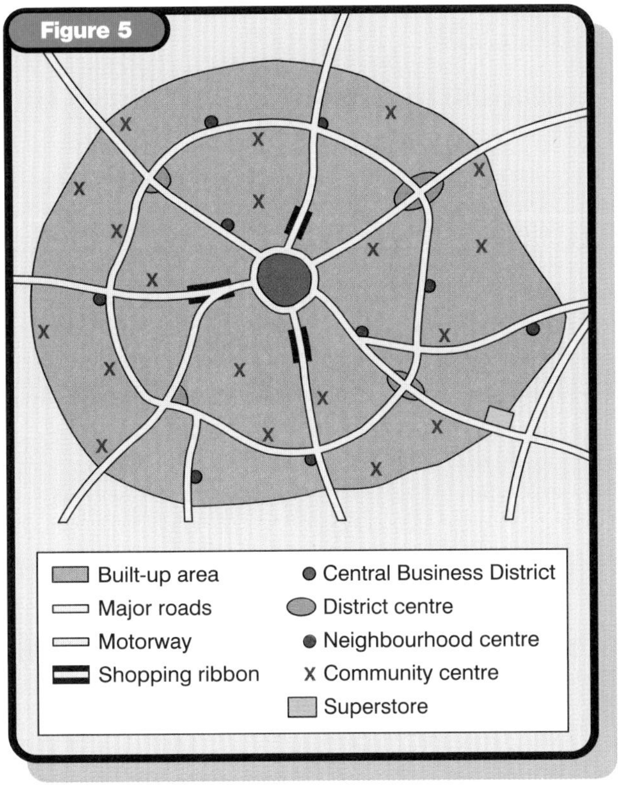

Patterns of shopping centres in a city

The new retail parks and superstore developments do not fit into the hierarchy very well. They are large and draw people away from city centres and from local and district shopping areas. Usually they are in locations which are easily accessible by car so people often travel long distances to them. They sell a wide range of goods and often have entertainment functions like cinemas. Therefore, they compete with the established shopping centre hierarchy rather than being part of it.

Inner city decline

Inner city areas can be the most deprived areas in the country. The features of inner city areas include poor housing, declining industry, low incomes and high unemployment. Redevelopment has affected not only housing but also industry.

Different development programmes have been set up to help regenerate inner city areas, including Inner City Partnerships and Inner City programmes. These involve central government, local government and business. Large-scale schemes have included Urban Development Corporations. Some examples are:

- The Black Country in the West Midlands, where particular problems were derelict land dating back to the last century, poor transport networks and the decline of much metal-working industry.
- In London the Docklands Development Corporation was set up to deal with areas affected by dock closures. The problems included the large areas of water, the former dock buildings, the run-down environment and high unemployment. The solution here has been a high-profile change to the image of the area. The new office developments and highly priced residential accommodation have been criticised by local people because they ignore local needs.

Population patterns

Population patterns within cities are affected by:

- the growth zones and their features
- the changes in these zones.

The general population changes which have affected large cities and surrounding regions are shown on page 64. Five points to remember:

1 The city centre has very few people.

2 The inner city still has a relatively high density of population, in spite of the effects of redevelopment. It does vary, however, and on the whole this zone is still losing population.

3 The suburbs, especially the older suburbs, have a much lower density of population. Even these areas are losing people in big cities.

4 The lower densities in outer areas are partly due to the greater amount of open space.

5 Ethnic minorities tend to cluster in particular areas, especially in the inner city, but this pattern is changing as people establish themselves and move to other areas.

review

All the features of this unit and the last one are linked together. Make a revision plan separating each section. But remember to make use of every section in an examination answer.

Issues and changes

There are very many issues which concern cities and most importantly the people who live in cities. This unit looks at some of these. Many of them overlap with the last two units.

Inequalities

There are big differences in levels of income and quality of environment.

Inner city areas suffer some of the worst problems (*see* previous unit). But some large outer-city council estates have the same low incomes, high unemployment and deteriorating environment.

This pattern occurs in British cities, but similar features can be found elsewhere. Look at the map of Paris (Figure 6) and the map of Atlanta, venue of the 1996 Olympic Games, on page 59.

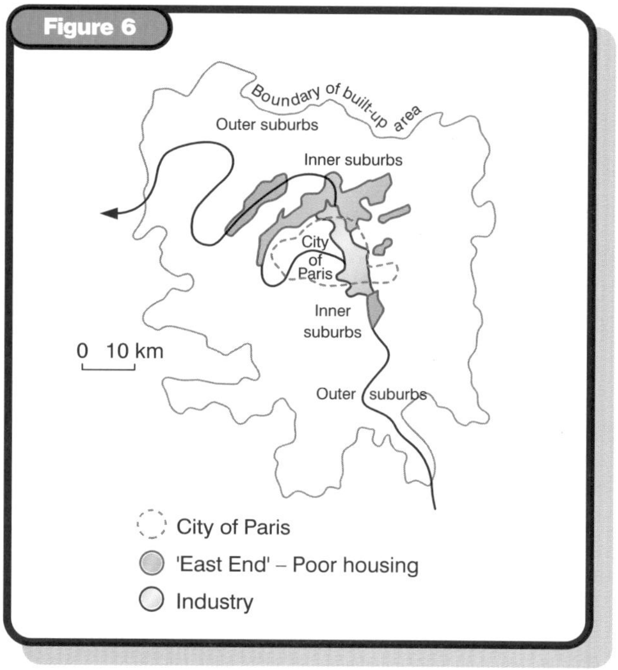

Poor housing in Paris

Planning

New towns

In the United Kingdom, **new towns** were built to reduce congestion and to improve housing and living conditions. The first were built around London after 1945, such as Basildon. Others have been built throughout the country, for example Peterlee, Cwmbran and Milton Keynes. People and industry were encouraged to move to them. Most were based on existing settlements.

Many new planning ideas were developed in the new towns, including:

- pedestrianised shopping centres
- neighbourhood housing areas centred on local shopping, social and educational services
- limiting traffic within residential areas
- separating through roads from local roads
- separating housing and industrial areas.

Other **expanded towns**, like Swindon were based on towns which were already sizeable. They were also built to relieve congestion in major cities and provide housing to meet a growing demand.

Planning in the Paris region

Figure 7 shows the location of new towns around Paris. They were established to relieve congestion and housing problems in the city of Paris.

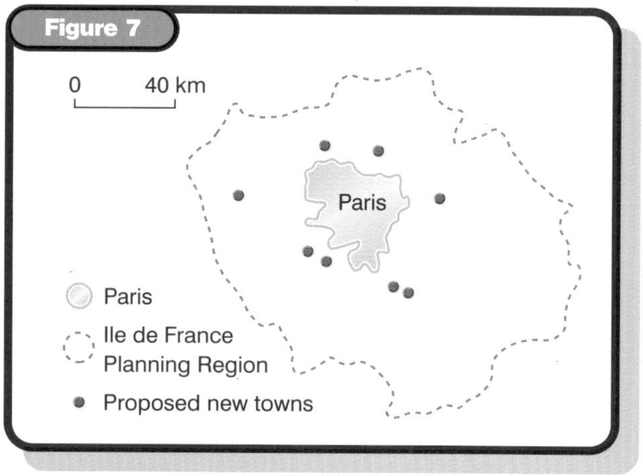

New towns in the Paris region

Figure 8

	Area				
	Islington	Liverpool	Leicester	Solihull	Eastbourne
Population ('000s)	154.8	449.5	272.1	195.7	83.5
Population density per hectare	110.7	40.1	36.9	11.2	18.4
% of pensionable age	15.1	19.0	18.0	17.1	23.0
% born outside UK	25.0	3.4	19.0	4.6	6.6
% male unemployment	17.2	20.8	13.9	7.8	9.6
% households with 2 or more cars	7.2	9.4	12.5	34.3	17.2
% households with 1 or more persons per room	4.8	2.4	3.8	1.5	1.4
% households without bath or shower	0.3	0.4	0.3	0.1	0.2
% households without inside WC	0.1	0.3	0.2	0.1	0.1

Selected census statistics

Inequalities and statistics

Figure 8 shows selected features from different districts in the United Kingdom. These figures are for quite large areas so the worst and the best are hidden.

Task

(a) Study Figure 8 and pencil in W for worst and B for best against the appropriate figures.

(b) Do the figures indicate which areas have more poor housing, more unemployment and are the most crowded?

(c) Which area has the greatest proportion of elderly people? What are the implications for social, welfare and health services?

(d) Which sets of figures could be used as an indicator of wealth?

Exam tip

These are the kinds of figures you could be given in an examination question.

review

This unit overlaps other units, especially the previous two. When you make a summary refer to other related material, like that on inner cities.

Cities in less developed countries

Most of the fastest growing cities in the world are in less developed countries. There are so many 'million' cities now that a map of '10-million' cities is easier to use (Figure 9). The causes for this rapid growth are:

- migration from rural to urban areas
- high birth rates and low death rates.

Features of cities in less developed countries

- very rapid growth
- high densities
- squatter settlements
- modern CBD
- industrial areas
- different class residential areas
- traffic and pollution problems
- housing problems
- employment difficulties.

Figure 9

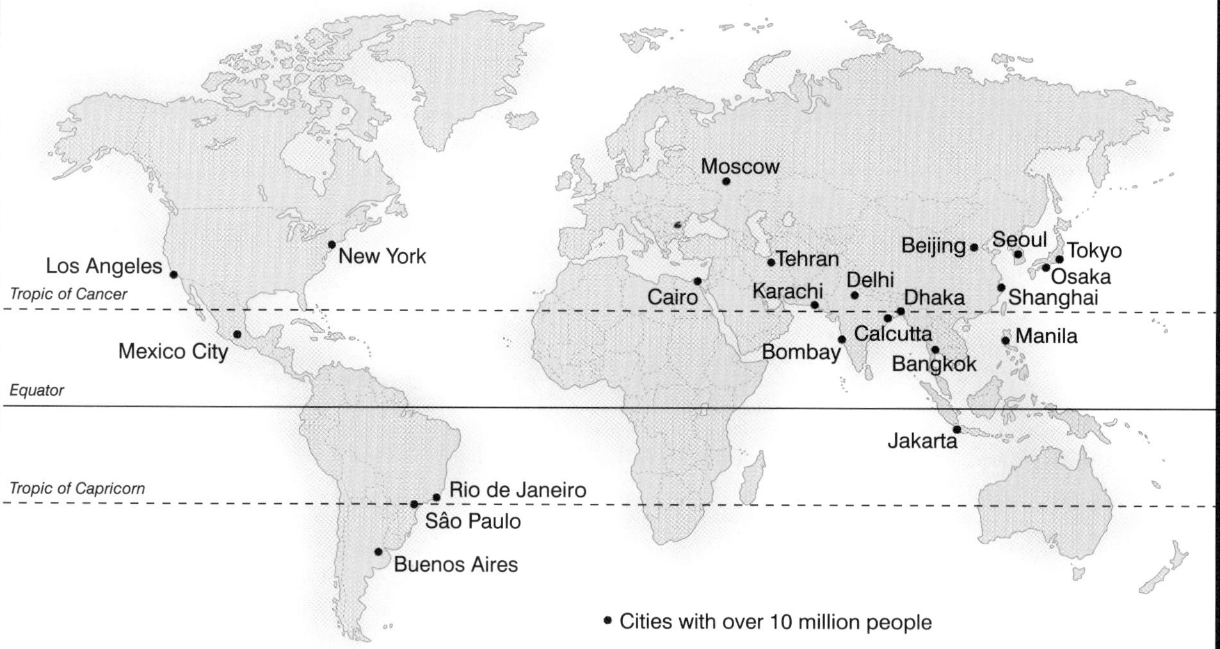

10 million cities in the year 2000

Patterns within the cities

Patterns within the cities vary. All cities have general concentric zones of growth. The CBD in the centre has modern shops and office blocks like any city in the world.

Squatter settlements are found in most areas but are mainly on the outskirts. These squatter settlements are known by different names in different countries, for example bidonvilles (in former French colonies), favelas (Brazil) and barriadas (Colombia).

Case study

Mexico City

This is one of the major cities of the world in size and rate of growth (Figure 10).

Importance of the city

The reason for the rapid growth is **the importance of the city**. It is the centre of government and the centre of economic power as well. The region has always received the greatest share of the country's resources. As a result it has a great deal of industry. A quarter of all workers are in industry, which is very good compared with many cities in less developed countries.

Population growth

Population growth has brought a huge growth in area (Figure 11). It has produced housing and employment problems. A large proportion of homes are without their own water supplies and lack sewerage facilities. As services improve new squatter areas grow, also needing the same facilities.

Apart from industry, most people are in low-paid service jobs, such as, gardeners or domestic servants. The informal sector is especially important. But apart from being low, the income is very unreliable.

Inequalities

There are great **inequalities**. The majority receive less than the official minimum wage. This shows itself in the pattern of housing areas.

The small wealthy part of the population occupies a small part of the city in the south-west (Figure 12). Most of the city is covered by low-income housing:

1. Flats which have been divided up to accommodate more people;
2. Large squatter settlements or colonias;
3. Government housing schemes. These were only available to families with a certain income level and at least a third of the population are too poor to qualify for this housing.

Figure 12 shows a complicated pattern. But you can pick out the pattern of inequality:

1. The poor are concentrated in the north and extreme east.
2. The poor are found everywhere around the edge of the city.
3. The rich are concentrated in the south-west.
4. The small middle-income area is next to the high-income areas and also occupies only a small area.

Environmental problems

The city has several **environmental problems**, including:

1. water supply problems;
2. surface subsidence in the city centre caused by over-pumping of water from aquifers (water-bearing rocks);
3. earthquake risk, made worse by building on the soft deposits of the former lake bed;
4. air pollution, caused by the great concentration of industrial and traffic emissions in a city surrounded by high mountains. Air pollution is trapped by the ring of mountains and the temperature inversion which develops.

Figure 10

Year	Population
1900	370 000
1930	1 000 000
1960	5 000 000
1970	8 500 000
1995	16 000 000

The growth of Mexico City

Figure 11

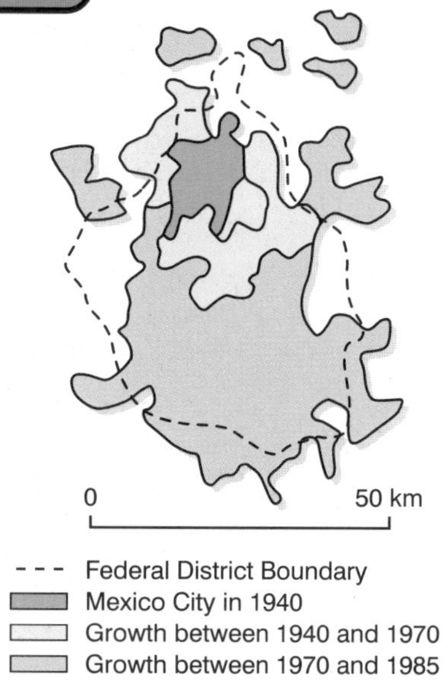

The growing area of Mexico City

Figure 12

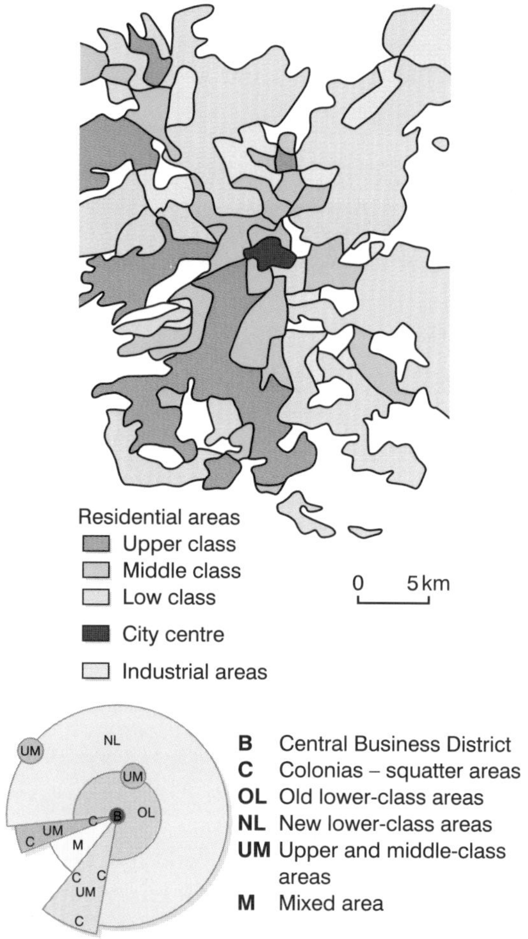

Pattern of land use in Mexico City

Test yourself

1 Make a large copy of the inset model in Figure 12.

Add labelling to it. Cover these points about Mexico City:

- population growth
- area growth
- employment and wages
- housing
- inequalities.

2 Make two Mind Maps reviewing the similarities and differences between cities in more developed and less developed countries. Take some time over this; you will have to look back over the last three units as well as this one. Allow at least 30 minutes to list:

(a) similarities between cities in less and more developed countries;

(b) differences between them.

review

Check that you now know the general features of cities in less developed countries, and how to use Mexico City as a case study.

Remember to do an extra review.

8

Transport

preview

What you need to know

- Factors affecting the choice of routes
- Features of different kinds of networks
- Types of journeys
- The importance of distance
- Types of transport
- Their advantages and disadvantages
- Problems associated with them
- Why urban areas suffer from traffic congestion
- What problems this causes
- Measures to deal with problems

Routes, networks and journeys

Routes

'Route' has two meanings:

1. The line followed by a road, railway line, ship or aircraft.
2. The path followed by an individual or a vehicle on a journey.

In both cases there are factors which affect the choice of a route.

1. Individual routes take a **straight line** unless forced to deviate.
2. Obstacles or difficulties make routes take an avoiding detour. This is a **negative deviation**.
3. Attractions also cause routes to take a detour, but towards the feature. This is a **positive deviation**.

Networks

A **network** is made up of a series of route links joining a number of places. They vary in complexity or completeness (Figure 2).

Figure 1

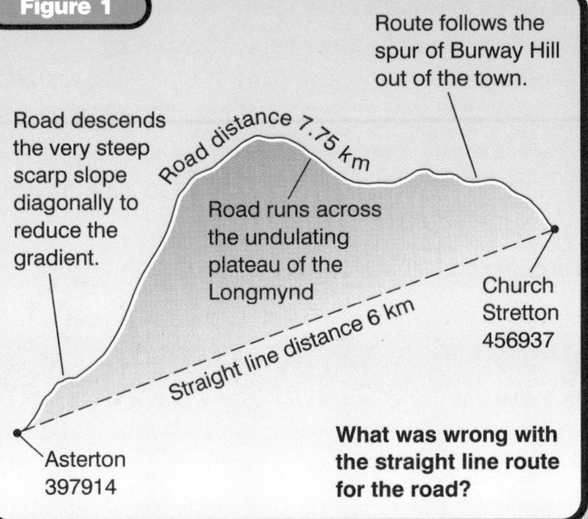
Route follows the spur of Burway Hill out of the town.
Road descends the very steep scarp slope diagonally to reduce the gradient.
Road distance 7.75 km
Road runs across the undulating plateau of the Longmynd
Church Stretton 456937
Straight line distance 6 km
Asterton 397914
What was wrong with the straight line route for the road?

Route across the Longmynd (*see* OS map extract, page 82)

Figure 2

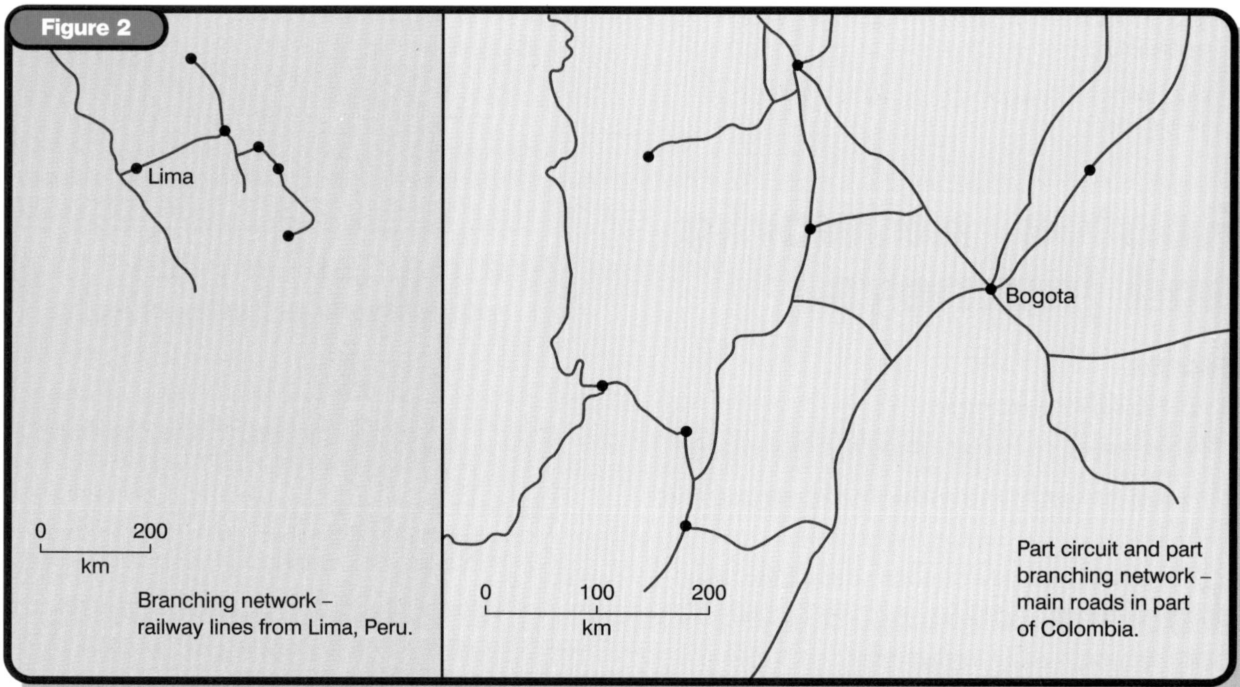

Types of network

More complete networks have more circuits and a higher level of **connectivity**. This means that places are better connected.

The more links there are on a network the more **accessible** individual places become.

Figure 3

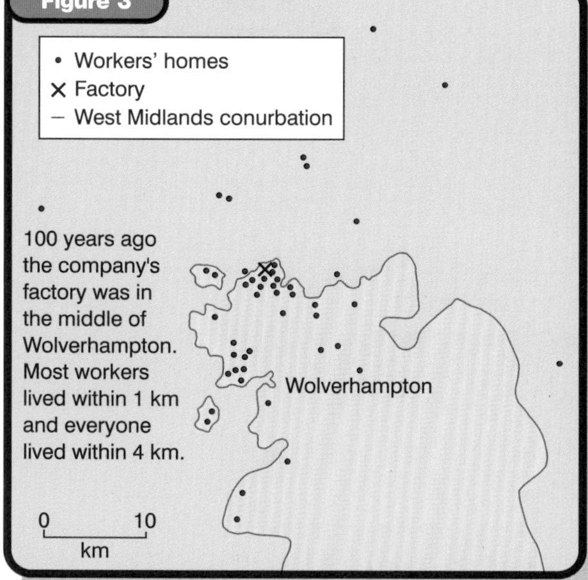

Changing journeys to work

Journeys

Two kinds of frequent journey are particularly important:

- journeys to work (including school!)
- shopping journeys.

Notice that the changes are tied in with changes in locations of industry and other businesses including shopping. Both journeys to work and shopping journeys have been affected by developments such as:

1 Groups of superstores or 'shed shops'.

2 Major 'out-of-town' shopping centres.

3 Leisure facilities on the sites of 1 and 2.

4 Industry and business parks on the edges of cities.

Task

Study Figure 3.

1 Make a list of the changes in journey patterns brought about by the new developments listed above.

2 How are increases in car ownership linked to these developments?

3 What transport network changes might have helped the changes?

review

Remember:

- Route choice is affected by positive and negative factors
- Networks vary in complexity and completeness
- Journey patterns change as a result of changing business locations

Types and growth of transport

Distance

Transport is how we overcome **distance**. But it can be measured differently:

1. Linear distance is measured in kilometres or miles.
2. Time distance is measured in journey time.
3. Cost distance is measured in money terms.

For different purposes each one might be more important.

Task

Match up the most useful distance measures to these.

1. Moving gravel to a construction site from a gravel pit.
2. Planning a day's walking route.
3. Motor parts' supplier delivering to local garages.

Types of transport

Different types of transport have advantages and disadvantages for moving goods or people over different distances.

Water	Large quantities carried at low cost; good for bulky and low value products. Very efficient in energy use. Change of transport needed to take goods on from port.
Rail	Moves large quantities cheaply and quickly; good for bulk products. Efficient in energy use. With most products needs other transport to complete journeys, slowing journey time.
Road	Fast and flexible; good for local delivery of small- to medium-sized products. Causes traffic congestion and major pollution problems especially in cities. New roads generate more traffic as well as using up large amounts of land.
Air	Fast; useful for any goods which are valuable in relation to their weight. Goods (and people) need to be taken on by other means of transport. Major airports tend to cause traffic congestion and to cause major local noise problems.

Airport location

Airport location is something that causes controversy and conflict.

Airports need:

1. Good transport links with centres of population.
2. Access to a large workforce.
3. A large area of generally flat land.

Controversy and conflict occur because of:

1. Loss of farmland, both to the airport and to linked housing, roads and airport services like hotels and catering suppliers.
2. Direct effects on local communities and environment, with noise, demolished homes, construction, increased traffic both short and long term.
3. Wider effects on transport routes.
4. Disagreements between different groups (local and national). Supporters would point to increased employment and the beneficial effects on the local economy. Opponents would focus on the harmful effects.

Route problems

Land routes are also the focus for controversy. The many years of disagreement about the route of a high-speed railway between the Channel Tunnel and London is an excellent example.

Look at other chapters of the book!

There is material to do with transport under Towns and cities, Settlement, Industry and Pollution.

The same applies to other topics. All aspects of geography are linked together.

review

Make a summary Mind Map.

Urban transport and journeys to work

Problems of urban transport

Urban transport has to move goods and people around in areas which are tightly packed with people and buildings in a limited space. The problems of urban transport are concerned with:

- movement
- environment.

Movement

Movement problems are caused by **traffic congestion**, resulting in long delays. The causes of congestion are:

- rising numbers of road vehicles;
- increased numbers of private cars;
- through traffic;
- lack of offroad parking places;
- morning and evening rush-hour traffic peaks;
- mixed traffic types (cars, buses, delivery vehicles);
- roads leading towards the city centre;
- central areas with narrow roads.

Environment

Environmental problems caused by traffic are:

- air pollution;
- noise;
- vibration and building damage;
- accidents and injury to people;
- poor visual environment;
- loss of land and buildings to new road schemes.

Solutions

Solutions are all linked to issues of:

- road and rail transport;
- private and public transport.

Roads

These are some of the measures used to deal with traffic problems:

1. By-passes and ring-roads to keep through traffic out of towns and cities.
2. Inner ring-roads to keep traffic out of central areas, but often these just involve signposting and taking heavy traffic through residential areas.
3. Building urban motorways to speed up flow.
4. Pedestrianising streets in the CBD to create more pleasant environments for shoppers.
5. Using one-way systems to keep traffic moving.
6. Providing parking outside the CBD, with park-and-ride schemes.
7. Traffic calming (e.g. 'sleeping policemen' road humps and traffic islands narrowing road widths) to slow traffic especially in residential areas.
8. Limiting the times when large lorries can make deliveries of goods in central areas.
9. Using separate bus lanes to speed up public transport.

Rail

Underground railway systems are extremely efficient ways for people to move about cities. London's Underground system is well known. In Hong Kong the Mass Transit Railway allows rapid movement when road traffic is at an almost complete standstill. Two major cities with underground systems are Tokyo and Moscow. The Tokyo system is well known for packing people into the trains, while the Moscow system is renowned for the architectural beauty of its stations.

Railway systems carry large numbers of passengers. In many cities around the world 'rapid transit light railways' are being developed. In the UK an example is the Tyne and Wear Metro. Integrating such projects with bus services is seen by many planners as the most efficient way for city transport to work.

Private and public transport

Cars are convenient and car owners tend to avoid using public transport. Where congestion is bad and parking in central areas difficult, people are more likely to use public transport. However, reductions in private car use needs cheap fares and efficient services.

Changing trends

More complicated patterns of journeys to work and for shopping make solving the problems of urban transport more difficult. Public transport that is based on journeys to and from the central area is not suitable for the changed conditions. Integrated transport systems are needed to allow easy cross-city journeys.

Test yourself

Draw a simple model of a large city (look back to the sections on cities if necessary).

Label the model using the material in this unit.

Remember, keep the labelling short!

review

Check that you now know:

- Why urban areas suffer from traffic congestion
- What problems this causes
- What measures could deal with the problems
- The effects of changing work and shopping trends
- Problems of urban transport

Figure 4

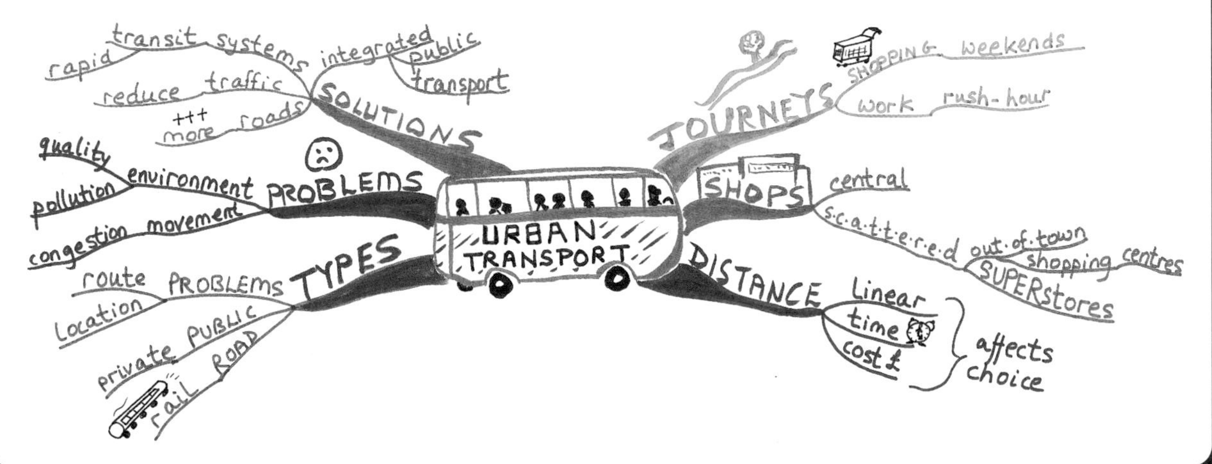

Sample question 3 — Foundation

a) Study Figure 1 which shows projected world population growth.

(i) What was the total world population in 1990? [1 mark]

(ii) What is the projected total world population in 2025? [1 mark]

(iii) In which parts of the world is the population unlikely to change much between 1990 and 2025? [1 mark]

(iv) Give two reasons why population in some parts of the world will grow considerably. [2 marks]

(v) Give two reasons why population in some parts of the world will not grow much. [2 marks]

b) Study Figure 2 which shows migration of people to and within the European Union.

(i) What is 'migration'? [1 mark]

(ii) From which country within the EU did most people migrate? [1 mark]

(iii) Give two reasons why people migrate from one part of Europe to another. [2 marks]

(iv) From which country outside the EU did most migrants come? [1 mark]

(v) Which EU countries received most migrants? [2 marks]

(vi) What problems sometimes occur in countries which have encouraged in-migration? [4 marks]

Figure 1

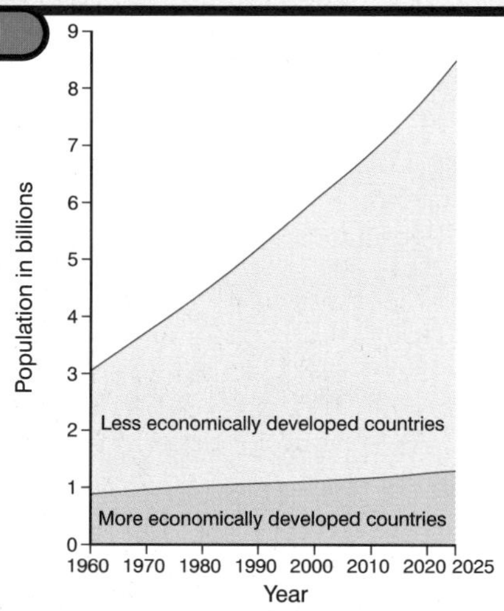

Figure 2

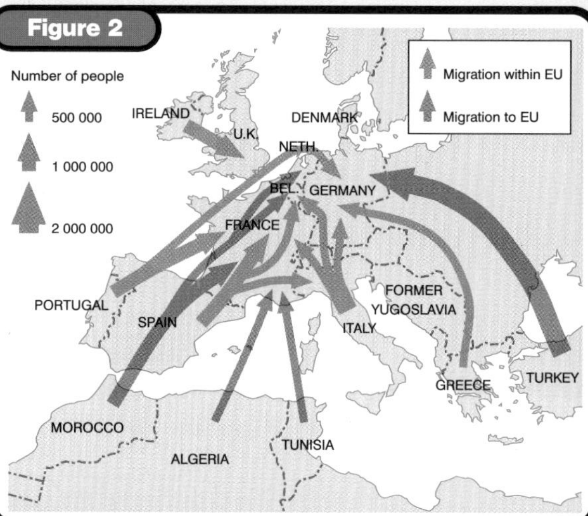

Suggested answer

a) **(i)** 5.2 billion

(ii) 8.5 billion

(iii) The more economically developed countries.

(iv) High birth rates and falling or low birth rates produce high growth rates; where birth rates are falling the increases are still large because the population is relatively young (more people in child-rearing age group); low standards of living encourage larger families as a means of increasing family income.

(v) Low birth rates and low death rates produce low growth rates; higher standard of living gives benefits to people with smaller families; greater career opportunities generally; higher standards of health care reduces infant mortality (more babies survive); generally easier access to family planning.

b) **(i)** Movement of people from one area to another.

(ii) Italy

(iii) Opportunities in destination country (jobs mainly); shortage of workers in destination country, especially for low-paid, 'dirty' jobs; lack of opportunity in home region (often long-term poverty and unemployment).

(iv) Turkey

(v) Germany and France

(vi) Racial and cultural tensions or problems; discrimination against migrants; expectation of better conditions by migrants; unemployment when there are economic problems; poor housing; lack of rights for migrants.

9 Using Maps and Photographs

preview

What you need to know

- **Use OS maps as a source of information on various geographical topics**
- **Identify and locate features on OS maps**
- **Identify features on photographs**
- **Relate features shown on photographs to maps**
- **Describe and explain the physical and human features shown on OS maps**
- **Describe and explain the physical and human features shown on photographs**

Start by looking at the Ordnance Survey map extract (Figure 1 on page 82).

1 What is the scale of the map? (Always check the scale.)

2 What types of features does it show? First make a list of as many features as you can. Then put them into types or groups; use the unit headings of this book for the groups.

3 Make a Mind Map to summarise the kinds of information an OS map shows.

Remember

You get more from a map the more you look at it, so spend some time doing just that. Use the table of map symbols (Figure 2 on page 83) to find ones you don't know or don't remember. Whenever you revise any topic come back to the map to see how the work you have revised fits with the map.

Locating places

Grid references

Use grid references to locate places accurately. Use six figures for a point. For example, there is a car park at 421954. Make sure you have found it. Use four figures for something taking up an area of land. For example, the woodland in square 4689. (Remember, for a four-figure reference use the grid lines that intersect in the south-west corner of the square.)

Distance and direction

Locate places in relation to each other by distance and direction. So Boiling Well is 3.5 km north-west of Little Stretton. Try a few directions and distances of your own.

Outline maps

Locate places on an outline map. Use Figure 3 and add ten places or features. Here are two to start with: All Stretton, and the level crossing at Marshbrook. Notice that the outline is not the same scale as the map extract.

Change about 07' (2 mils)E
Grid North
True North
The figures in blue along this side of the map are EASTINGS and must be quoted first when giving a grid reference
SHREWSBURY
39
40
41
42
43
44
45
46
47
Shropshire Way
New Leasowes Fm
Tumulus
Wilderley Hill
Picklescott Hill
Leasowes Bank Fm
409
Thresholds
297
Picklescott
Motte & Bailey
Smethcott
Old Mill Fm
Walkmills
Fields Fm
129
Castle Hill Fm
Gatten Lodge
99
Waterfall
Betchcott Hills
Betchcott
Castle Bank Motte & Bailey
Betchcott Hollow
Woolstaston
PH
Lee
399
Stitt Fms
Gatten
Tumulus
413
The Portway
Hodghurst
147
Stitt Hill
98
Castle Ring
Ratlinghope Hill
Shropshire Way
Darnford Brook
Darnford
228
Brook Ho
289
Cross Dyke
Settlement
Hawkham Hollow
The Villa
Dryhill
Womerton
Lower Wood
High Park Ho
265
Holly
298
High Park
Highfield
167
Dudgeley Fm
Heath Ho
Cross Dyke
Ratlinghope
Tumulus
Robin Hood's Butts
Tumuli
445
Plush Hill
Inwood
163
Bridges
Manor Ho
PH
Overs
Belmore Fm
Wild Moor
Tumulus
Worsley
Castle Hill
Coppice Fm
96
Mott's Road
Woodnall
All Stretton
Botvyle
Haddon Hill
The Batch
New Ho
Coates
Priory Cottage
425
Shooting Box
Tumuli
LONG MYND
Nover's Hill
Caer Caradoc Hill
95
504
Cow Ridge
Bodbury Hill
Bodbury Ring
Carding Mill Valley
Three Fingers Rock
Medlicott
Tumuli
Pole Bank
516
Boiling Well
Resr
NT
Cross Dyke
Devil's Mouth
Burway Hill
CH
Sch
Ashbrook
189
New House Fm
Cwms
Helmeth Hill
317
Adstone
94
Tumulus
Pole Cott
Long Synalds
Nature Trail
Church Stretton
Cwms
Stanbatch
Narnell's Rock
Hotel
B4371
MP
Gaer Stone
Moorhouse
Robury Ring
Wentnor Prolley Moor
Tumulus
Hazler
93
Jack Mytton Way
The Portway
Round Hill
Ashes Hollow
347
Hazler Hill
345
Cross Dyke
Tumuli
Ashes
Brockhurst Castle
Cemy
ROMAN ROAD
Ragleth Wood
Asterton Prolley Moor
Callow Hollow
Hotel
Dryhill Fm
Ragleth Hill
Jack Mytton Way
Coffin Brook
92
Well
Tumulus
Yapsel Bank
Callow
Little Stretton
MS
PH
Grove Cott
Gliding Club
Packetstone Hill
Packet Stone
Waterfall
Ragdon
Chelmick
Asterton
Synalds Tumulus
Minton Batch
The Hough
Wks
Minton
Manor Fm
Motte
Birtley
Handless
Tumuli
Knolls
Shooter's Knoll
Oakwood
Hatton
Tumulus
90
New Ho
Swiss Cott
Priors Holt Hill
Marshbrook
Inn
LC
Acton Scott
Working Farm
Hall
Myndtown
Priors Holt
Hattongrove Fm
Churchmoor Hill
Hamperley
B4370
156
Shropshire Way
Whittingslow
dismantled railway
89
Black Knoll
380
Pillocksgreen
232
Cwm Head
268
ROMAN ROAD (course of)
Churchmoor Hall
Jack Mytton Way
Churchmoor Rough
Marsh Fm
Henley
Henley Common
Blakemoor
88
Hillend Fm
Brokenstones
Bushmoor
Wolverton

1:50 000 Scale Landranger® Series Map
CONVENTIONAL SIGNS

Ordnance Survey®

ROADS AND PATHS Not necessarily rights of way

Service area M1 Junction number 3 Elevated	Motorway (dual carriageway)
	Motorway under construction
Unfenced Footbridge	Trunk road
A 40 (T) Dual carriageway	Main road
	Main road under construction
B 284	Secondary road
A 855 Bridge B 885	Narrow road with passing places
	Road generally more than 4m wide
	Road generally less than 4m wide
	Other road, drive or track
	Path
	Gradient: 20% (1 in 5) and steeper, 14% (1 in 7) to 20% (1 in 5)
	Gates Road Tunnel
Ferry P Ferry V	Ferry (passenger) Ferry (vehicle)

PUBLIC RIGHTS OF WAY (Not applicable to Scotland)

- Footpath
- – – – – – – Bridleway
- –·–·–·–·– Road used as public path
- –+–+–+–+– Byway open to all traffic

Public rights of way indicated by these symbols have been derived from Definitive Maps as amended by later enactments or instruments held by Ordnance Survey on (date) and are shown subject to the limitations imposed by the scale of mapping. Later information may be obtained from the appropriate County or London Borough Council.

The representation on this map of any other road, track or path is no evidence of a right of way

Danger Area Firing and Test Ranges in the area. Danger! Observe warning notices

WATER FEATURES

	Marsh or salting
	Lake
	Canal, lock and towpath
	Canal (dry)
	Aqueduct
	Footbridge
	Normal tidal limit
	Lighthouse (in use and disused)
	Beacon
	Slopes
	Cliff
	Flat rock
Mud	Low water mark
	High water mark
Sand	
Dunes	
	Shingle

RAILWAYS

	Track multiple or single
	Track narrow gauge
	Freight line, siding or tramway
a b	Station (a) principal (b) closed to passengers
LC	Level crossing
	Embankment
	Cutting
	Bridges, Footbridge
	Tunnel
	Viaduct

ROCK FEATURES

outcrop cliff 550 600 scree

HEIGHTS

50	Contours are at 10 metres vertical interval
144	Heights are to the nearest metre above mean sea level

Heights shown close to a triangulation pillar refer to the station height at ground level and not necessarily to the summit.

1 metre = 3.2808 feet

GENERAL FEATURES

ruin	Buildings
	Public buildings (selected)
	Quarry
	Spoil heap, refuse tip or dump
	Coniferous wood
	Non-coniferous wood
	Mixed wood
	Orchard
	Park or ornamental grounds
	Electricity transmission line (with pylons spaced conventionally)
> – –> – –>	Pipe line (arrow indicates direction of flow)
	Radio or TV mast
	Places of Worship { with tower / with spire, minaret or dome / without such additions }
○	Chimney or tower
	Glasshouse
	Graticule intersection at 5' intervals
Ⓗ	Heliport
△	Triangulation pillar
	Windmill with or without sails
	Windpump/Wind Generator

ABBREVIATIONS

P	Post office
PH	Public house
MS	Milestone
MP	Milepost
CH	Clubhouse
PC	Public convenience (in rural areas)
TH	Town Hall, Guildhall or equivalent
CG	Coastguard

ANTIQUITIES

VILLA	Roman
Castle	Non-Roman
⚔ 1066	Battlefield (with date)
∴	Tumulus
+	Position of antiquity which cannot be drawn to scale

The revision date of archaeological information varies over the sheet

BOUNDARIES

–+– –+– +	National
–○– –○– –○–	London Borough
–●– –●– –●–	District
NT	National Trust
	County, Region or Islands Area
	National Park or Forest Park
NT	always open
NT	limited access, observe local signs

NTS (in red or blue) National Trust for Scotland

TOURIST INFORMATION

🅵 ⓘ	Information centre, all year/seasonal
	Selected places of tourist interest
	Viewpoint
🅿	Parking
✕	Picnic site
Å	Camp site
	Caravan site
▲	Youth hostel
⚑	Golf course or links
	Bus or coach station
✆	Public telephone
✆	Motoring organisation telephone
PC	Public convenience (in rural areas)

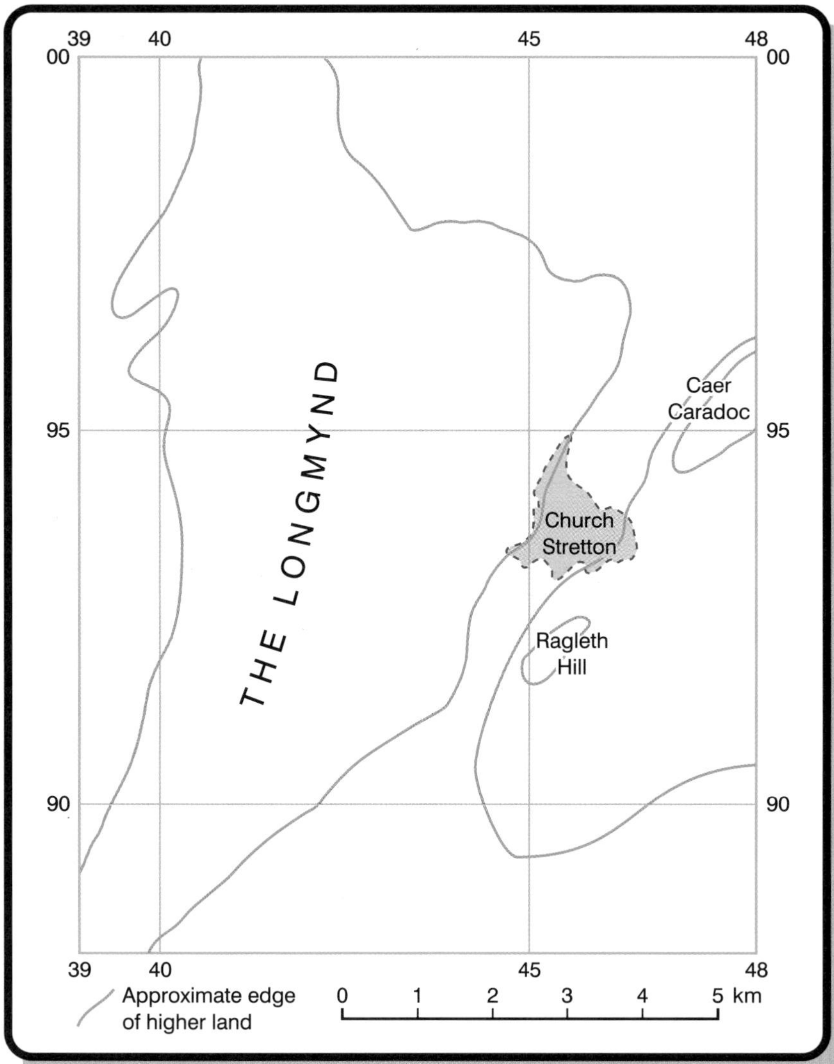

Outline map of the area

Identifying features

Physical features

Figure 4 shows the shapes of different landforms and the contour patterns that go with them. To remind you, contours are the lines which join places of the same height. Examples of them can be found on the map extract (Figure 1). Spend some time looking at the map and see how many landforms you can find.

Task

Look at the photograph (Figure 5). It shows some of the physical features in Figure 4. Add their names to the arrows on the sketch made from the photograph (Figure 6).

Contours

You have been using height and shape to identify features. Look at the contours in different parts of the map (Figure 1). Find places which are flat (no contours), gently sloping (contours far apart) and steeply sloping (contours close together).

Figure 4

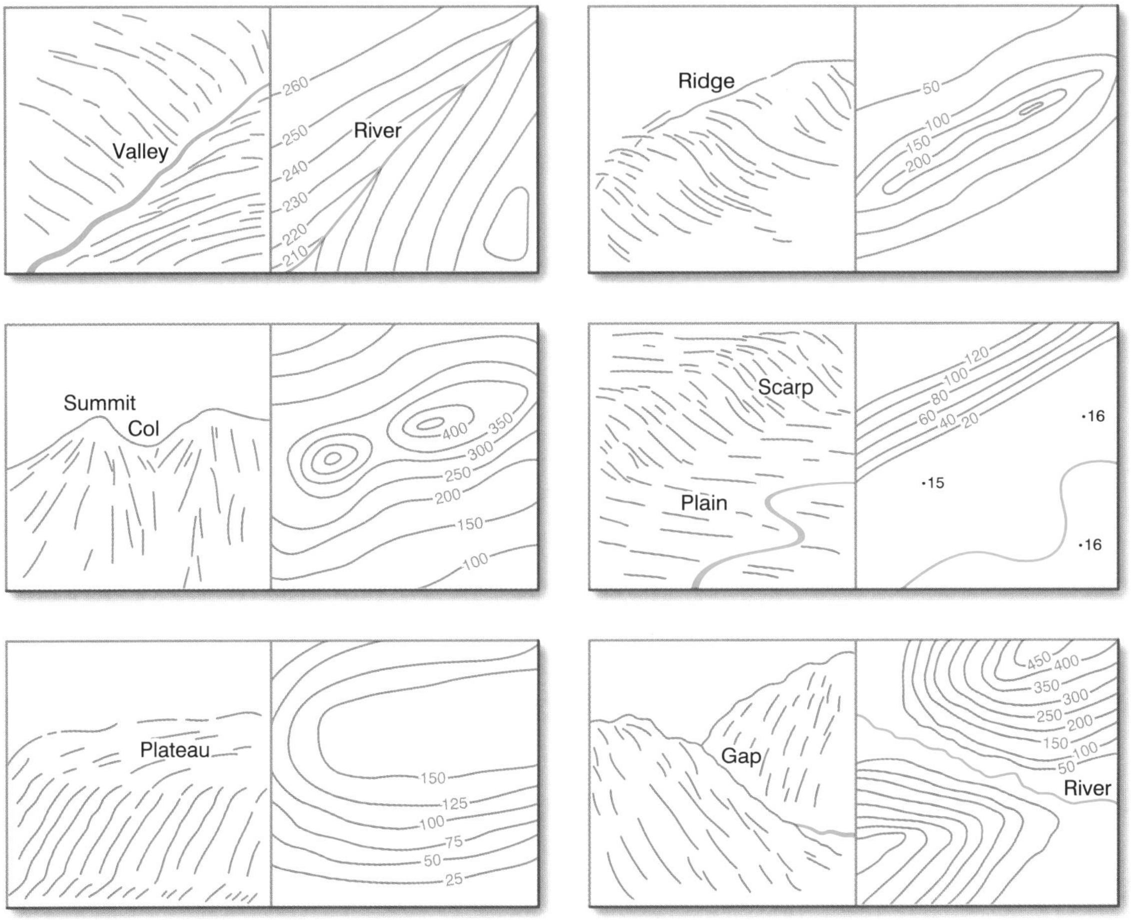

Landforms and contour patterns

Figure 5: Photograph taken from 477954

Figure 6

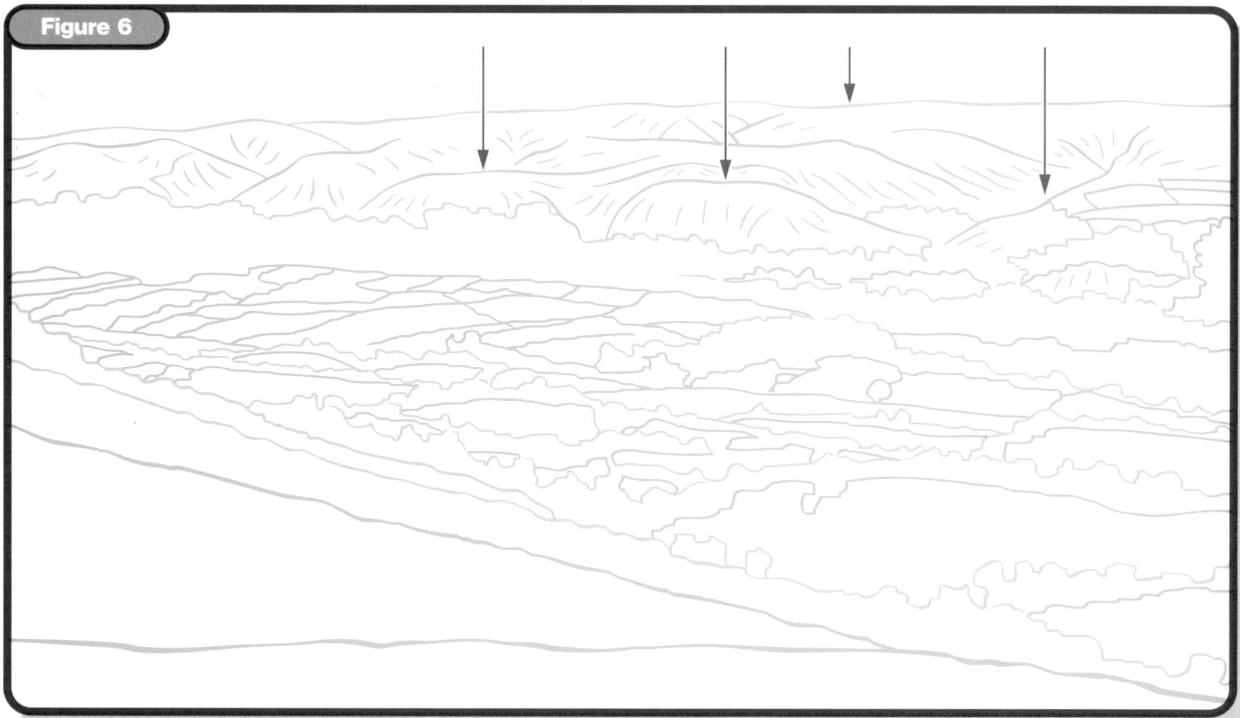

Sketch based on Figure 5

The more you look at contours the more sense they will make. Compare the photograph (Figure 5) with the area on the map. Notice how the two relate to each other.

Height is also shown by spot heights and some triangulation points (usually called trig points). Find these at 471970 and 415944.

Cross-sections

Contours are used to draw a cross-section across a map. This shows you the shape of the land along a line. Figure 7 shows the shape of the land along a line running east to west.

Task

1 Find the end points of the section on the map.

2 Add these labels to the cross-section:

- a road and a railway line
- scarp slope
- Little Stretton
- Yapsel Bank
- Callow Hollow
- Ragleth Hill
- unfenced minor road
- The Longmynd

Little Stretton is at the southern end of the Church Stretton valley; label the valley.

3 What would a cross-section from Caer Caradoc to Ratlinghope look like?

Human and economic features

The map shows evidence of:

- settlements
- tourism
- routes and transport
- some kinds of land use
- conservation.

Study the key to map symbols (Figure 2) to see what else might be useful. Notice that you cannot tell if land is arable land, pasture land or open moorland. Your only evidence is the abbreviation Fm for farm. Even that does not tell you what sort of farmland.

Test yourself

You can apply your knowledge of geography to identifying and explaining map features. Here are some examples of links between topics and map reading.

Transport

Explain the route followed by the railway and the A-road. The B-road east from Church Stretton follows a gap in the hills.

Figure 7

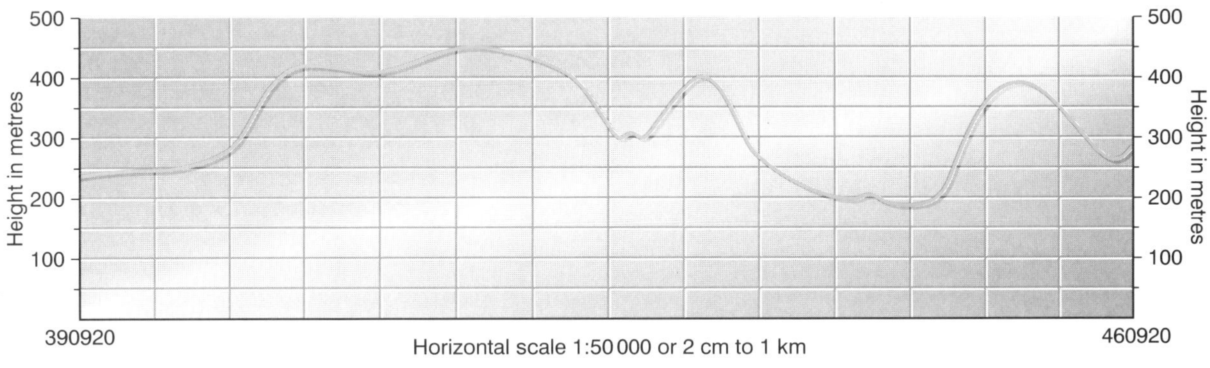

Cross-section along northing 92

Settlement
Give an example of dispersed settlement. Give examples of a hamlet, village and town. What are the differences between each type of settlement?

Describe and explain the site and form of All Stretton. What evidence is there of ancient settlement in the area? Describe and explain the importance and form of Church Stretton.

Tourism
What activities and land uses are related to leisure and tourism?

Conservation
What small amount of information is there to do with conservation of the landscape?

Land use
What different land uses are shown on the map? Give an example of each one, with its grid reference.

review

This unit has reminded you about aspects of map reading and map use. The best way to review the subject is by using maps. Spend a few minutes looking at the map at the same time that you review a related topic. Better still, get an OS map of your local area and spend time using it.

Look back over the chapter and complete the Mind Map (Figure 8).

Figure 8

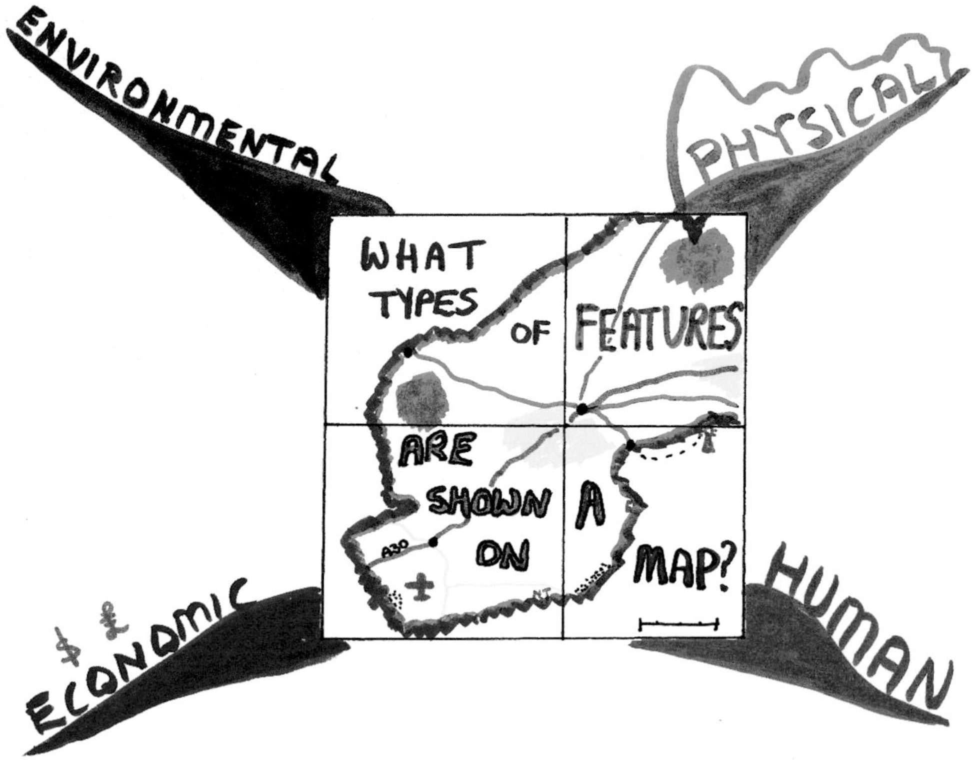

10 Agriculture

preview

What you need to know

- Subsistence farming systems
- Commercial farming systems
- Factors affecting farming systems
- Patterns of land use
- Factors affecting land use patterns
- How farming has changed
- How the countryside has changed
- The effects of the changes
- Features and problems of farming in less developed countries
- Increasing agricultural production
- Agribusiness

Types of economic activities

Economic activities are usually grouped as:

★ **Primary activities**, which include farming, fishing, forestry, mining and quarrying.

★ **Secondary activities** cover manufacturing industry.
  - Basic industries
  - Heavy industries
  - Assembly industries
  - High technology

★ **Tertiary activities or services** include the distribution wholesaling, retailing and transport; finance; personal and professional services; and public services.

★ **Quaternary services** are concerned with research and development and the processing and handling of data. Their presence is an indicator of a highly developed economy.

Types and systems of farming

Check what you know

Do you know what these are?

subsistence farming

shifting cultivation

bush fallowing

intensive subsistence farming

nomadic herding

commercial farming

pastoral farming

mixed farming

plantation farming

Subsistence farming

The term **subsistence farming** is used for the types of farming where the family's basic needs are met from their land. It is mostly found in less developed countries.

Virtually everywhere, some production is sold because cash is needed to pay, for example, for education, health care or tools.

Types of subsistence farming

- ★ **Shifting cultivation**. Small areas of forest are cleared and cultivated for two to five years and then abandoned when the soil's fertility has been lost. The vegetation will be left to regrow. This system is possible only in areas of low population density.
- ★ **Bush fallowing**. This goes on where populations are too high for shifting cultivation. Areas of land are cultivated for a few years and then abandoned but for only a few years. The land will be farmed again while the area is still 'bush'.
- ★ **Intensive subsistence farming**. The most intensive version of this is rice farming in south-east Asia, where very small plots are cultivated extremely carefully giving high yields.
- ★ **Nomadic herding**. This is still found, for example, in areas of tropical grasslands in Africa, especially the drier parts. It is being squeezed out by a combination of pressures from the environment (droughts), governments (border problems) and population (increased settled farming).

Commercial farming

Here farm production is for sale. Crops or animals can be destined for food or industry. There is a great variety of types.

Pastoral farming

This primarily involves cattle rearing for meat or milk, and sheep rearing for meat and wool. **Extensive** rearing means there are low densities of animals grazing on large holdings, as in the

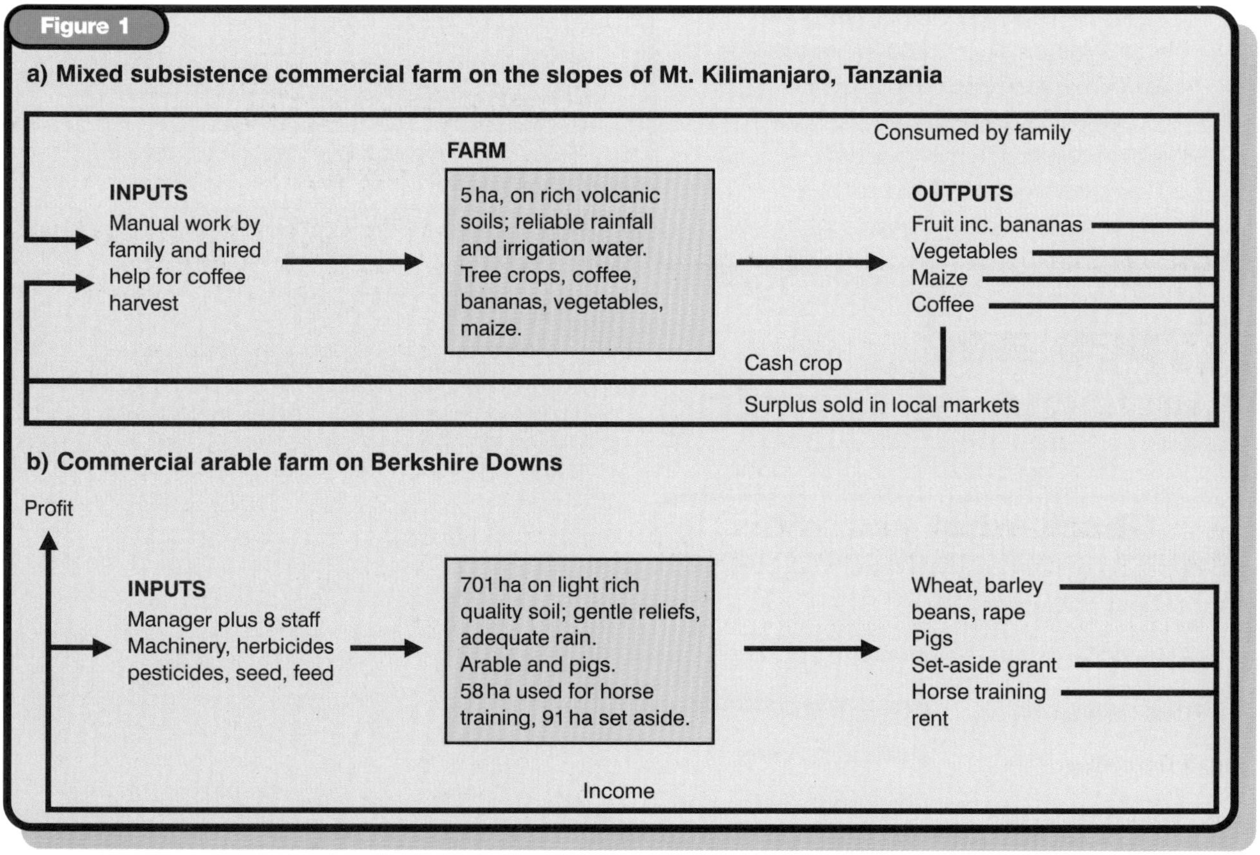

Farm systems

sheep and cattle stations of Australia. **Intensive** rearing means that large numbers are produced on small areas of land. They are fed on specially grown or bought fodder and the animals are, perhaps, kept indoors.

Arable farming

This is crop production. It varies from highly intensive production on smallholdings to equally intensive production on large farms. Commercial crop production is almost always **capital intensive**. Large sums are spent on machinery, fertilisers and pesticides. The labour force is usually small.

Mixed farming

Although there is a trend for farms to specialise, mixed farming is still the most common type, with a mixture of crops and animals.

Plantation farming

This is large-scale crop production in tropical areas. Workers may have small plots on which to grow their own food, otherwise they have to depend on irregular work and very low wages. Many plantations are owned by large transnational companies based in North America or Europe.

Exam tip

Farming systems are often shown in diagram form (Figure 1). They are useful ways to summarise the workings of a type of farming system or just one farm.

Test yourself

Rearrange the following statements under the headings:

(a) subsistence farming

(b) commercial farming.

- bush fallowing
- large-scale crop production in tropical areas
- mixed farming is still the most common type
- crop production
- extensive rearing
- very small plots are cultivated extremely carefully giving high yields
- found especially in the drier areas of tropical grasslands in Africa
- intensive rearing
- shifting cultivation

review

Check that you can summarise the types of subsistence farming systems and types of commercial farming systems on a Mind Map. Remember to include the elements affecting farming systems.

Patterns of land use

Patterns of land use vary at world scale, national scale and local scale (Figure 2).

World scale

The most productive areas are those with environmental advantages (look at the Climate unit, pages 39–40).

The map also highlights more developed countries, especially the USA, as big producers. So level of development as well as the environment is important.

National scale

The map of Tunisia shows an obvious environmental effect. Agriculture and rainfall are closely related. However, the major cities and the bulk of the population are in the north and north-east. This is also important. Farming is more intensive in these areas, so more is produced from the same amount of land.

Figure 2

(a) Major food producing areas of the world

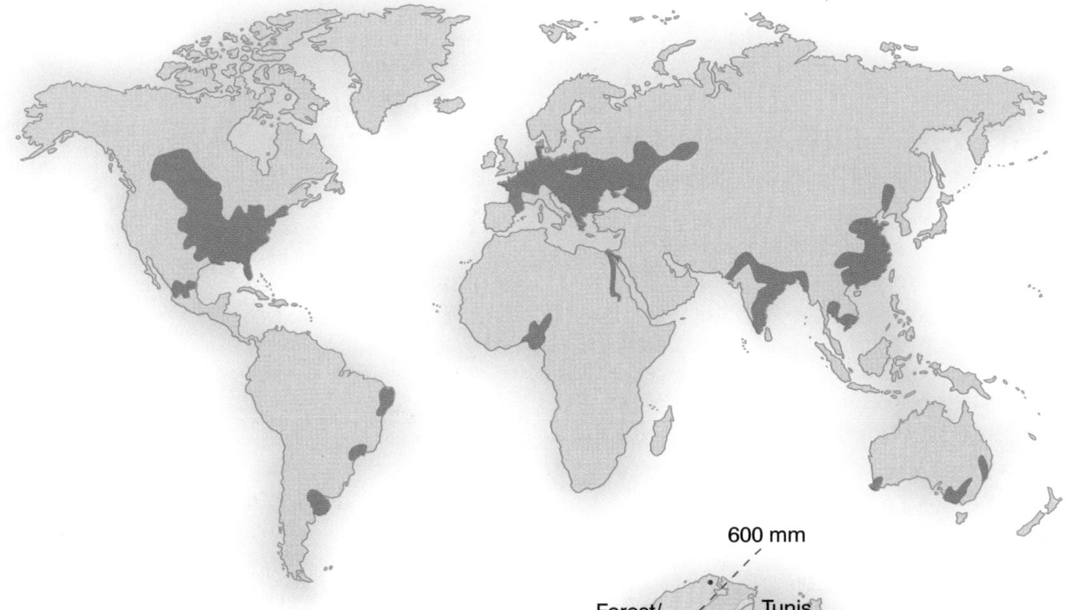

(b) Farming in Tunisia

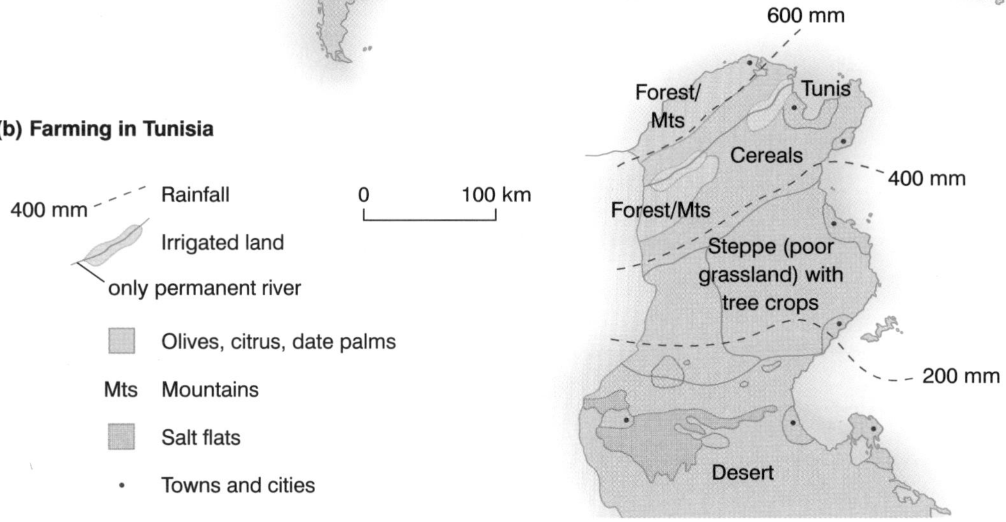

(c) Land use in the Vale of Evesham

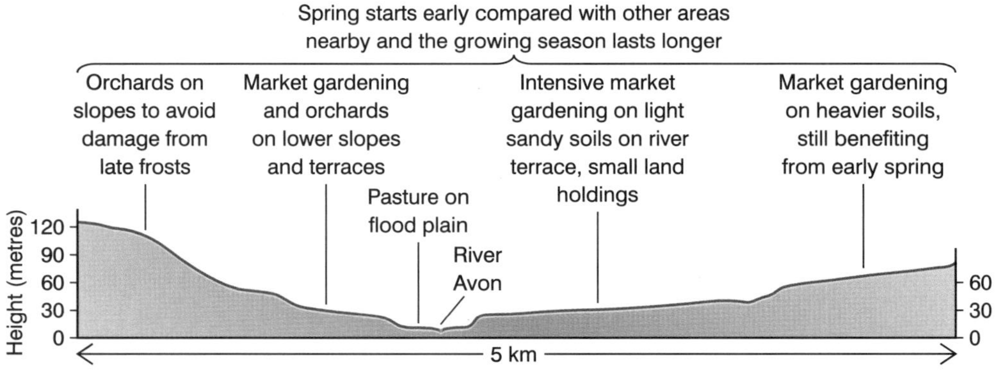

Agricultural land use patterns

Figure 3

Physical or environmental factors

Climate –	temperatures length of growing season months free from frost or frost risk rainfall total seasonal distribution of rainfall
Relief –	height of land slopes drainage
Soil –	drainage properties texture fertility

Human factors

sizes of farms
methods of farming
levels of technology
distance from markets
transport facilities
level of education and training
marketing organisation
availability of advisory services
banking and insurance
demand and competition
government influences

Factors affecting land use

Local scale

In the Vale of Evesham, in the Midlands, orchards are on higher and more sloping land, market gardens and greenhouses are on level terraces and land on the flood plain of the river is pasture. (Note that the small intensively worked holdings mark this district out from surrounding areas.)

Factors affecting land use patterns

The examples in Figure 2 show different reasons for **patterns of land use**. They include:

- climate
- slope
- soils
- nearness to cities and centres of population
- size of land holding.

Figure 3 gives a fuller list of factors affecting land use.

Task

Look at Figures 2 and 3. Decide which factors are likely to be **relevant** to each example in Figure 2. Pencil in the letters for the examples by the items in the lists. You will use some of them every time.

Figure 4 shows a simple model of land use patterns. It assumes that all the features of climate, relief and soils are the same throughout the area. There is still a definite pattern of zones of different land uses.

The pattern is related to these features:

- **nearness to market** – the city is the market for all production in this region.
- **intensity of farming** – near the city means easier, cheaper and quicker to get produce to market, but that means the land is more expensive, so it has to be farmed more intensively to be worthwhile. This is why market gardening forms the inner ring. The land is farmed less and less intensively as distance from the city increases.

Figure 4

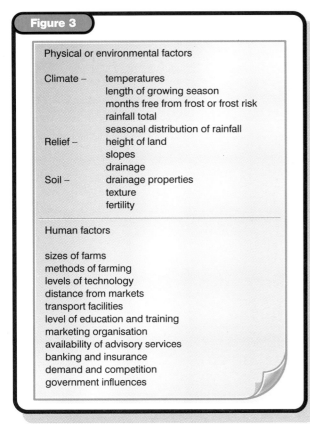

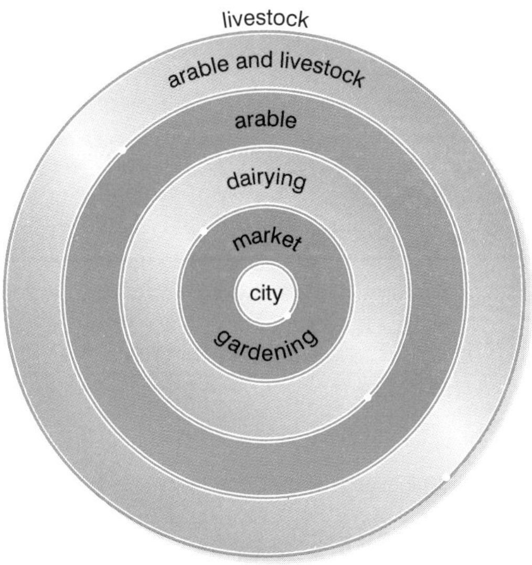

Model of agricultural land use

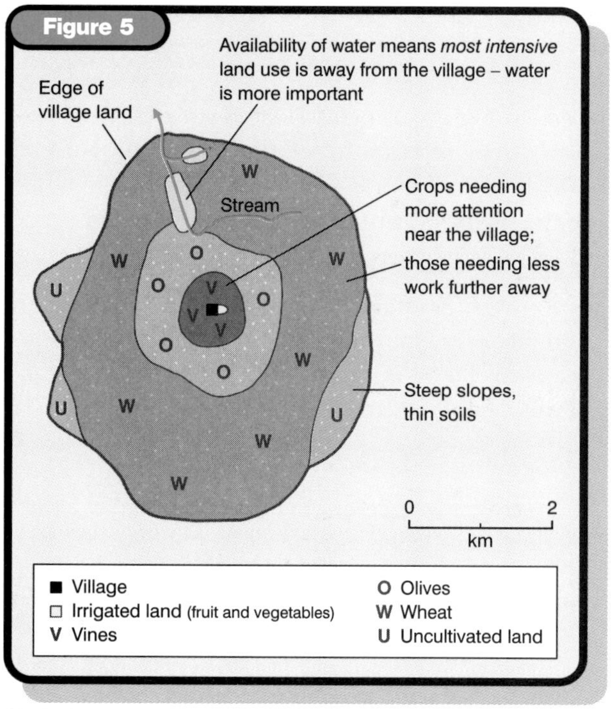

Physical and human factors affecting land use around a Cypriot village

Figure 6

Figure 5 shows the pattern of land use in an area where there are also differences in relief, soils and climate. The pattern has changed. You can make the pattern more and more complex by adding other factors. For example, the river could also be used for exporting crops to another city. How would the pattern differ? What land use would you expect to find along the river?

Test yourself

How many points can you make from the photograph (Figure 6)?

Arrange them under:

- types of land use
- patterns of land use
- factors affecting land use.

review

Check that you now know how patterns of land use can be seen at world, national and local scales. You should also know how the factors affecting land use can be grouped as physical factors and human factors.

In 'Test yourself' you have applied all the ideas to one simple case study.

The Mind Map (Figure 7) is based on Figure 3. Use any of the case studies in this unit and add its details to your own copy of the Mind Map.

Figure 7

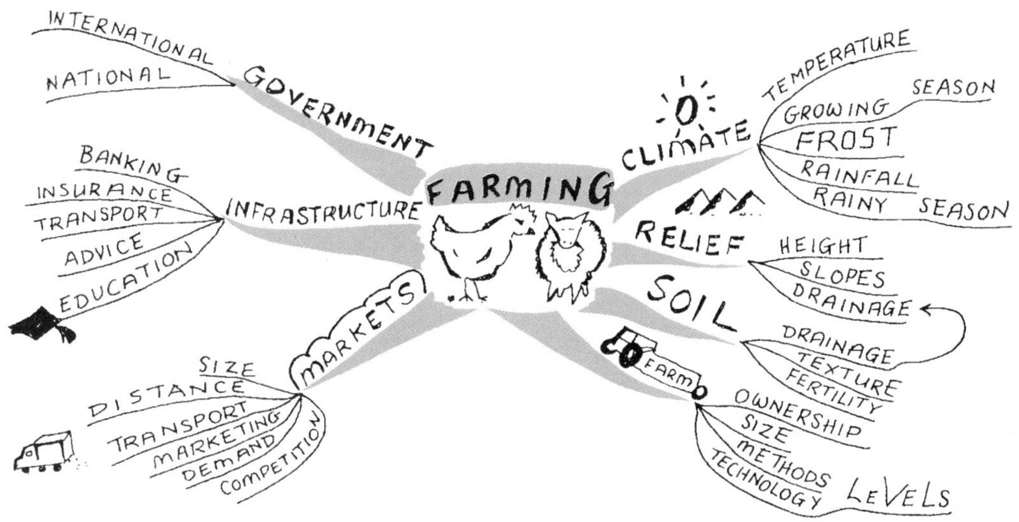

Factors affecting farming

Changes in farming and the countryside

Changes in farming

Since the 1940s there have been many changes in farming:

- fall in the farming workforce from 6% to 2% of the total
- increase in mechanisation
- more efficient machinery
- technological changes including pesticides, herbicides and fungicides
- fall in the number of farms by amalgamations
- increase in the average size of farms
- increased production of all types of crops and animal products
- changes in land use (e.g. from pasture to arable due to land drainage)
- changes in landscape (e.g. hedge removal).

Task

Which of the changes actually brought about a fall in the workforce?

Exam tip

Work through the case study on page 96 and pick out items which match the list of general changes in farming. Knowing an actual example helps you to remember the general point. In an examination answer use the example to emphasise your point.

You can use the same case studies to answer many different questions. This one could be used to deal with changes in farming, farm systems and factors affecting farming.

Case study

Farm on the Berkshire Downs

This study illustrates almost all the changes that have affected British farming. It also includes some of the more recent developments.

Background

One large farm made by amalgamating five separate ones.

Total area – 701 hectares (ha).

Soils – loam soils of light, medium and rich quality on mainly chalk base.

Relief – gently undulating downland.

Local climate – exposed, but still potential to grow range of crops.

1950

32 staff – 20 farm workers, 3 shepherds,

3 gamekeepers, 6 estate staff.

Land use – 620 ha mainly arable (wheat and barley plus peas, lucerne, clover and mustard).

800 sheep

Machinery – tractors and combine harvesters were used.

1993

8 staff – 3 arable men, 4 pigmen, 1 general maintenance.

Land use – total arable 629 ha (wheat 310 ha, barley 65 ha, beans 53 ha, rape 50 ha, set-aside 91 ha), pig land 14 ha.

Total area farmed – 643 ha.

Remaining land used as horse gallops.

Changes

Staff ratio (arable)

1950 1 to 31 ha

1993 1 to 210 ha

Reasons for changes

Crops

Cereals, mainly wheat, became more profitable under the Common Agricultural Policy (CAP) which made it more profitable to grow cereals. Labour costs were lower with cereals due to mechanistion.

Peas, grown at one time, were dropped due to the closure of the factory and harvesting difficulties.

Potatoes, grown in the 1960s, were dropped because no casual labour was available and the soil too stony for machines.

Sugar beet was dropped due to transport costs to the sugar beet factory at Kidderminster.

Livestock

Sheep rearing was given up.

Pigs were introduced in 1950s and, with changes, continued and expanded to 600 sows.

Labour

Mechanisation. One modern combine does all the work.

Technology

Weeds and leaf diseases are now controlled by herbicides and fungicides.

Land use

Set-aside is land taken out of cultivation because of over-production. Farmers receive a payment for this land.

Diversification means that farmers look for an alternative income from their land. This is because farm prices are not being supported by government in the same way as in the past. Here, land is used by local racing horse trainers as training gallops.

Landscape

Unlike many arable farming areas there have been few changes; no hedge removals as the area has always been mainly open downland.

Figure 8

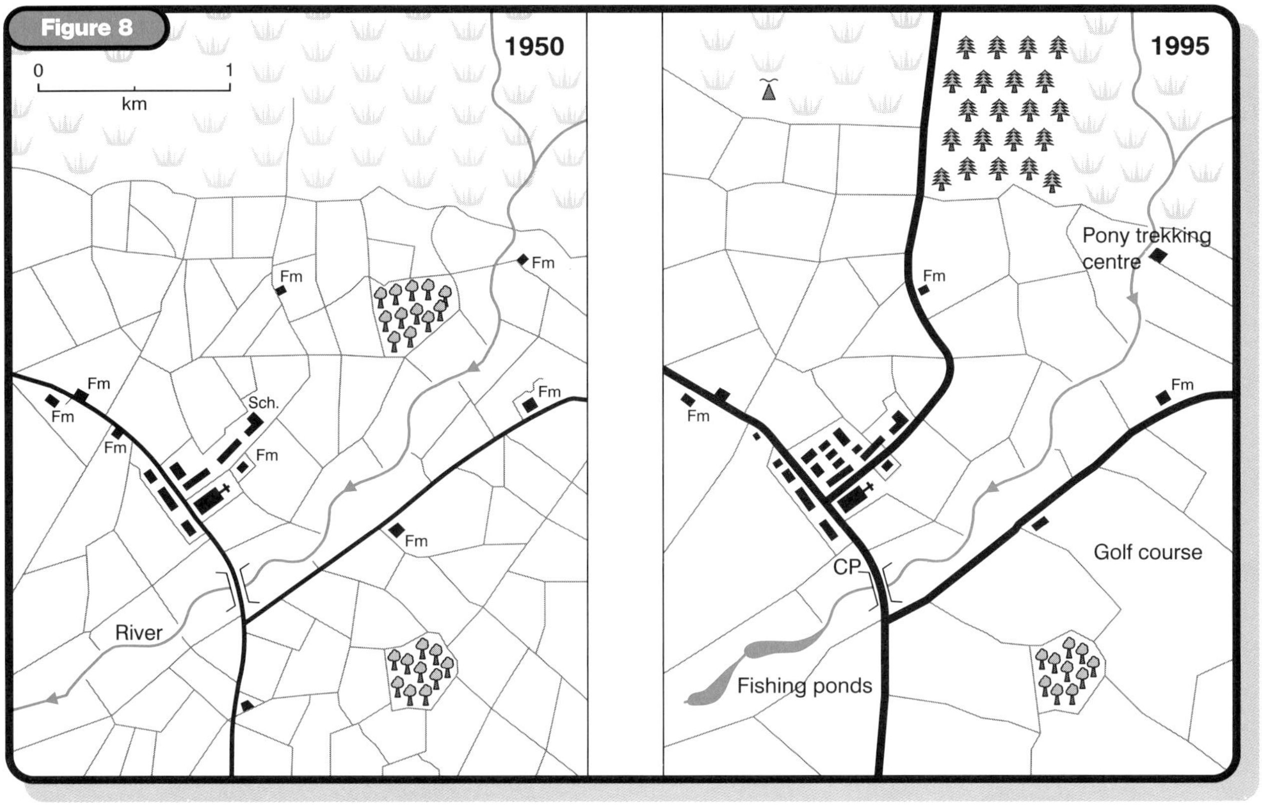

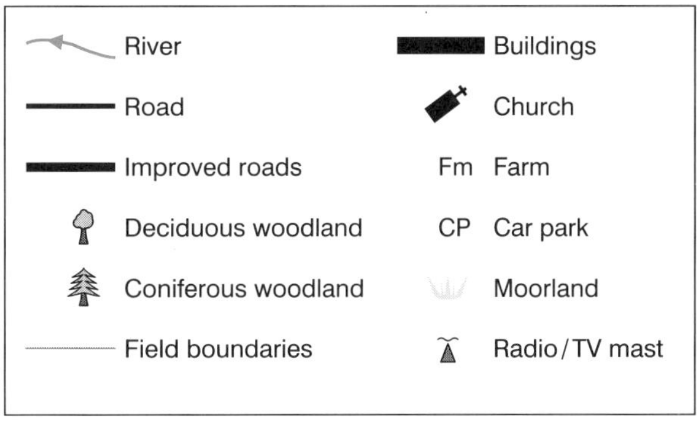

1950

1995

Pony trekking centre

Golf course

Fishing ponds

Changes in the countryside

Changes in farming have brought about changes in the countryside affecting:

* people
* the landscape.

Changes affecting people

Look back at the chapter on Settlement and the section on changes in rural areas (pages 63–4). It links the changes in farming to:

* population changes
* rural communities
* services in villages.

Changes affecting the landscape

Figure 8 shows the kinds of changes in the rural landscape. Some of them are directly related to the changes in farming. Others are related to more general changes, like increased car ownership, road improvements and the growth of tourism.

←	River	▬▬	Buildings
───	Road	◆✝	Church
▬▬	Improved roads	Fm	Farm
🌳	Deciduous woodland	CP	Car park
🌲	Coniferous woodland	⩗	Moorland
----	Field boundaries	⛰	Radio/TV mast

Changes in the countryside, 1950 to 1995

review

Check that you now know:

■ How British farming has changed

■ How changes have affected a farm

■ What impact changes have had on people in the countryside

■ What impact there has been on the landscape.

Farming and food problems

Agriculture in less developed countries

The main features are:

1 **The importance of agriculture**. In less developed countries overall, 61% are employed in agriculture.

2 **Low production levels per worker**. Great skill is used in obtaining high yields from small areas of land. This is done by very intensive work with very little equipment. The result is low total production per worker. Low production means money cannot be made to buy better equipment.

3 **Urbanisation**. This is changing the situation in the countryside. Cities attract people from the countryside and provide a market for farming produce.

4 **Dependence on export crops**. Prices for crops exported fluctuate greatly and they rise more slowly than prices of industrial products. For many countries agricultural products are the only export.

Reasons for low levels of production

1 **Lack of capital**. Capital is needed to buy equipment, fertiliser, storage facilities, irrigation, etc.

2 **Lack of land**. This is partly as a result of population pressure, but partly because only a small area can be farmed with simple equipment.

3 **Malnutrition**. The low standard of living itself limits work. This is part of 'the vicious circle of poverty'.

4 **Environmental problems**. These cause difficulties in some regions especially semi-arid regions. The major difficulties are linked to population pressures.

5 **Poor infrastructure**. Isolation of many rural areas means that surplus crops cannot be sold.

6 **Landholding systems**. Many very small farms means that even with great effort there is a limit to production. The relatively small number of larger landowners are the ones who benefit most from changes.

Food production trends

- Total agricultural production of less developoed countries has increased.
- There are differences between major regions (Figure 9).

Figure 9

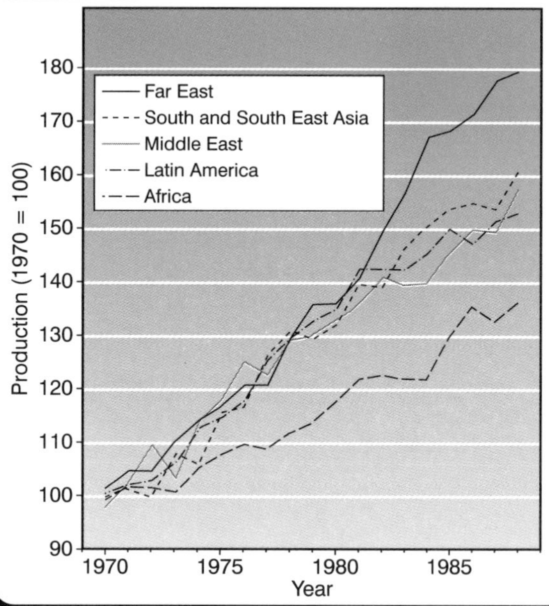

Changes in total agricultural production in less developed regions

- Food production per person has also increased overall.
- Food production per person varies between major regions (Figure 10).

Task 1

In examinations you usually have to interpret data given to you. Make sure you do what is asked. They are easy marks.

(a) Write down three points about the trends in total agricultural production (Figure 9).

(b) Write down three points about the trends in food production per person (Figure 10).

Food supplies

Within countries actual lack of adequate food supplies is affected by:

- poverty and differences in incomes;
- whether or not individuals have land to farm;
- environmental hazards, like floods or hurricanes.

Figure 10

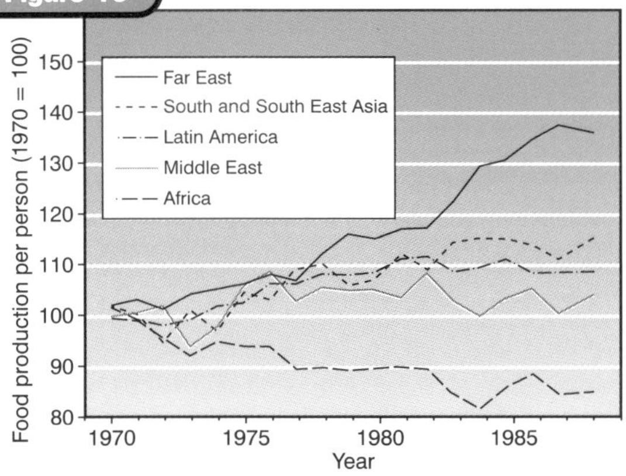

Changes in food production in less developed regions

Increasing food production

Increases in food production have been a result of:

1 Increasing the area of cultivated land

- Clearing forest land.
- Expanding irrigation into land grazing land and unused land.
- Colonising new areas, for example, the Amazon basin.

2 Increasing crop yields

- Irrigation, to increase the production from existing arable land.
- Use of fertilisers.
- Use of high-yielding varieties (HYV) of cereals, especially rice and wheat (the Green Revolution).

Other ways of increasing production and yields include both small-scale changes and major developments.

1 The use of **intermediate or appropriate technology**. Examples are locally made food stores, wind pumps which can be made and maintained locally, or the use of bio-gas for heat and power.

2 **Agricultural reform** which is a large-scale process. The most important feature is land reform, dealing with land ownership so that small farmers and landless people benefit. It also involves developing agricultural advice services, making cheap loans available and improving communications.

Figure 11

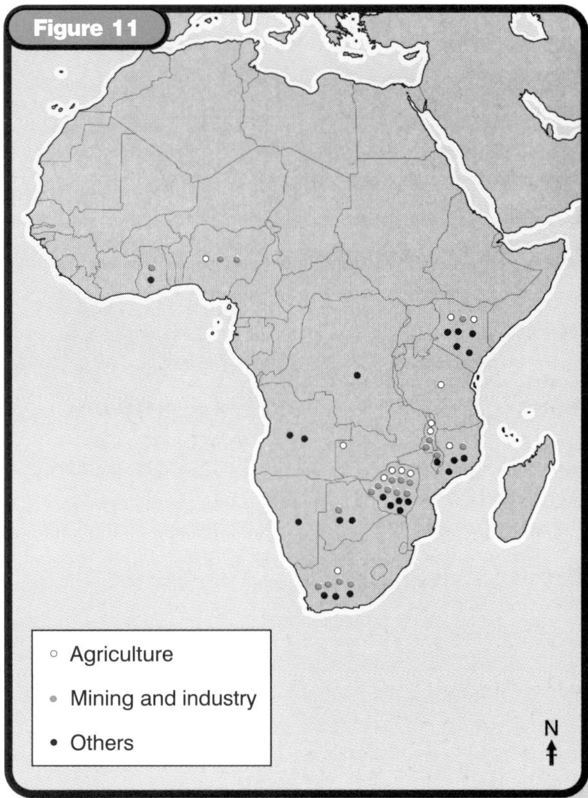

A multinational's operation in Africa – Lonrho

Agribusiness

Export crop production is linked to large plantations. On these the land is generally devoted to one crop, such as rubber, sugar or cotton.

Many plantations are owned by **multinational companies** which are based in the developed world. They control not just production on the plantation, but also processing, packaging, transport, marketing and distribution.

These multinational companies operate in many different countries and are involved in other activities besides agriculture (Figure 11).

Task 2

Make lists of the advantages and disadvantages of export crops to the less developed countries when they are controlled by foreign-based companies.

review

Spend time making a large Mind Map using this list of headings. Try to take it in at a glance. The summaries give you the background for dealing with case study material.

Don't forget your review timetable.

1. Agriculture in less developed countries
2. Reasons for low levels of production
3. Food production trends
4. Increasing food production
5. Agribusiness

Sample question 4

Higher

a) Study Figure 1 showing changes in the typical English farming landscape.

- **(i)** Name three changes in the landscape. [3 marks]
- **(ii)** Describe and explain changes which led to an increase in farm production. [4 marks]
- **(iii)** Explain why conservationists opposed some of the changes. [4 marks]

b) Figure 2 shows the changes in the number of occupied dwellings in a valley on the Welsh–English border.

- **(i)** What does 'rural depopulation' mean? [1 mark]
- **(ii)** How does Figure 2 show that rural depopulation has taken place? [2 marks]
- **(iii)** Explain the reasons for rural depopulation and suggest how the loss of population has been halted. [5 marks]

Figure 2

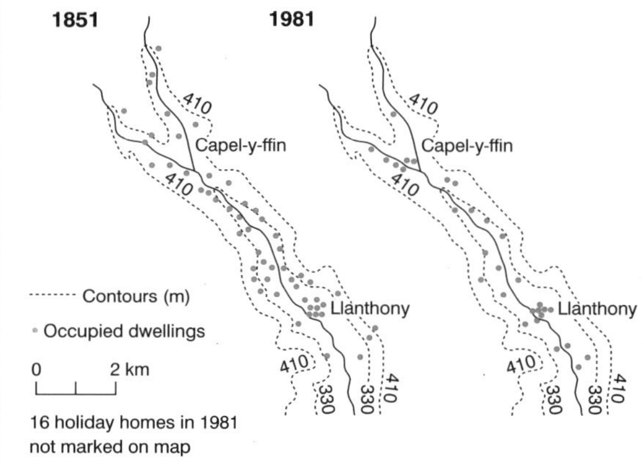

Figure 1

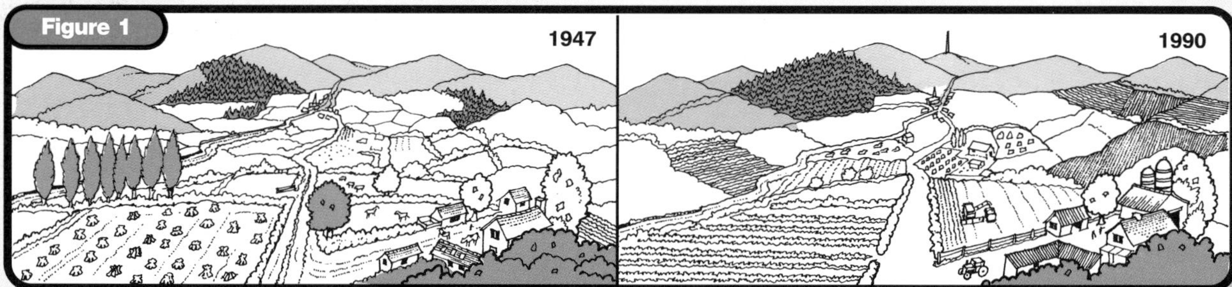

Suggested answer

a)
- **(i)** Larger fields, fewer hedgerows, more arable land, less grassland, larger farm buildings, hilly areas forested.
- **(ii)** Larger fields made mechanisation easier; removal of hedgerows increased area of land available; more arable crops used chemical fertiliser and pesticides increasing yields; more arable crops produced fodder for intensive animal production.
- **(iii)** Loss of wildlife habitats and flora by removal of hedgerows and use of pesticides and herbicides; pollution of rivers and groundwater by fertilisers and pesticides.

b)
- **(i)** Loss of population from rural areas.
- **(ii)** Many fewer dwellings in 1981; shows abandonment of homes and farms.
- **(iii)** Changes in farming, requiring fewer workers; larger farms means fewer farms; lack of other opportunities in countryside, especially more isolated areas; attraction of urban areas with wide range of services. Possible reasons for the loss being halted include development of tourism, providing accommodation for visitors and activities, like pony trekking.

11

Industry

preview

What you need to know

- The factors affecting industrial location
- Applying them to case studies
- Multiplier effects
- Changes affecting old, heavy industrial regions
- Factors behind the growth of high-technology based regions
- What are NICs?
- Where are they?
- Why has industry grown so quickly?

Location of industry

The location of industry is affected by many factors (Figure 1). The importance of each factor varies.

The case study on pages 102–3 shows the importance of many of the **factors of location**.

Multiplier effect

The case study shows how the **multiplier effect** works.

TWR Steering Systems employs a lot of people. They spend money locally and that helps create jobs in various services, like retail and leisure activities.

The factory provides work for other businesses. Many of its suppliers are even moving to an industrial park next door. This brings more jobs and more income to the area. The new firms will provide work for other businesses, too.

Figure 2 is a multiplier model, showing how one development **multiplies** its effect in an area.

Exam tip

The factors of location can be applied to any example. The difference is that the importance of the factors vary.

Any new economic activity has an effect that multiplies in an area.

Figure 1

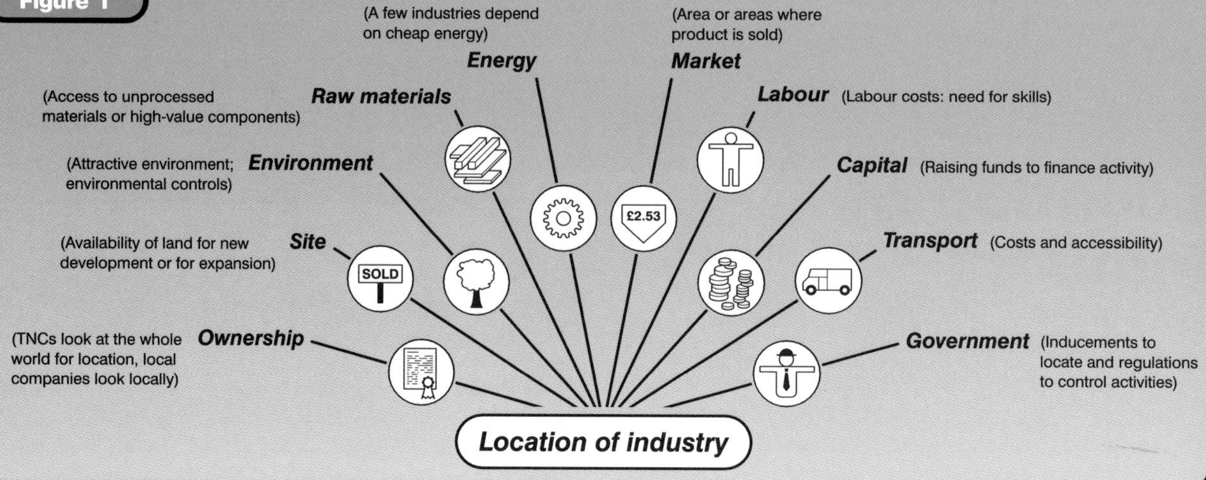

Factors of location

Case study

TRW Steering Systems — an engineering factory in South Wales

The information given here describes the factors which have affected the **location** of this factory. The information is not given in any particular order. This is because the different factors have changed in importance over time.

Task 1

Study the information and give each section a heading. Refer to Figure 1 to help you. Don't use a heading more than once, but for some sections you will have to use two.

______________. An industrial park next to the factory is going to house seven or eight of the firms which make parts for the steering systems. This will make delivery of parts much smoother.

______________. The factory, which makes power steering systems for major car manufacturers occupies a large site on the floor of the Vale of Neath at the village of Resolven.

______________. The original factory was set up here during the Second World War to make aircraft parts. After the Second World War a company based in Luton took over as part of the government scheme to move industry from the crowded south-east.

______________. 850 people work at the factory in an area which used to depend on coal as the main source of jobs.

______________. Resolven is close to the transport routes along the coast of South Wales and on a route leading directly to the Midlands. It is well placed for transporting finished products to factories elsewhere in this country and for shipment overseas.

______________. New owners in 1960 brought new investment. In 1965 the new company became part of an American corporation, TRW Steering Systems, which operates on a worldwide scale.

______________. Increases in car production meant greater demand for steering systems. The company's market is worldwide. It supplies Honda, Volvo, Nissan, Ford and Rover.

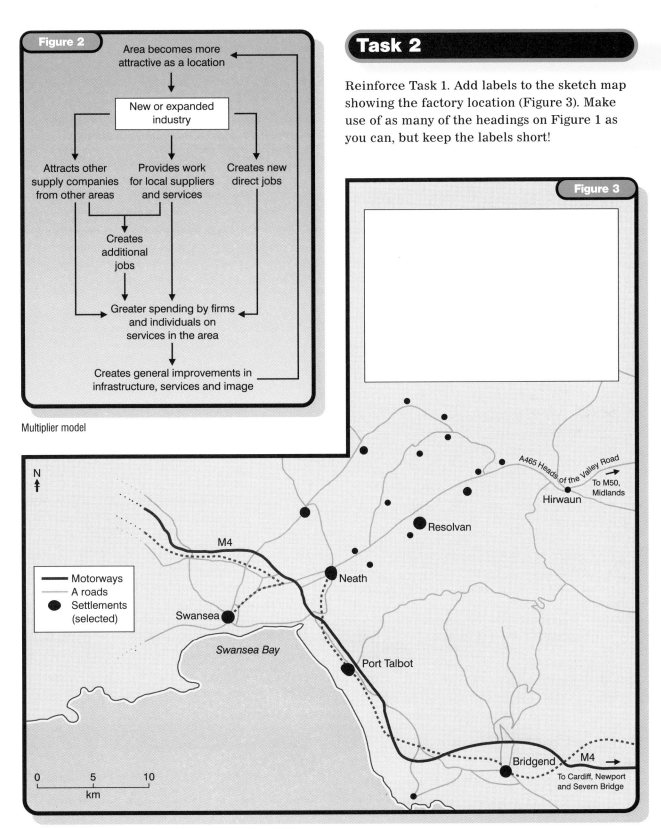

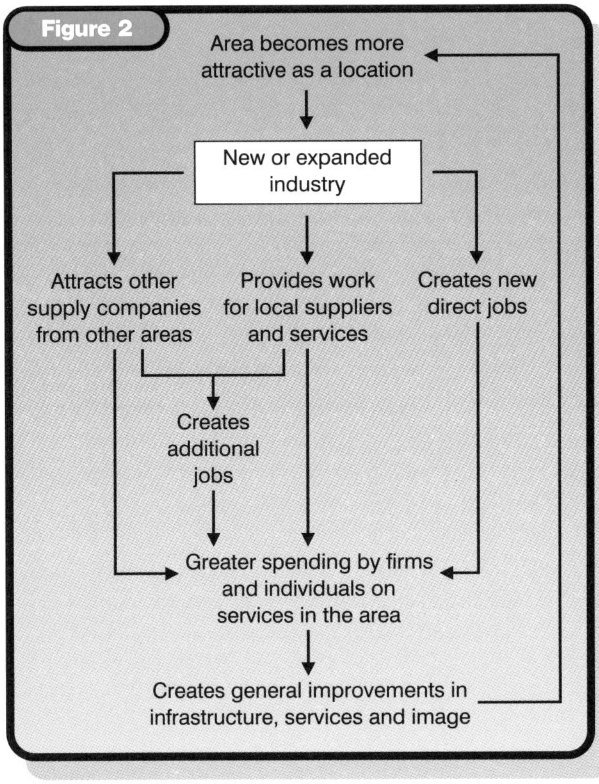

Multiplier model

Task 2

Reinforce Task 1. Add labels to the sketch map showing the factory location (Figure 3). Make use of as many of the headings on Figure 1 as you can, but keep the labels short!

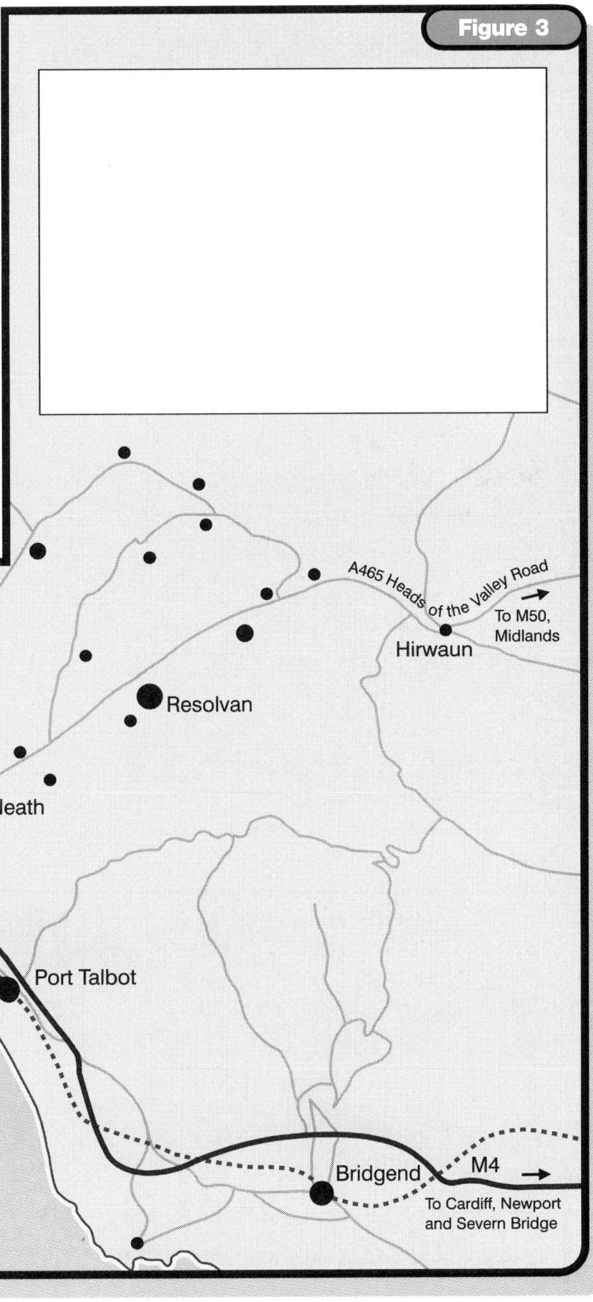

TRW Steering Systems – location

Changing patterns of industry

Growth, decline and recovery

The Ruhr conurbation in Germany is a good example of both **industrial decline** and **industrial growth** (Figure 4; *see also* page 67).

There are actually **three phases of change**:

1. Original **growth** of coal, iron and steel, chemicals and textiles. Coal, as fuel and raw material, and iron ore were found in the Ruhr coalfield itself. The river Rhine and canals were the means of transport. They brought other raw materials to the region and transported finished products away.
2. **Decline** of the old, heavy industries as raw materials became worked out and the competition from coastal works.
3. **Regeneration** of the region. More specialised and modern steel plant is able to compete because there is a large market of steel-using industries. Chemical industries based on oil instead of coal are important. Other light, high-value industries like pharmaceuticals have grown rapidly.

Note that the latest changes were accompanied by **environmental and planning improvements** (*see* page 67). These make the area more attractive to modern industrial development.

Remember

There are three phases – growth, decline and regeneration. Now note down what happened and why in each phase.

Note: similar changes have happened in almost all coalfield areas. The differences are usually in the third phase.

Case study

Rotterdam

Rotterdam in the Netherlands shows the attractions of a break-of-bulk location.

Rotterdam-Europoort is one of the largest industrial areas in the Netherlands. The Port of Rotterdam expanded about 25 kilomtres towards the sea and enormous areas of land were reclaimed for dock and industrial use. Amongst these developments were five major oil refineries and a large number of petro-chemical plants.

The reasons for this growth were:

1. Rotterdam was one of the few ports able to take large ocean-going bulk carriers.
2. It is at the mouth of the Rhine, giving water access to large areas of Europe.
3. It is also at the focus of road and rail networks, giving excellent access to markets throughout Europe.
4. Large areas of land could be reclaimed for industrial use.

Heavy industrial growth

Industries depending on the import of large quantities of raw materials are pulled to coastal locations, like Rotterdam. Here they gain from manufacturing at the **break-of-bulk** point where the raw material is unloaded. It can be processed and then transported on as finished products.

Modern industrial growth

New industrial regions have developed in recent years. In the USA, Silicon Valley near San Francisco (Figure 5) grew very rapidly as a centre for the electronics industry.

Exam tip

Time yourself over the next task. Take about ten minutes. Don't worry if you do take longer, but get some practice on actual exam questions.

Case study

Silicon Valley

The reasons for the growth of new high-technology industry here were:

1. Stanford University produced large numbers of highly qualified people in the electronics field.
2. The university established the Stanford Industrial Park for high-technology firms.
3. There was already a great deal of research-based industry in the area, especially the aircraft industry.
4. Research and development centres were set up here by several major companies.
5. The attractive environment was an inducement to employees.
6. All the above factors meant there was a huge concentration of people highly qualified in the skills needed for high-technology industry.
7. Once some small firms had achieved success it became easy for others to raise the capital they needed to start in business.
8. By the mid-1980s there were over 700 electronics-related companies in the area. This shows the importance of accessibility to labour and skills for a high-technology industry.

Figure 4

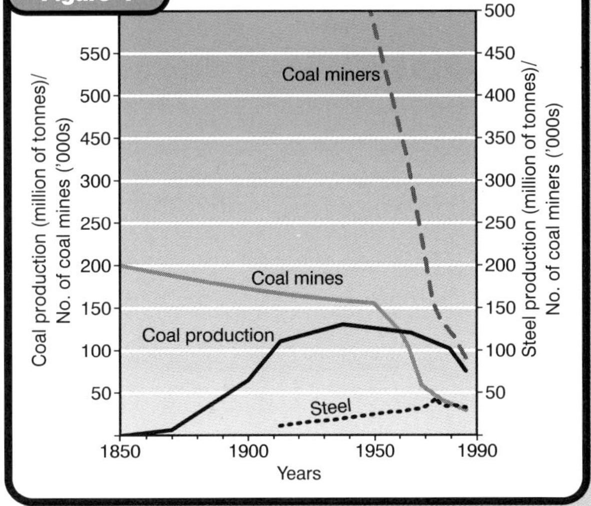

Decline and change in the Ruhr

Figure 5

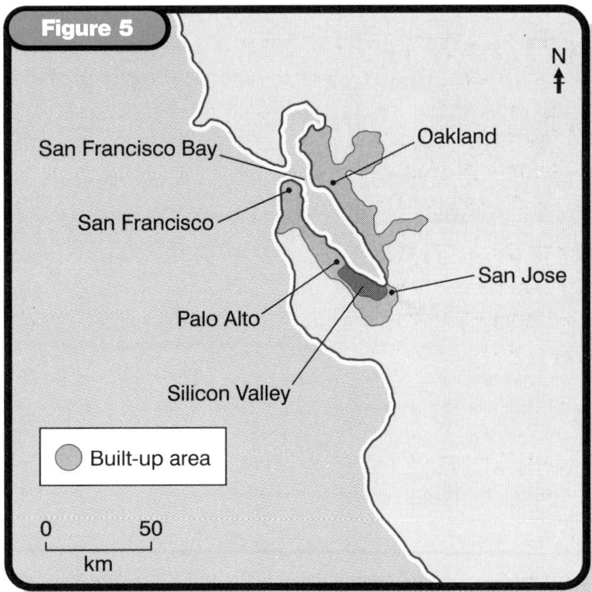

Silicon Valley, California

Task 1

Study the information about Silicon Valley.

Make a list of the items that would fit the multiplier effect as a way of explaining the growth of high-tech industry here.

Task 2

Look back at Figure 1 (page 102).

Study the information about Silicon Valley again. Make a copy of the diagram. Cross out the factors which are not important. Add very brief notes to the factors you have left.

review

The unit is based on case studies. They illustrate the kinds of developments that are common in old industrial areas and in new areas.

You have made summaries of each case study. Review them regularly.

Growing industrial regions

On the world scale, new industrial regions are developing. Countries around the **Pacific Rim** are particularly important with **Newly Industrialised Countries** (NICs) joining established industrial giants like Japan and the USA (Figure 6).

The NICs are individual countries where industry has developed rapidly. Not all of them were classed as less developed; some were at the poorer end of the more developed group of countries. They include some large countries. Brazil, for example, has become one of the world's major car producers. Others are small countries, like South Korea.

In each country the earlier industries depended on cheap labour. Production methods were less controlled giving poor working conditions and environmental problems. The early industries have been replaced by more modern high-technology ones. In some cases there is more emphasis on services, especially financial services, for example Singapore.

The growth of industry in the NICs is due to a number of factors. One or more of the following might be important in a particular country.

1. **Transnational** companies (TNCs), also called **multinational** companies (MNCs), have relocated manufacturing to these countries. This is usually because of cheaper labour costs and fewer regulations controlling industrial development. (TCNs are international businesses which have factories and offices in many countries, but their headquarters are almost always in a more developed country.)
2. Local **capital** (money) has been used to develop industry. Initially, goods like textiles and relatively simple industrial products were produced. With growth, capital has been invested in more sophisticated products. By developing the most modern industrial plants companies in the NICs are able to compete with longer established companies elsewhere in the world.
3. Governments have encouraged industrial growth. In some countries, special industrial zones have been created where development is allowed largely without controls. One example is the Shenzen Special Economic Zone in southern China immediately next to Hong Kong.
4. Special customs and trade agreeements allow goods to be imported and exported without paying duty. The **maquiladora** industry of Mexico is an example. US firms locate just across the border in Mexico and are allowed to import raw materials and to export finished products free of any customs duty. The attractions are low wages and little control of production methods.

Figure 6

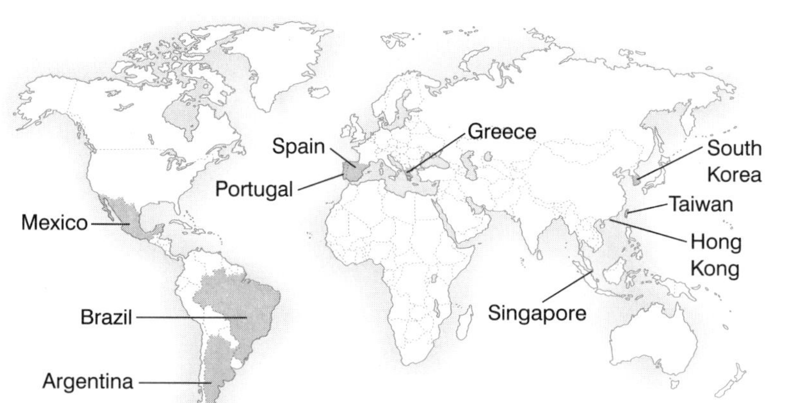

Newly industrialised countries

review

Draw a Mind Map using the four points above. Develop it using case studies you have learnt about.

12

Tourism

preview

What you need to know

- Factors affecting tourism
- Environments favouring tourism
- Tourism brings gains
- Tourism brings problems
- Tourism causes conflicts
- Importance of tourism in development
- Benefits of tourism for less developed countries
- Problems of tourism for less developed countries

Growth of tourism

Tourism is the world's fastest growing industry. It is now an activity which takes in the entire world.

The majority of tourists are from more developed countries. This is because time and money are necessities for tourists.

Domestic tourism

In the United Kingdom mass tourism started during the 19th century. It was mostly **domestic tourism**, that is, tourism within the country. For most people it involved day trips by train. Paid time off work became normal after 1938; only then did mass travel to the seaside for summer holidays really become possible.

Seaside resorts were the great attraction and they still are, but the pattern of tourism has changed. With greater choice and greater car ownership people are more flexible in their choice of type, time, length and destination of holiday. The result is that seaside resorts are not the only destination any more (Figure 1).

International tourism

International tourism on a mass scale started during the 1950s. As incomes rose and holidays became longer so the destinations and types of holidays became more varied. Air travel was a major factor in making the spread of international holidays possible. Now **mass tourism** is accelerating.

Most developed countries have well-established tourist industries. Specific parts of the countries are the main destinations, like the 'Costas' in Spain or the mountains in Austria (for summer as well as winter holidays). Major cities and rural areas also have their attractions for many people and draw many tourists.

Figure 1

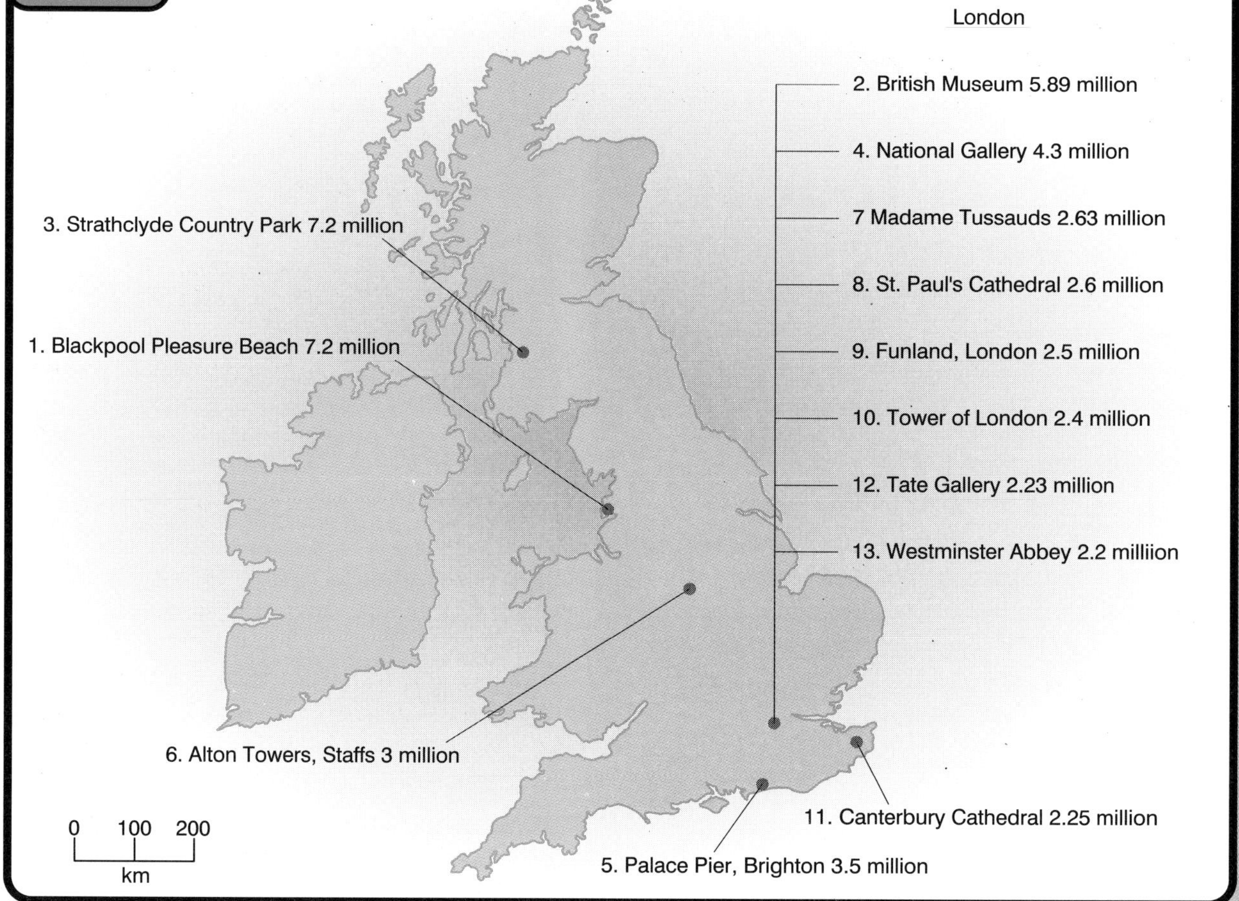

What attracts tourists? Top UK tourist attractions 1994

In less developed countries tourism is growing and where tourism is already established it is a major earner of **foreign currency**. In Egypt it brings in over 60% of foreign earnings and in Morocco the figure is 30%. In The Gambia, the very small tourist industry produces 10% of the country's total GNP.

In many less developed countries tourism is very patchy. Development concentrates in particular places. The local effect is great, but other areas may be completely unaffected. Much depends on where foreign companies want to build.

Resources for tourism

For tourism to develop there must be the right attractions or environments. These can be thought of as the **resources for tourism**.

Climate

Climate affects comfort and the kinds of activities that are possible. Holidays depending on sun have to avoid rainy seasons and cold regions. Winter sports holidays depend on reliable snow. Places which have only a short season of suitable conditions have problems in making enough money and problems of seasonal unemployment.

Coasts

Sun and sea go together for many holidays. Wide, flat and safe sandy beaches are the preference for many tourists and for developers. Water sports may require quite different conditions.

Figure 2

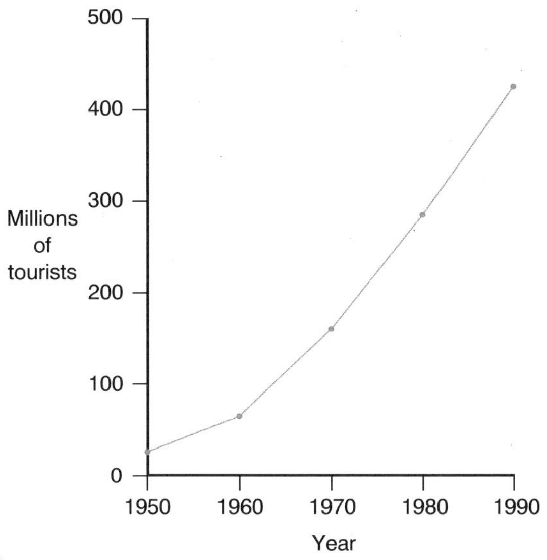

Growth in international tourism

Landscapes

The landscape of a country is the focus for many people. The attractions can be:

- spectacular landforms, like the Grand Canyon;
- activity holidays, like climbing or paragliding;
- touring to see a variety of natural and human landscapes;
- to get away to somewhere peaceful, far from the noise and rush of urban life;
- natural history holidays for bird watchers or people interested in wildlife generally.

History and culture

Many people are interested in:

- historical evidence of past cultures, such as the remains of Greek and Egyptian civilisations;
- the art and architecture of particular countries;
- the traditional ways of life still found in many areas.

In Europe the regions which have most of these resources are in the Mediterranean countries. The source of most of the international tourists is in the north, and their destination is the south, of Europe.

Figure 3

Tourism involves different purposes:
Religion – pilgrimages to holy places.
Business – travel is part of some people's work.
Family – visiting relatives or friends who have emigrated.
Sport and other interests – cities compete to hold major sporting events or cultural festivals because of the number of visitors they bring.
Holidays – rest, recreation, activities and interests mean that there are many types of holiday.

Why do people travel?

Other resources

Figure 1 shows specific attractions to tourists. Some of these are actually purpose-built tourist developments – like the Center Parcs of Britain and northern Europe, for example – which could be located anywhere. EuroDisney is an example of a theme park, another purpose-built tourist development. However, since developments like this cost large sums of money to build, the most successful ones need:

1 to be accessible to a large population, like Alton Towers in Staffordshire, within easy reach of the Manchester, Birmingham and South Yorkshire conurbations;

2 to have some of the other resources for tourism, especially good weather, if enough visitors are to be attracted, such as Disney World in Florida.

Test yourself

Make a Mind Map to review and summarise the unit. It breaks into two main sections and they break down into parts as well. Use that as a framework for learning.

Syllabus check

What case studies does your syllabus ask for?

The unit gives you general points. If your syllabus demands particular case studies, add their details to your summaries.

Problems with tourism

Advantages and disadvantages

In developed countries tourists tend to cause **problems** because:

- there are too many in one place

or

- there aren't enough tourists.

Too many tourists

This is a problem in '**honeypot**' areas like the Lake District. The motorway network makes the area very accessible to all the main population areas of the country (Figure 4). The tourist resource is the landscape, which offers many opportunities for different kinds of holiday (*see* page 109).

The Lake District has about 12 million visitors a year.

The **problems** it faces as a result include:

- traffic causing congestion on the narrow roads and parking problems;
- pollution partly from traffic but also from boating, especially on Windermere;
- threats to wildlife and vegetation, particularly by people on the lake shores disturbing wildlife and damaging habitats;
- erosion of footpaths on the mountains requires expensive work to repair them, apart from being unsightly.

Tourism does bring **benefits** to the area, however. They include:

- tourist spending on accommodation, meals, gifts and traditional arts and crafts. About 30% of the area's jobs are directly in tourism;
- environmental protection has increased with the increase in visitors who make it easier for conservation organisations to raise funds;

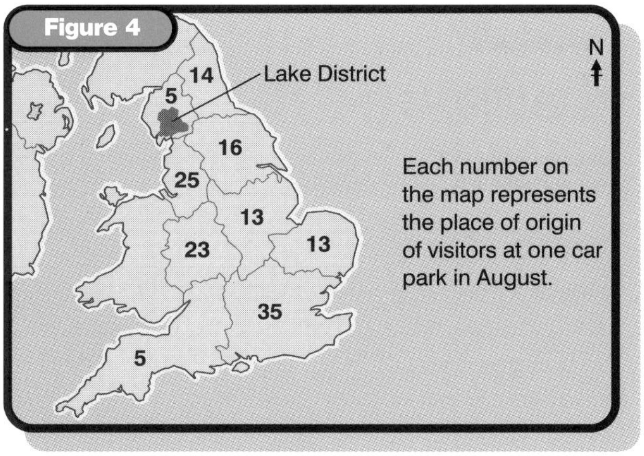

Distances travelled to the Lake District

- services in the local area are supported by visitors so that bus services used by tourists at busy times are still available for local people for the rest of the year;
- village shops which would close without the visitors are able to stay open.

Not enough tourists

Seaside resorts have always had the problem of a short summer season with virtually no tourists for the rest of the year. The problems became worse with holiday patterns changing and more people going abroad for their main holiday.

Many seaside resorts have invested in indoor facilities like sports, leisure and entertainment centres. Others have tried to spread the visitor season by building conference facilities to attract business travel as well as holiday travel.

Test yourself

For any tourist resort or area you have been to or which you have studied, make a 'problems and benefits' list.

review

Summarise the material in a Mind Map so you can review it easily and quickly.

Tourism in less developed countries

Gains

There are many **gains from tourism** for less developed countries. Five are listed below. Brainstorm to try to add more gains to this list, based on your own knowledge and experience.

1. **Employment**. Direct employment in hotels and restaurants is available to local people, as is work on construction. This is important as alternative work is limited. Employment as guides and drivers is an obvious benefit.
2. **Indirect benefits**. The tourists are a market for locally made craft goods like carvings. Local farmers and fishermen are sometimes able to sell their produce to hotels.
3. **General infrastructure improvements**. To attract tourists new and improved roads are needed. Airport improvements and better air services make other activities possible. An example is the export of vegetables and flowers from West Africa to Europe.
4. **Foreign funds**. Finance for local developments that would bring more tourists, including training of hotel staff.
5. **Foreign currency**. The industry brings foreign currency which is needed to pay for imports.

Losses

There are many **disadvantages** too.

1. **Imports.** Much of the produce used in hotels is imported, giving little benefit to local farmers.
2. **Foreign owners.** Hotels owned by foreign companies often put their own people into the senior jobs.

Figure 5

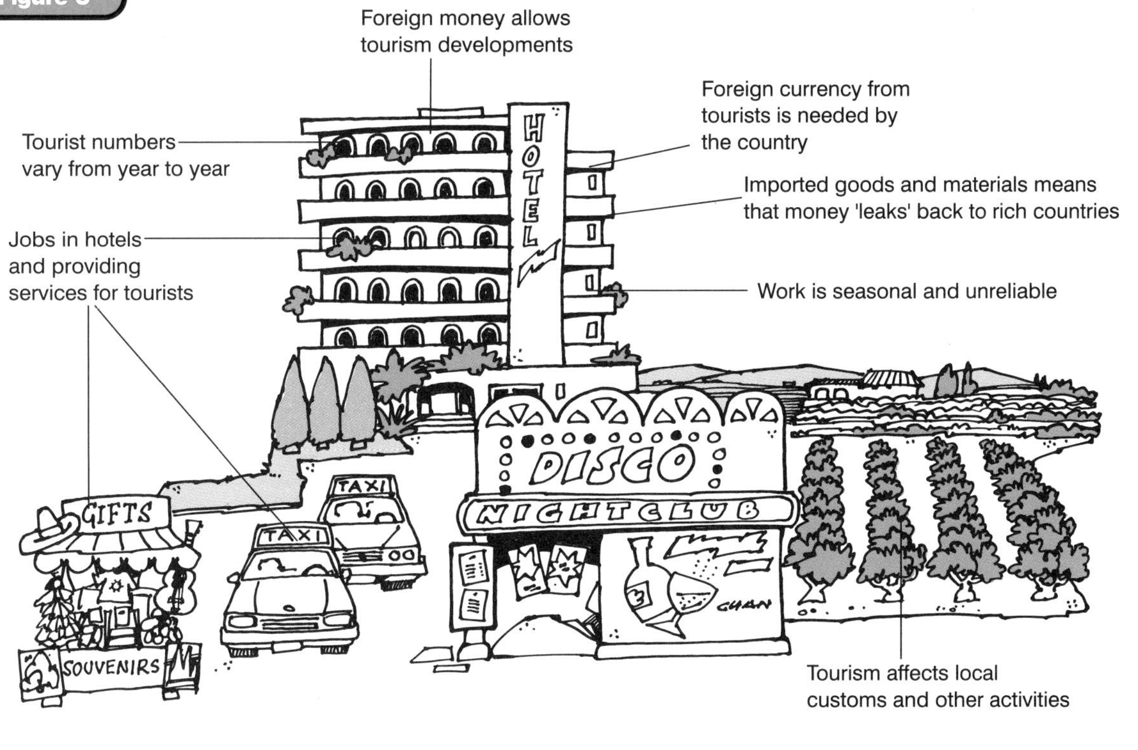
Foreign money allows tourism developments
Foreign currency from tourists is needed by the country
Tourist numbers vary from year to year
Imported goods and materials means that money 'leaks' back to rich countries
Jobs in hotels and providing services for tourists
Work is seasonal and unreliable
HOTEL
DISCO
NIGHTCLUB
TAXI
TAXI
GIFTS
SOUVENIRS
Tourism affects local customs and other activities

As part of your review add extra labels

Hotel Sunseeker

3 Unreliable work. Work is unreliable, with short seasons and tourist numbers varying.

4 Vulnerability. Heavy reliance on tourism makes a country vulnerable.
- **(a)** Political and economic events elsewhere in the world can have disastrous effects on tourist numbers.
- **(b)** Similar events in the countries themselves are even worse. After terrorist attacks on tourists in Egypt, visitor numbers plummeted.
- **(c)** If another region becomes more fashionable or is even cheaper, tourist numbers drop.

5 Destroys way of life. Tourism destroys local customs and ways of life.

6 Other economic activities. Tourist developments damage other areas of the economy. In Thailand, golf courses are using enormous amounts of irrigation water. Farmers have been starved of irrigation water and rice production has fallen.

7 Money leakage. Money spent by tourists does not stay in the country. Imported goods have to be paid for, profits are returned to companies' home countries, loans from abroad have to be repaid. 60% of Thailand's tourist income is estimated to 'leak' back to the developed world.

Test yourself

Look at Figure 5. Check each item of labelling. Give a tick if it is a gain to the country and a cross if it is a loss.

You can use the finished picture for future reviews.

review

Check that you now know why tourism is an activity with gains and losses.

The issues in less developed countries are not the same as in more developed countries.

Sample question 5

Higher

Study Figure 1, showing National Parks in England and Wales.
- **(i)** Which National Park is most accessible to very large numbers of people? Give reasons for your answer. [3 marks]
- **(ii)** Large numbers of visitors to National Parks may lead to conflicts of land use. Describe the land use conflicts which can occur in National Parks. [7 marks]

Suggested answer

- **(i)** Peak District. It is surrounded by major urban areas and almost surrounded by motorways giving access from further afield.
- **(ii)** Tourism and farming, quarrying, industry, military training, water supply, forestry, local towns and villages. There can be conflicts between any of these and tourism, either with these interfering with tourism or with tourism interfering with them. Develop individual points and, if possible, name examples you have studied.

Figure 1

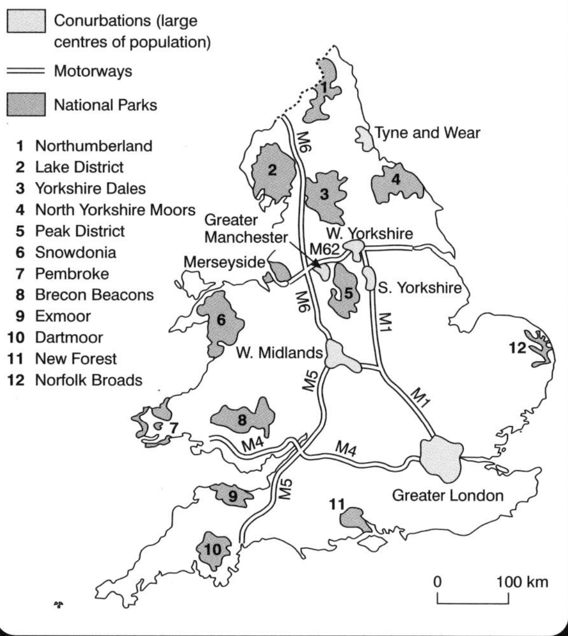

13

Trade

preview

What you need to know

- The importance of trade
- The patterns of world trade
- Changes in trade patterns
- The meaning of dependence and interdependence
- The role of transnational companies

Trade patterns

The importance of trade

Trade between countries is important for several reasons:

- Resources are not distributed evenly around the world.
- The demand for resources is not evenly spread, either.
- The distribution of manufacturing is uneven.
- Differences in types and quality of products create a demand in other countries.
- Trade produces wealth and jobs.

Task

Brainstorm a few more points to add to the list above.

Imports and exports

Trade involves **imports** and **exports**. Imports are goods coming from overseas; exports are goods which are sold to other countries.

Services also form part of trade. These include:

- tourism
- financial services
- sea transport
- air transport.

Statistics for imports and exports are given by:

1. Value, usually given in US dollars in tables of international statistics.
2. Percentages, to show the relative importance of different groups of exports or imports to a country.

Figure 1

(a) UK exports and imports (by value)

	£ million Exports	£ million Imports
1955	3 073	3 386
1975	19 185	22 441
1995	135 200	145 727

(b) UK exports and imports by commodity (% of total value)

	Exports	Imports
Food, beverages and tobacco	7.5	9.6
Basic materials	1.7	3.5
Fuels	6.2	4.8
Semi-manufactured goods	26.2	23.7
Manufactured goods	47.6	50.3
Others	10.8	8.1

UK trade statistics

Patterns of world trade

There are two main points:

1 World trade is not distributed evenly.

2 It is dominated by the developed countries.

Figure 2 shows exports and imports for developed countries, less developed countries, oil producing countries and the 30 least developed countries. The difference between the developed countries and the less developed countries is great. Check back to the chapter on Population (pages 50–9) to see how the populations of those two groups compare. This shows just how the developed world dominates trade.

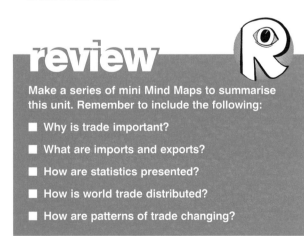

75% of exports from developed countries go to other developed countries. With less developed countries 60% of their exports go to the developed world.

Figure 2

	Millions of US dollars Imports	Millions of US dollars Exports
Total world trade	3 716 705	3 632 090
Developed countries	2 535 248	2 538 789
Less developed countries	1 091 065	998 254
OPEC	153 325	182 809
Least developed countries	90 393	95 047

World trade

Most exports of developed countries are manufactured goods. Developing countries have also increased the proportion of their manufactured exports. However, nearly 50% of their exports are made up of primary products. The poorest of the developing countries rely very much on primary-product exports. In some cases these make up almost all their exports.

How patterns of trade are changing

1 The Pacific Rim region is becoming one major trading bloc. Trade is growing rapidly between the established developed countries like the USA, Japan and Australia, the newly industrialised countries like Taiwan, Hong Kong, South Korea and Singapore (also called the Asian Tigers), and the other rapidly developing countries of the region, especially China.

2 In Europe the trend has been to increase trade within the region. In 1948, 48% of trade was within Europe, now it is more than 60%.

review

Make a series of mini Mind Maps to summarise this unit. Remember to include the following:

- Why is trade important?
- What are imports and exports?
- How are statistics presented?
- How is world trade distributed?
- How are patterns of trade changing?

Dependence and interdependence

Dependence

All countries depend on trade to a greater or lesser extent. **Dependence** becomes a problem when countries rely too much on one product. Less developed countries which rely on primary products are vulnerable in four ways:

1. They rely on demand from more developed countries which is where most exports go. A fall in demand can mean an enormous fall in income from exports if one primary product makes up 60% of a country's exports.
2. Prices also vary with demand. A fall in demand also means a fall in price so exporters of primary products are hit twice; total exports fall and the price falls.
3. Primary product prices rise and fall much more than prices of manufactured goods. These wide fluctuations make development planning difficult in less developed countries.
4. Prices of manufactured goods tend to increase over time more than prices of primary products. The result is a bigger gap between income from exports and payments for imports, so many less developed countries need to export more to pay for less. On average, between 1960 and today, primary product prices (apart from oil) have halved. This means that countries have to export twice as much to pay for the same imports.

Figure 3

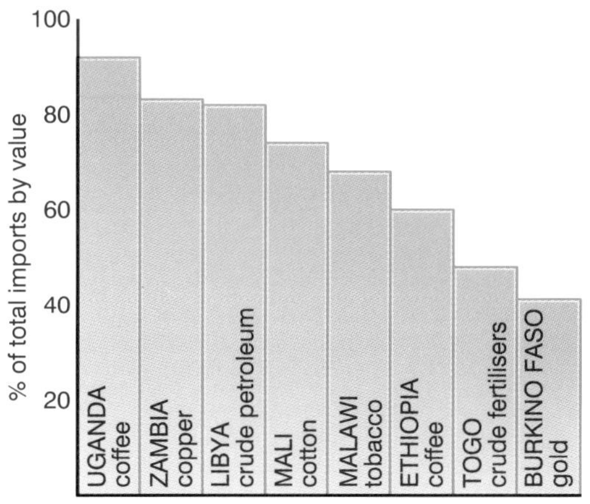

Dependence on a single export product

Figure 4

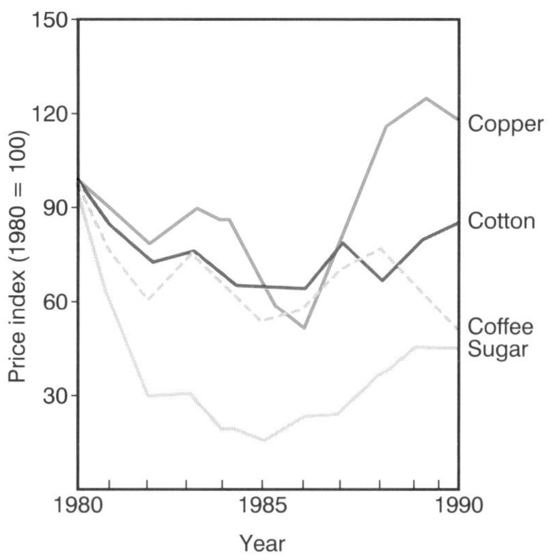

Changes in some primary product prices (1980–90)

Interdependence

Trade involves **interdependence**, where countries depend on other countries. The more trade there is, the more interdependent countries become.

Task

Check your home for products from other countries. Include different categories of things. Stop when you get to 20 countries. This should prove that we are all interdependent and trade is what makes us so.

Transnational companies (TNCs)

Transnationals (TNCs), which are also called multinationals (MNCs), are companies which operate on a worldwide basis. They are mostly run from more developed countries; they are very large and very wealthy. In fact, the sales of any TNCs are greater than the total GNP of many countries.

Figure 5

TNC	Country	Sales ($ millions)	Employees
General Motors	USA	125 126	761 400
Royal Dutch/Shell	UK/Neth	107 204	137 000
Exxon	USA	105 885	104 000
Ford	USA	98 275	370 400
IBM	USA	69 018	373 816
Toyota	Japan	64 516	96 849
IRI	Italy	61 433	419 500
BP	UK	59 541	116 750
Mobil	USA	58 770	67 300
General Electric	USA	58 414	298 000

Top ten transnationals

These major companies are very important in world trade. They are involved in 70% of the world's trade. A large part of this trade is actually between different parts of the same company. For example, in the aluminium industry most mining, refining and smelting is controlled by four transnationals (Alcan, Alcoa, Kaiser and Reynolds) and they control the movements between each stage of the industry and therefore control most trade to do with the industry.

Test yourself

In the oil industry TNCs are involved in every stage of the activity. Brainstorm a list of as many parts of the oil industry as you can – in particular, think about what is made from oil.

Exam tip

Practising this kind of brainstorming will help you to do the same thing in your examination. It will help you to use your general knowledge – you know far more geography than you think you do!

review

Check that you now know about the significance of dependence, interdependence and TNCs.

Remember that it helps to draw on your general knowledge. These ideas will help you to understand case studies.

14 Development

Development preview

What you need to know

- Features of less developed countries
- Topics important to development issues
- The difficulties or obstacles to development

Development themes

Before you start

Most of the work to do with development and less developed countries is included in other units. This is because every topic in geography is important to studies of development.

Task

(a) Before looking at the other units in the book do a brainstorm on each topic to check how much you already know. You will have studied them at Key Stage 3, even if you haven't done them yet in your GCSE course.

(b) Make a mini Mind Map for each topic.

Now you can look through the pages listed below. Mark the sections to do with less developed countries by drawing a frame around them with highlighter; that way, you will be able to find them easily.

1 Inequalities or differences in development at global, national and local scales – *see* pages 57–9.

2 Agriculture – *see* pages 98–9.

3 Industrial development – *see* pages 106 and 111–12.

4 Urbanisation – *see* pages 72–4.

5 Trade problems – *see* page 115.

6 Population – *see* pages 53–6.

Contrasts in wealth

The contrasts in wealth at world level are shown on Figure 1. There are three points to note:

1 There is a great difference in wealth between the richest and the poorest countries. This is called the **development gap**.

Figure 1

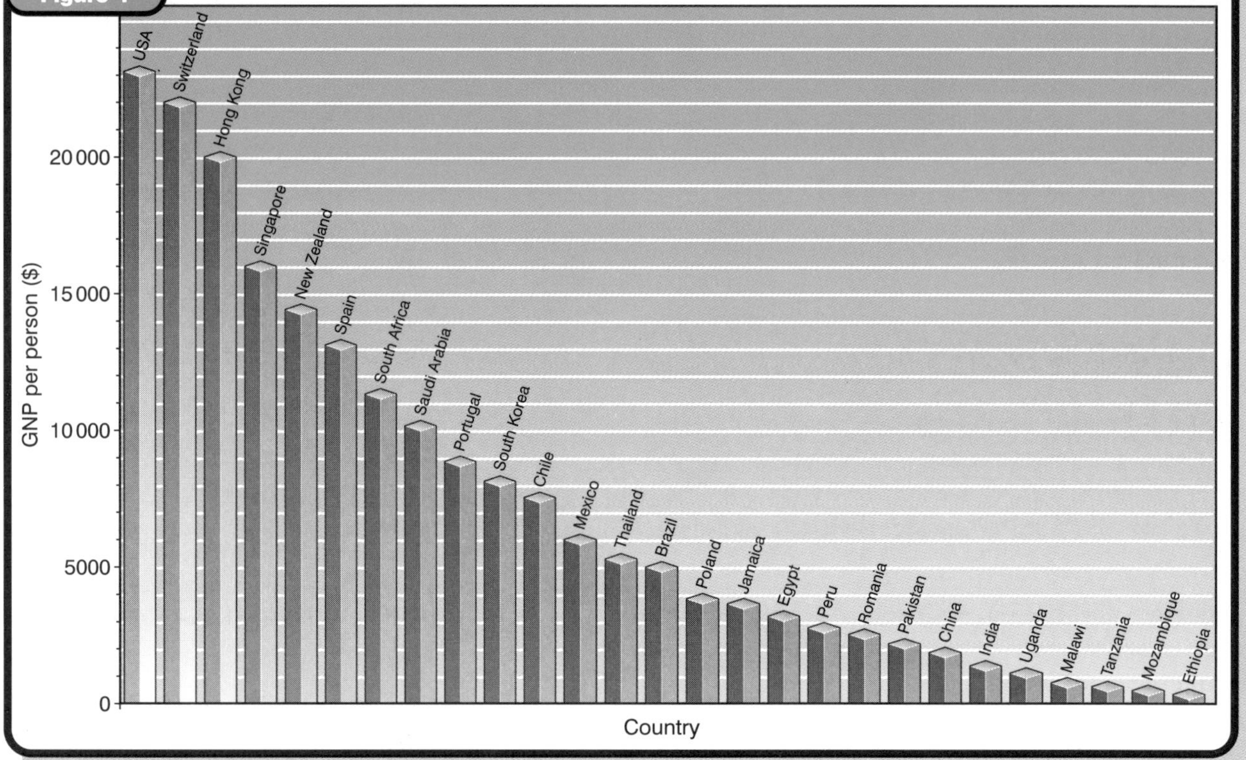

Average Gross National Product per person ($) 1992

2 There is no actual 'gap', in that there are countries with low, middle and high incomes.

3 The bar chart is based on average incomes. In all countries there will be a spead of incomes from low to high. In less developed countries, however, the richest have incomes well above the average figures, while the very much larger poorer section of the populations have incomes well below the average.

Gross National Product (GNP) or wealth is one way to compare countries. Many other **indicators of development** are used to give a clearer picture (*see* page 59). The **Human Development Index** is another way of making comparisons.

Internal and external agencies

There are very many organisations involved in dealing with problems of development. They are of different types:

- ★ **Intergovernmental.** The United Nations is the highest-level intergovernmental organisation. It has many sections which are concerned with issues of development. These include the United Nations Development Programme (UNDP), the Food and Agriculture Organisation (FAO) and the World Health Organisation (WHO). One of the most important is the World Bank. Other intergovernmental organisations are regional, like the European Union, which allocates funds for development aid. Some are based on former colonial links like the British Commonwealth or the Franc Zone which includes former French colonies.
- ★ **Governmental.** These are departments of the governments of individual countries.
- ★ **Non-governmental** organisations (NGOs) which include aid charities, groups of activists and independent research institutes.

All of these are involved in programmes of development. NGOs and intergovernmental organisations have to work with governmental bodies. In any one less developed country there could be projects run by agencies of the United Nations, other intergovernmental organisations, by government departments, and by a number of NGOs.

Exam tip

There are frequently items in the news to do with development and the different agencies working in the field. Every time one is mentioned make a note of it, what it is doing and where. You will quickly build up some examples to mention in examination answers.

Development difficulties

Many explanations have been put forward for the problems of less developed countries.

Environment

Many less developed countries are in semi-arid areas. For example, the countries of the Sahel region, immediately south of the Sahara Desert in Africa, have far less reliable rainfall than countries nearer to the equator. Periodic droughts result in lost crops. Soil erosion can follow and can be particularly bad if farmland has been extended into more marginal areas.

Natural hazards affect less developed countries more than the more developed countries. This is partly because of their location and partly because they are less developed:

- tropical storms cause great problems, including flooding as well as wind damage;
- many less developed countries are in regions prone to earthquakes and volcanic activity;
- many countries are unable to afford the early warning and protection schemes that richer countries have;
- at the simpler level, poorer quality building structures and materials result in greater damage and, hence, greater casualties.

Task

Other parts of this book provide more points to add to the above list. First, see if you can brainstorm any more points; then decide which units are likely to be helpful; then find the extra points. Do the same for other parts of this unit.

Population

The units on Population deal with the problems that are linked to:

- population growth
- population structure.

Another population related issue is health.

- Undernourishment and malnutrition produce deficiency diseases; this makes people less able to fight off infectious diseases.
- Tropical areas have widespread diseases which are debilitating (cause weakness) and which cause millions of deaths. Malaria is one example and bilharzia is another.
- Low incomes often make it impossible for people to buy the medicines which would prevent, for example, bilharzia being contracted.
- The distribution of health care is usually uneven, with limited access for people in rural areas.

Manufacturing industry

Many less developed countries depend on primary resources. (*See* the units on Trade). Associated with this is the limited growth of manufacturing industry. Development of manufacturing industry helps development by:

- reducing the amount of manufactured goods which are imported;
- providing job opportunities;
- **diversification** of the economy so that there is a greater variety of economic activities. This makes the country's economy less vulnerable to changes in world trade;
- processing raw materials produced by the country before export provides a greater export income.

It is often difficult to develop manufacturing industry because:

- in a poor country the market for manufactured goods is too small for the industry to be profitable;
- competition from established industrial countries makes it difficult for industries to become established;
- lack of a skilled workforce;
- lack of the capital needed to establish industry.

Much industry that does grow is owned by foreign companies from the developed world. These are often large transnational companies (TNCs), and as profits are returned to the parent country the less developed country does not benefit fully. TNCs are also likely to move to other countries if conditions change, such as the introduction of tighter environmental controls.

Trade, aid and international investment

These are all linked. The particular problems of trade are dealt with in other units. Here it is linked to aid and international investment.

Aid is a major issue because there are different views on its value. There are two kinds of aid.

1. Official aid to less developed countries comes from intergovernmental agencies of the United Nations or from individual governments. The latter are often for particular projects and often linked to trade with the donor country.
2. Non-governmental organisations (NGOs), or development charities, like Oxfam and Intermediate Technology provide small but growing amounts of aid.

Points made against aid policies include:

- much official aid is tied to purchases from the country providing aid;
- a large proportion of aid funds is used to pay salaries of consultants from the country providing the aid;
- the result of these is that the receiving country does not get the full benefit of the aid.

In favour of aid are these points:

- it benefits both sides as the donor country receives export orders and the receiving country is able to develop;
- aid can support the growth of development programmes already set up;
- emergency aid is vital to deal with natural disasters and refugee problems.

International investment by commercial banks is another way of meeting the need for capital for development projects. Major projects, especially for developing the infrastructure (e.g. transport systems) require large amounts of capital. Commercial loans are an alternative to using income from exports. However, repayments have to be made to a timetable and interest rates vary. The results have been disastrous for some countries, with almost all export earnings being used to repay interest on loans.

Other investment, especially directly by overseas companies, has been mentioned above. Much economic activity is, in fact, controlled by overseas companies. In agriculture, for instance, many of the plantations producing export crops are in fact owned by overseas companies.

review

Make a Mind Map to summarise this unit. Use this one as a base.

Figure 2

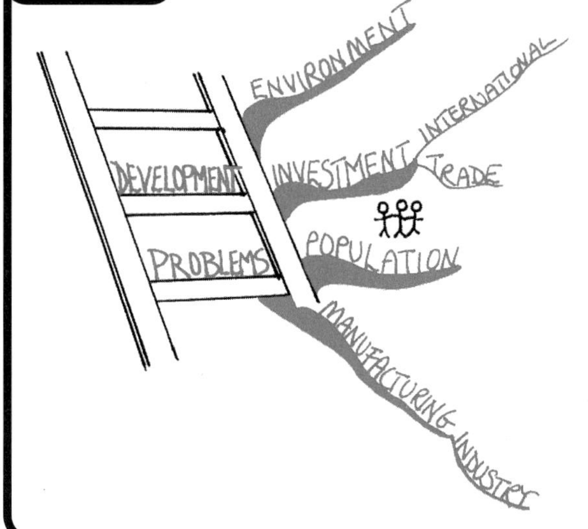

15 Resources

preview

What you need to know

- The types of resources
- Sustainable resource use
- Development of energy resources and location
- Exploitation of resources
- Environmental impact
- The reasons for conflict
- Location of water supplies
- Problems with water supply
- Conflict over reservoir building
- Multiple use of reservoirs
- Water and development problems
- Development of energy resources
- Types of renewable energy resources
- Factors affecting the location of renewable energy sites

Types of resources

Resources are useful natural materials or objects, like iron ore, timber or coal. They are exploited by people and used as energy sources or raw materials for manufacturing industry.

Land and landscapes are also considered as resources. Land, especially soil, is the resource for agriculture. Landscape is regarded as a resource for tourism as well as general recreation.

Renewable or flow resources

These are resources which renew themselves naturally, like water supplies, or can be replaced, as when forests are replanted.

Non-renewable or stock resources

Once used they cannot be replaced. Metal minerals and fossil fuels are **non-renewable**. Other minerals like gravel can, in theory, be **recycled**.

Exploitation

Resource development affects the environment. It may be extremely damaging, destroying local ecosystems and societies as well as creating regional problems.

Exploiting resources creates **conflicts** when the new developments cause problems for other uses and activities.

Sustainable use of resources

Sustainable development

This means using resources that are needed now, but without harming prospects for the future.

Figure 1

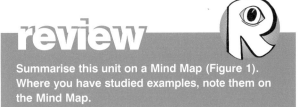

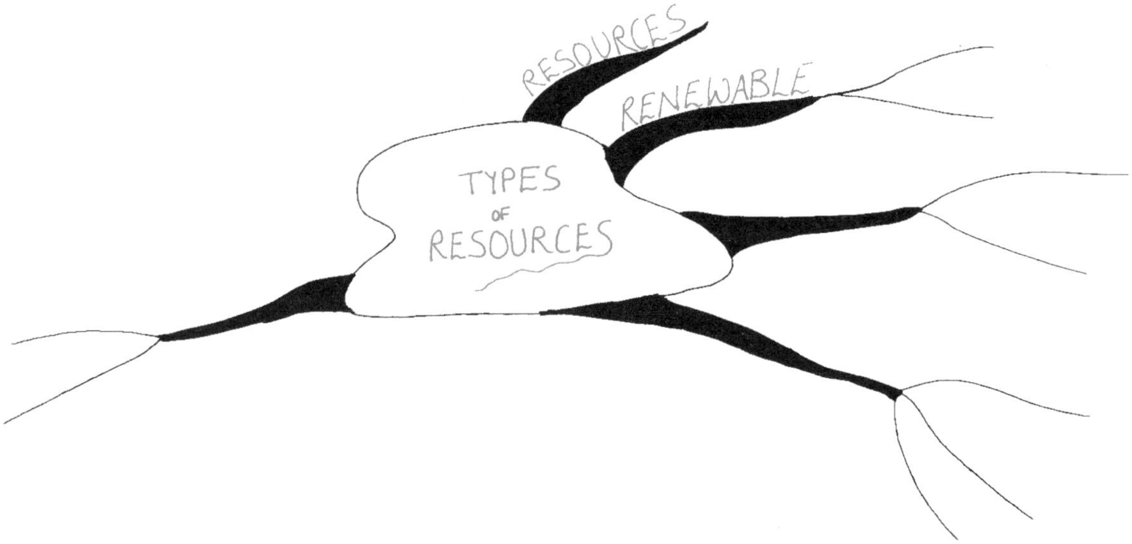

Recycling

This involves reclaiming and reusing materials from manufactured goods that have reached the end of their life.

Substitution

Here one metal is substituted for another. Aluminium can be used in some electrical applications.

Conservation

This includes recycling, substitution and any means of reducing the demand for resources.

Levels of development and resource use

The more developed countries use 90% of the world's resources but they have only 30% of its population. Two things are happening which change the situation:

1 In the more developed world public pressure and a stable population is gradually resulting in more sustainable approaches being taken. Energy consumption, for instance, is fairly constant and even likely to fall slightly.

2 In less developed countries more resources are going to be used due to rising population and increased development. Energy use itself will rise in line with development.

review

Summarise this unit on a Mind Map (Figure 1). Where you have studied examples, note them on the Mind Map.

Factors affecting patterns of exploitation

Development

Mineral and fossil fuel resources are found in specific locations. Not all locations are ideal for development.

- Accessible deposits are exploited before less accessible deposits.
- As resources are used up less accessible deposits are developed.
- Large deposits are exploited before small ones.
- Richer quality deposits are used before poorer quality ones.
- Of the less accessible deposits, those which are easy to extract or mine are used first.
- New techniques allow the exploitation of resources previously unworkable.
- Scarcity encourages the search for new resources.
- New exploration technology aids the discovery of new resources.

The above factors are to do with distance and the economics of mining. Other factors can be important:

- **Transport technology**, such as bulk carriers enabling low-value, bulky products to be transported at low cost.
- **Economic factors**, such as world demand and therefore world price levels.
- **Political factors**, such as controls put on development by a particular government.
- **Environmental issues**, such as the impact on the local natural environment.

Figure 2

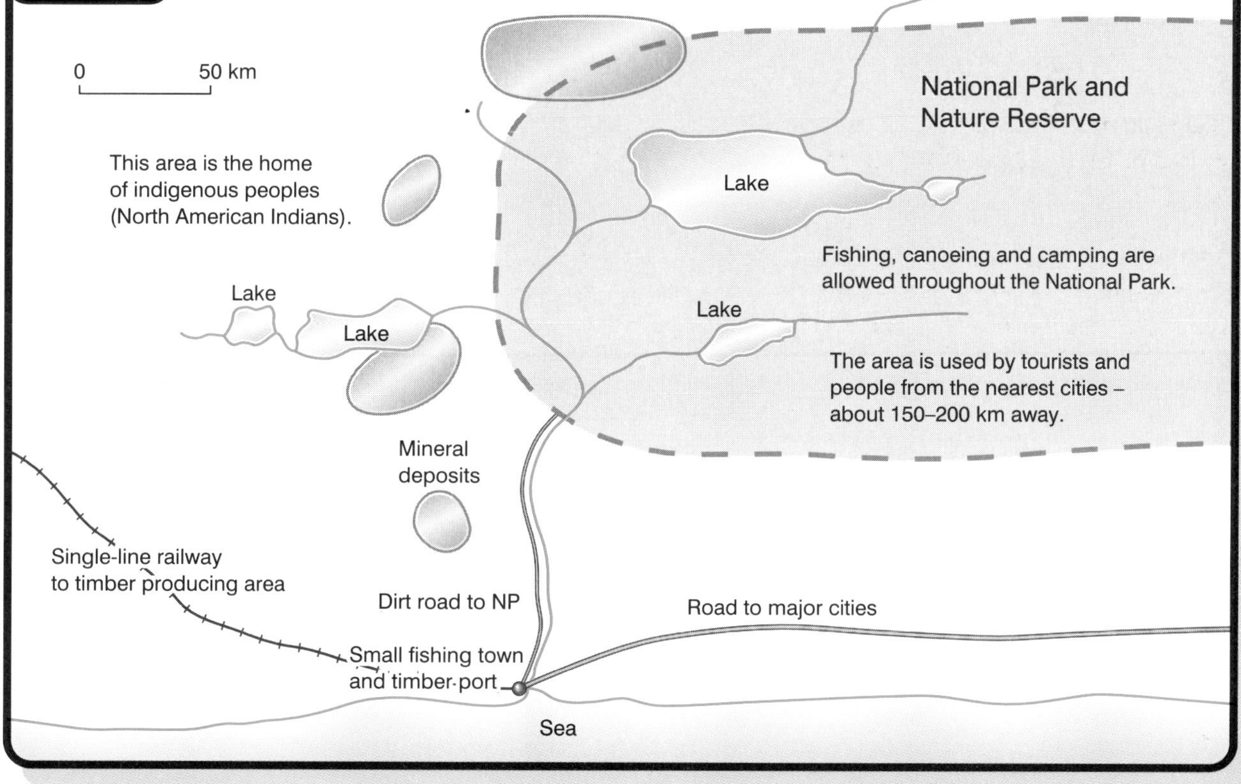
0 50 km
National Park and Nature Reserve
This area is the home of indigenous peoples (North American Indians).
Lake
Lake
Lake
Lake
Fishing, canoeing and camping are allowed throughout the National Park.
The area is used by tourists and people from the nearest cities – about 150–200 km away.
Mineral deposits
Single-line railway to timber producing area
Dirt road to NP
Road to major cities
Small fishing town and timber port
Sea

Factors affecting development

Task 1

Answering these questions will reinforce your understanding.

Figure 2 shows an area with mineral deposits.

(a) Label the deposits in the order in which they are likely to be developed.

(b) What facilities would have to be built before some of the deposits could be exploited?

(c) What kinds of environmental effects would the spread of mining have?

(d) Using information on the map list the groups who would probably object to the developments.

Mining methods

Quarrying

This is the usual method for obtaining hard rock, like limestone. Most is broken down into gravel and sand.

It has a great environmental impact. Visually, quarries intrude on the landscape. Dust and noise from the operation and from lorries travelling through the local area of the quarry disrupt local life.

Gravel dredging

(a) This method is used to obtain sand and gravel from deposits at or near the surface.

Because the areas are low lying, usually in wide river valleys, the workings become flooded after extraction and cannot be returned to farming.

(b) It is also used to extract minerals (generally heavy metals, like tin) deposited in river gravels.

There are environmental problems because there is so much waste since only the metal mineral is wanted.

Underground mining

Used where the mineral or fossil fuel is found in lodes, veins or seams. Usually requires greater capital investment.

Waste or spoil from mining builds up as large tips in the locality or is dumped in large holes such as old quarries. The waste causes a greater environmental problem than the mining itself. Water pumped from the mine may also cause problems. Subsidence causes surface damage, including damage to buildings and roads.

Opencast mining

If deposits are close to the surface they can be extracted by huge diggers.

Overlying soil and rock (overburden) has to be removed first. If removed carefully the overburden can be replaced and the land returned to its former use after mining has finished.

The dust and noise from the mining and the disruption by the transport lorries has a severe effect on the local area, perhaps for many years.

Open-pit mining

Open pits are large, deep holes in the ground. They are generally used to extract metals, such as copper. They are worked on a massive scale. This is necessary because the grade of ore is usually poor. As a result there is an enormous amount of waste. A pit of 80 hectares (ha) needs to be on a site of 800 ha to allow for waste disposal.

Environmentally, the problems can be devastating for localities – destruction of natural ecosystems over a large area, disruption and pollution of rivers and underground water supplies, disruption of peoples' lives, health problems caused by dust, and visual scarring of the area.

Task 2

Make a Mind Map to show the different types of mining and their features.

Task 3

What are the environmental problems caused by extraction of minerals?

Make a list. Add them to your Mind Map in Task 2.

Try to include some additional problems.

Are there any examples in your local area or in areas you have visited? If so, make some notes about it to use as a case study.

Project idea 1

Mineral extraction in some form takes place in all parts of the country. An example could be used for a coursework project. These are some of the questions to think about.

Where is it? What sort of mining? What minerals? Who owns it? How much land is used? What are the environmental effects?

Project idea 2

Mineral extraction can be tackled another way. How is it important to a locality?

In many places coal mining has stopped with serious effects on local communities. This is one possible project.

In other areas, mineral extraction is an important source of jobs. Here you could study the importance of the activity to the local area as a whole.

Test yourself

To check your learning, complete the crossword (Figure 3).

Figure 3

Across

1 Charges make discoveries and exploitation possible (10)
3 Underground mining gets at ______, veins and seams (5)
6 A quantity of resource in the rocks (7)
7 For getting hard rock out (9)

Down

1 A heavy metal (3)
2 Big hole in the ground (4, 3)
4 Removing gravel (8)
5 Coal is a fossil _____ (4)

Case study

Selar, Cwmgwrach, Neath Valley, South Wales

Opencast coal mining in a quiet valley with ancient oak woodland.

The hole will be about 800 football pitches in area and 150 metres deep.

It has destroyed the site of an SSSI (*see* page 140), although the grassland has been relocated to a new site about 1 km away.

It will greatly affect people's health, says specialist in respiratory diseases.

For ten years or more there will noise, blastings and heavy traffic and general ugliness, disturbing the previous tranquillity.

With another opencast site proposed nearby, the village of Cwmgwrach will be all but surrounded by opencast workings.

Against – Wales Against Opencast group, local people and local action groups, Earthfirst! environmental activists, district council, parish council

For – government, county council, Celtic Energy (the development company)

Possible effects

Extra jobs – 200 jobs created directly and indirectly but others say that workers will be transferred from other sites as needed.

House prices – dropping quickly.

Projected profits – £50 million.

Future – in six years' time the land will be restored to deciduous woodland, mountain pasture and agricultural grazing land.

Local environmental issues

Proposals to develop mineral resources cause controversy and conflict. Different people and different groups of people have different attitudes towards such developments.

Figure 4

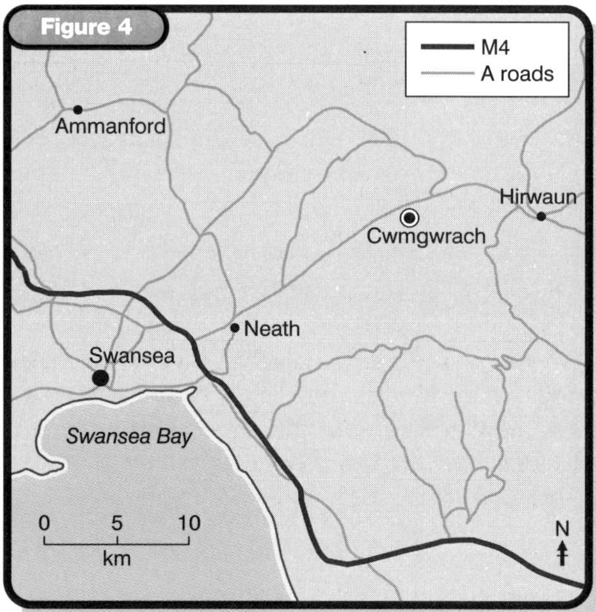

Location of Selar, Cwmgwrach

Task

(a) What are the objections to the opencast scheme?

(b) Who are the main objectors?

(c) What are the benefits of the scheme?

(d) Who are the main proponents of the scheme?

(e) Suggest reasons why the two groups have such opposing attitudes to the scheme?

review

Check that you now know:

- The factors that affect the location of mining
- The different methods of mining
- The effects of the mining methods
- The issues that arise from proposals to mine.

Water

Task 1

Skim through the unit quickly first, then start a Mind Map. Develop it as you work through the unit.

Remember case studies.

Water supply

Water supplies come from:

- **Boreholes**. They tap underground water-bearing rocks called aquifers.
- **Reservoirs**. These are mostly in upland areas; they store water. Pipelines or rivers are used to take the water to the areas of demand.
- **Rivers**. Water is taken out (or abstracted), and piped to and stored in a local reservoir.

Problems with water supply

Water supply and water demand do not match.

In Britain most rain falls in the north and west; most people live in the east and south. The areas of water surplus and water demand differ. This means there are large-scale transfers of water. Some examples are:

- Mid-Wales to the West Midlands
- Lake District to Manchester.

The areas which depend most on underground water and abstraction are in the south-east. Water treatment to clean the water returning to the river allows the water to be abstracted again further downstream.

Exam tip

Don't lose easy marks. For some marks you only have to pick out facts from the information on a map or diagram. Do it carefully. Task 2 will give you some practice. Notice that (d) and (e) go further than straight facts. With these use your geographical knowledge to make some reasonable suggestions.

Case study

The water supply system in South Wales

In the 1995 drought, water stored in the Elan valley reservoirs was released into the river Wye during July and August. It was taken out at Monmouth, cleaned at water works near Pontypool and supplied to Cardiff and other parts of south-east Wales (*see* Figure 5).

Task 2

Use the case study material and Figure 5.

(a) How many reservoirs or groups of reservoirs are there?

(b) Which rivers are used for water transfer?

(c) Which places are supplied with water transferred by river and pipeline?

(d) Which areas have a water surplus and which areas have a water deficit?

(e) Suggest reasons for the water surplus and water deficit.

Conflict over reservoir building

The construction of reservoirs has usually caused **controversy**.

Conflicts of interest focus on **demand for water** and the **local effects** of reservoir building.

Demand for water

- domestic use
- electricity generation
- industry
- agriculture.

Figure 5

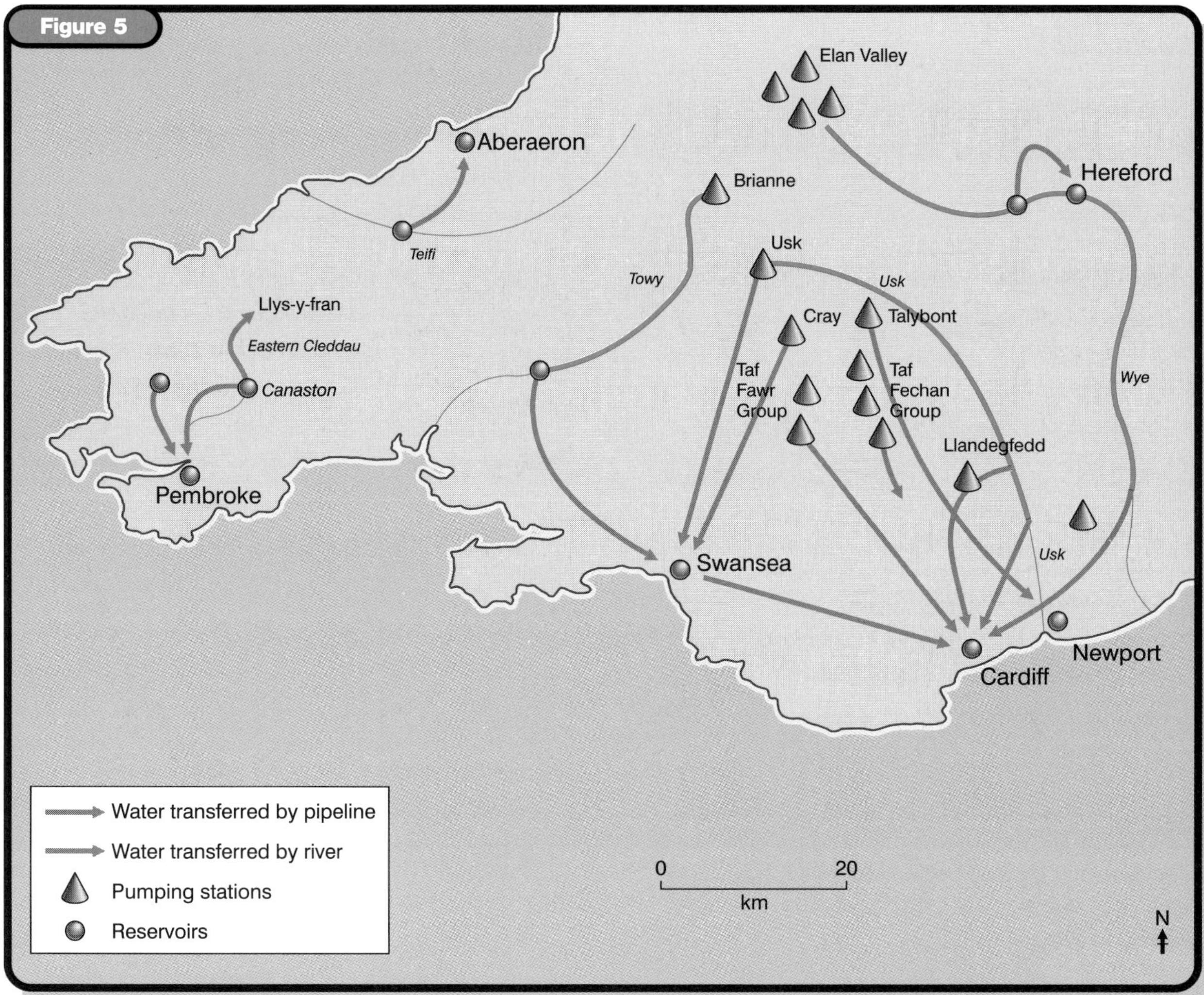

South Wales water supply system

Local effects

- Flooding of farmland, usually the best land in hilly areas, resulting in loss of farming jobs.
- Flooding of settlements, causing depopulation in rural areas and loss of services.
- Destruction of wildlife habitats.
- Disruption to normal life during construction.
- In lowland areas loss of large acreages of higher-grade farmland as these reservoirs are usually shallower.

Figure 6 shows the consequences of a proposal for a lowland reservoir in southern England as well as the reasons for building it.

Task 3

(a) Why are people worried about the lowland reservoir proposal?

(b) What direct effects will there be?

(c) What are the reasons for building the reservoir?

(d) What could be a local use for some of the water from the reservoir?

(e) What groups of people would be in favour of the project? Why? Are they local?

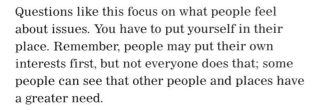

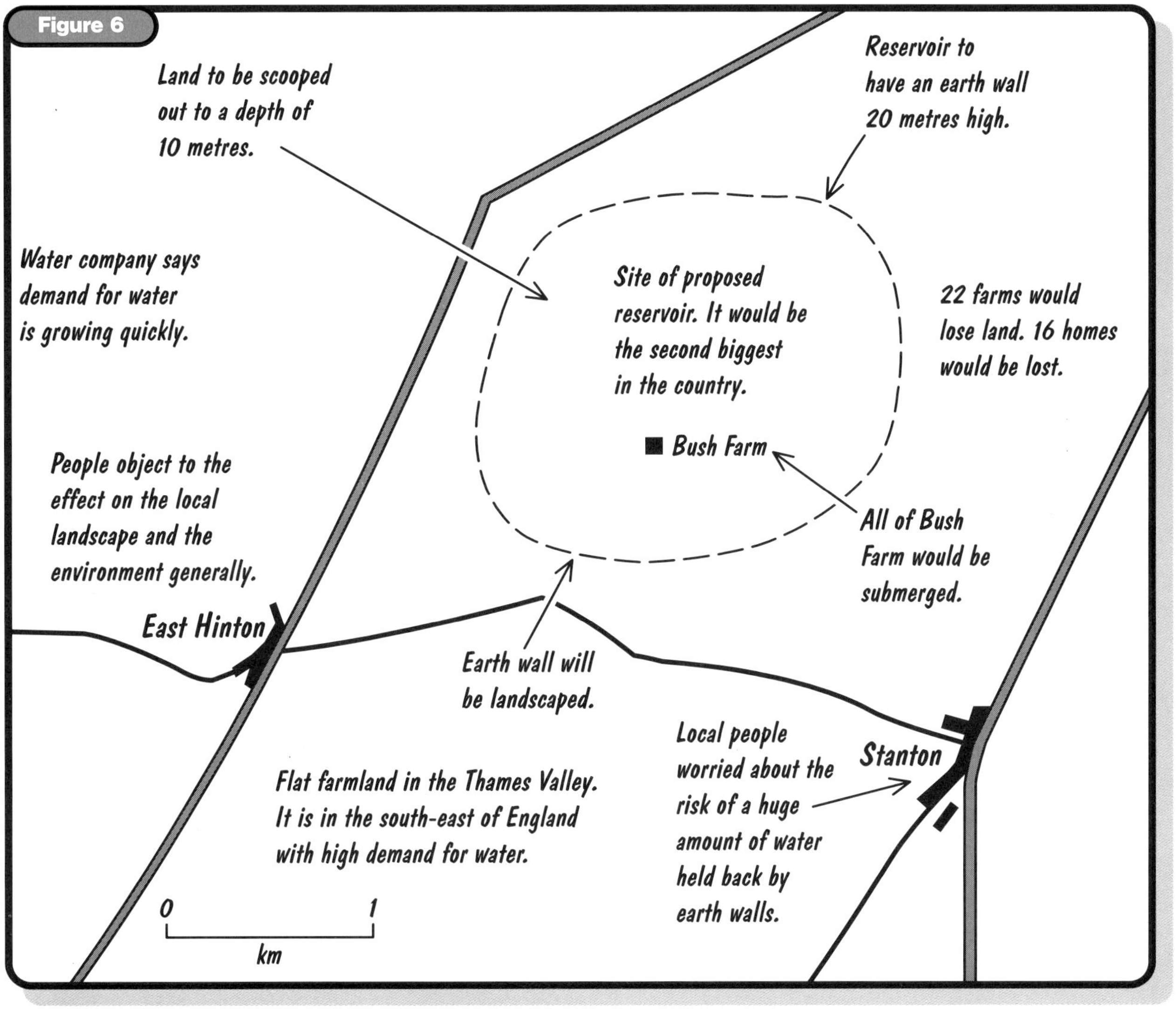

Figure 6
Land to be scooped out to a depth of 10 metres.
Reservoir to have an earth wall 20 metres high.
Water company says demand for water is growing quickly.
Site of proposed reservoir. It would be the second biggest in the country.
22 farms would lose land. 16 homes would be lost.
Bush Farm
People object to the effect on the local landscape and the environment generally.
All of Bush Farm would be submerged.
East Hinton
Earth wall will be landscaped.
Local people worried about the risk of a huge amount of water held back by earth walls.
Stanton
Flat farmland in the Thames Valley. It is in the south-east of England with high demand for water.
0
1
km

Lowland reservoir proposal

Exam tip

Questions like this focus on what people feel about issues. You have to put yourself in their place. Remember, people may put their own interests first, but not everyone does that; some people can see that other people and places have a greater need.

Whatever you say about people's views, try to give reasons.

Brainstorm to add your own views, based on your knowledge and experience. Make a mini Mind Map as a summary to help your revision.

Multiple use of reservoirs – management of resources

Using reservoirs for other uses besides water supply is an example of the **management of resources**.

In densely populated countries where there is great pressure on land this is essential.

Reservoirs have been planned for other uses as well as water supply. Recreation and conservation are the major ones.

Case study

The Euphrates River

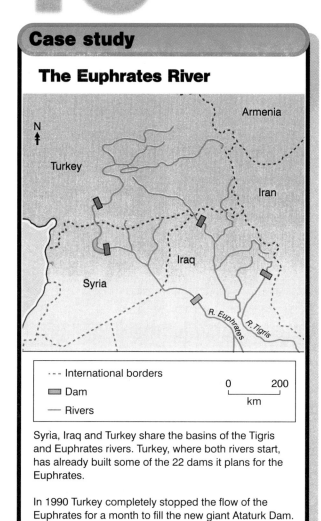

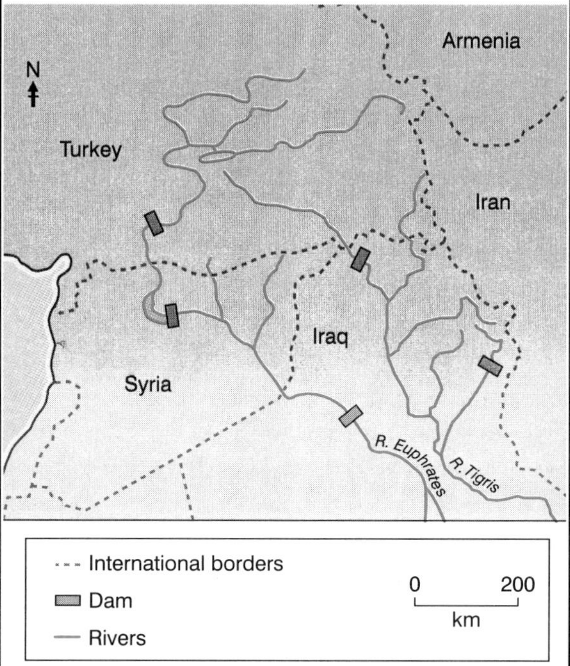

Syria, Iraq and Turkey share the basins of the Tigris and Euphrates rivers. Turkey, where both rivers start, has already built some of the 22 dams it plans for the Euphrates.

In 1990 Turkey completely stopped the flow of the Euphrates for a month to fill the new giant Ataturk Dam.

Turkey intends to turn an area one-third the size of Britain into 'the bread basket of the Middle East'. However, both Syria and Iraq depend on the flow of water of the river. Water is likely to be the cause of regional conflict in the future.

Reservoirs can have a range of facilities and activities:

- sailing, canoeing and windsurfing
- birdwatching, walking, nature trails
- picnic areas and car parks
- wildlife conservation and visitor centres.

Many activities are on land and in forests. This is because hillsides around reservoirs are often forested to reduce the amount of soil washed into the water.

Development issues

In more developed countries water problems are largely a result of wealth. Higher living standards result in greater use of water, whether for industry, power generation or in the home.

In less developed countries the availability or shortage of water is often a development problem. Here are some of the issues:

- **Clean drinking water** is a major means of eliminating disease.
- **Irrigation water** is essential in arid and semi-arid areas.
- **Irrigation water** is essential to maintain and increase food supplies.
- **Irrigation water** is essential for export crops.
- **Hydro-electricity** provides power but needs large amounts of capital.
- **Hydro-electricity** provides power for industrial development.
- **Political problems** – river basins crossing borders can be a source of conflict.

review

The topics covered in this unit fall into local, national and international scales.

Which parts of the unit belong to which scale?

Draw a three-armed Mind Map (one arm for each scale) and add headings from the unit to each arm.

You probably had to include some headings in more than one place. But you should find that thinking about it has helped you to learn it.

Energy

Types of energy resources

Fossil fuels

Fossil fuels are used as an industrial raw material, as fuel in transport, and to generate electricity.

Coal, oil and natural gas are all fixed resources. Once exhausted they cannot be replaced. Conservation or more efficient use extends their life.

(*See* page 123 for the factors affecting the location of fossil fuel development.)

Nuclear power

Uranium is needed in small quantities so exhaustion is not an issue. The negative points are safety in the case of an accident, and the safe disposal of radioactive waste. Nuclear power also needs large amounts of capital.

Hydro-electric power (HEP)

This is a renewable resource and is widely developed.

Advantages – low running costs, pollution free, cost of development can be shared with other schemes such as irrigation, recreation, water supply and flood control. The impact on the landscape can be a gain.

Disadvantages – high initial capital costs, flooding of farmland and valuable natural environment sites, trapping of river silt. The impact on the landscape may be seen as a loss.

HEP is often developed in mountainous regions. That is where high water supplies are usually found. The deep valleys provide better sites for dams.

Most HEP potential in developed countries has been put to use. In less developed countries its use is more limited due to the high capital costs. There are examples of major projects, such as the Aswan High Dam in Egypt and the Kariba Dam in southern Africa. However, small-scale or micro-hydro schemes are proving to be very significant locally.

Alternative energy sources

Wave power

Small schemes are in operation but they produce little power at the moment.

Tidal power

The Rance scheme in northern France has been in operation for a long time. It works with a barrage across the estuary with power being generated from the tidal flow through the barrage. Barrages have been proposed in several places in the UK. However, construction costs are extremely high and there is always a considerable effect on the environment of the river estuary to be considered.

Geothermal power

In volcanic areas there is immense potential. Underground water, heated by volcanic activity, produces steam which can be tapped to drive turbines for electricity production. Hot water can also be used directly in neighbourhood or even whole-town central heating systems. New Zealand and Iceland are two places where this has been developed.

There is also potential to drill down into deep rocks which, due to pressure, are still hot. By pumping in cold water, steam is produced which can be drawn up another borehole and used for electricity generation.

Solar power

Solar power will be significant as a supplementary source of energy in many areas of the world. It is already being used as part of district heating schemes. It can be part of an overall energy conservation system. In less developed countries it has been one way of bringing electricity to isolated areas.

Wind power

Wind turbines obviously depend on wind power which is not totally reliable. Where they have been developed, large 'wind farms' dominate the skyline in hilly or coastal areas. To make a really significant contribution there would have to be huge areas covered by wind farms. They cause conflict where they have been developed, partly due to their visual impact on the landscape and partly due to their noise.

Research and development

Throughout the world individuals, companies and governments are involved in research into alternative energy sources. The countries which are spending most are the USA, Japan and Germany. Sweden spends the most per person. Can you think why Sweden has such a great interest in alternative energy resources?

Conservation

This counts as an alternative source of energy because it makes existing power go further. Methods include:

- increase in power station efficiency
- use of waste heat from industry, incinerators and power stations in district heating
- burning of waste to generate power
- general increase in power efficiency of machinery and appliances
- building insulation
- better initial design of buildings.

Figure 7

Type	Location
Hydro-electric power	
Wave power	
Tidal power	
Geothermal power	
Solar power	
Wind power	

Types of location for different sources of renewable energy

Task 1

Work through all the material above and complete Figure 7 to summarise the types of location for different sources of renewable energy.

Task 2

What are the effects of developments in Figure 7 above on people and places? Think of both gains and losses or advantages and disadvantages.

review

Check that you now know what the different sources of energy are, their possible locations and some of their effects, both good and bad.

16

People and Environments

preview

What you need to know

- Processes and causes of soil erosion
- Management and conservation
- The meaning and causes of desertification
- Management of desertification
- Rain forest distribution
- Rain forest environments
- The importance of rain forests
- Environmental effects of rain forest removal
- Sustainable development in rain forests
- How landscapes and habitats are threatened
- Protection and conservation of landscapes and habitats

Soil erosion and desertification

Spend ten minutes reading through the unit, jotting down the headings. Set it out as a Mind Map.

As you work through the unit again more slowly, develop your Mind Map. Don't forget to add any case studies you have learned about.

Soil erosion

Soil erosion happens when soil is removed by wind or water. It is a serious problem. It happens in tropical and temperate areas, in more developed and less developed countries and in humid as well as arid regions.

Processes of soil erosion

Wind erosion

Wind blows away fine particles of soil. These are usually the very important organic parts of the soil.

Water

There are two processes of water erosion:

1 **Sheet erosion**, where water pours across the surface removing all the lighter loose material, leaving behind a stony surface.

2 **Gullying**, where the water is concentrated along a particular line and cuts into the ground. It removes soil as it cuts down and back. Gullying also lowers the water table so that even deep-rooted plants cannot reach the water supply (*see* Figure 1).

Deposition of wind- or water-borne material

This can swamp farmland and destroy crops. Rich, alluvial soils can be covered by coarse, gravelly soil material washed down on to low land.

Figure 1: Gullying in Tunisia

Causes of soil erosion

1 Overcultivation or growing crops without returning nutrients to the soil, especially organic material. The problem is worse with monoculture, where the same crop is grown year after year. This exhausts the soil. It loses its structure and breaks up into fine particles which are easily blown away.

2 Overgrazing by cattle, goats or sheep removes all vegetation, and trampling destroys the roots. In forests grazing can remove new shoots so forests die away.

3 Cultivating steep, bare slopes leaves the soil at risk when it rains. Sheet erosion or gullying can happen very quickly.

4 Removing hedgerows and trees which act as windbreaks. This increases the risk of wind erosion.

5 Leaving soil bare for long periods obviously increases soil erosion risks.

6 Clearing of forest cover leaves the soil open to rain and wind. This can be done by logging for timber, clearing the land for crop farming or grazing, or collecting firewood and fodder for animals.

Without the trees to intercept the rain, water erosion is more likely. As well as that, nutrients will be leached out (washed out) of the soil reducing its fertility.

Soil conservation and management

Soil erosion can be repaired or avoided by a combination of some of the methods in Figure 2.

Figure 2

1 Trees – planted as wind breaks to reduce wind erosion on ploughed fields. Planted on watersheds to slow down run-off from highest land on to farmland on lower slopes.

2 Terracing – on steeply sloping land this reduces run-off and therefore reduces soil wash. In areas of heavy rainfall gullying is a problem which terracing helps to avoid.

3 Contour ploughing – ploughing parallel to the contours instead of up and down the slope interrupts run-off.

4 Preventing gully enlargement – planting vegetation and building dams and weirs.

5 Crop management – ensure that soil is covered by a crop at the times of highest risk of soil erosion, and maintain cover crops like a tree crop to intercept rainfall.

6 Integrated rural development – all necessary soil conservation planned as part of one programme so the greatest benefits are obtained.

Soil conservation methods

Test yourself

Figure 3 is a 'before and after' soil conservation picture.

(a) Look at the 'before' part. Add to the labels to show how and why soil erosion is happening.

(b) Look at the 'after' section. Add labelling to show why the soil conservation methods have been used.

Desertification

This means that areas of the world are being turned into desert.

There are two causes of desertification:

1 Land degradation caused by using the land in a damaging way.

2 Climatic change in which areas become more arid.

Figure 3

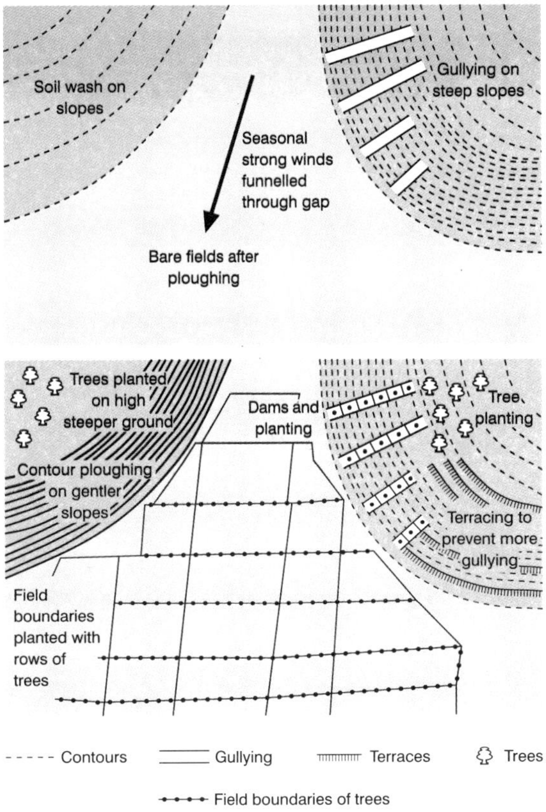

Before and after soil conservation

Of the world's surface, 30% is at risk of desertification, and over 1 billion people could be affected.

The causes of land degradation are the same as those for soil erosion described earlier, especially:

- overgrazing
- overcultivation
- cultivating steep bare slopes
- removing trees by collecting firewood
- waterlogging and salinisation (deposition of salt in the soil) happens with large-scale irrigation.

The processes are also the same as those for soil erosion, but with:

- the creation of moving dunes of sand by the wind blowing loose soil;
- the colonisation of grazing areas by plants of no use to animals.

Areas at risk

The risk of desertification is greatest in areas with a long dry season. These are the areas around the major deserts. They include:

- tropical grassland areas, especially the drier areas like the Sahel;
- Mediterranean type areas, such as parts of north Africa.

These areas are most at risk because:

1. They have relatively light rainfall combined with high temperatures. High evaporation rates means a long period of the year with dry soil.
2. Rainfall often varies considerably from year to year, with periodic droughts.

These reasons are not enough to cause desertification. Once rains return, areas which people thought were useless have been cultivated and become green once again. The real problem is a combination of population growth and greater pressure on the land.

review

How does population growth affect pressure on the land? Copy and complete Figure 4 to help you review this unit.

Figure 4

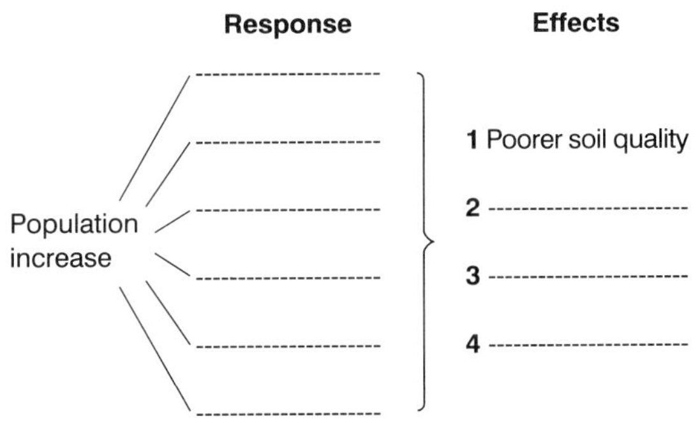

Rain forests

The distribution of rain forests is shown on the world map on page 46.

The typical rain forest has a variety of trees mixed together. It has a vertical structure of five different layers (Figure 5).

Rain forest environments vary with local features. Four of the variations are:

1. Mangrove forest along coasts and waterways.
2. Swamp forest in low lying and poorly drained areas.
3. Mountain forest where conditions change with height.
4. Heathland and grassland where local soil conditions produce their own environments.

Importance of rain forests

- **Biodiversity**. This means that there is an enormous variety of life in rain forests. For example in 50 hectares of Malaysia there are more tree species than in the whole of North America. Just as important as the number of species of plants and animals is the fact that there also are huge numbers of unknown species.
- **Economic value**.The rain forests have been the source of many plants which are now cultivated for industry or food, such as rubber and coffee.
- **Medicine**. 25% of pharmaceutical products (medicines) are based on rain forest products. New plants with a medicinal use are found frequently.
- **Flood protection**. Forests protect lower lands against flooding and silting. Deforestation in reservoir catchments has meant that so much silt is washed in that the life of a reservoir may be only 10 to 15 years, before the lake fills with silt.
- **Sustainability**. The rain forest provides the means for sustainable development in forestry, agriculture and tourism.

Figure 5

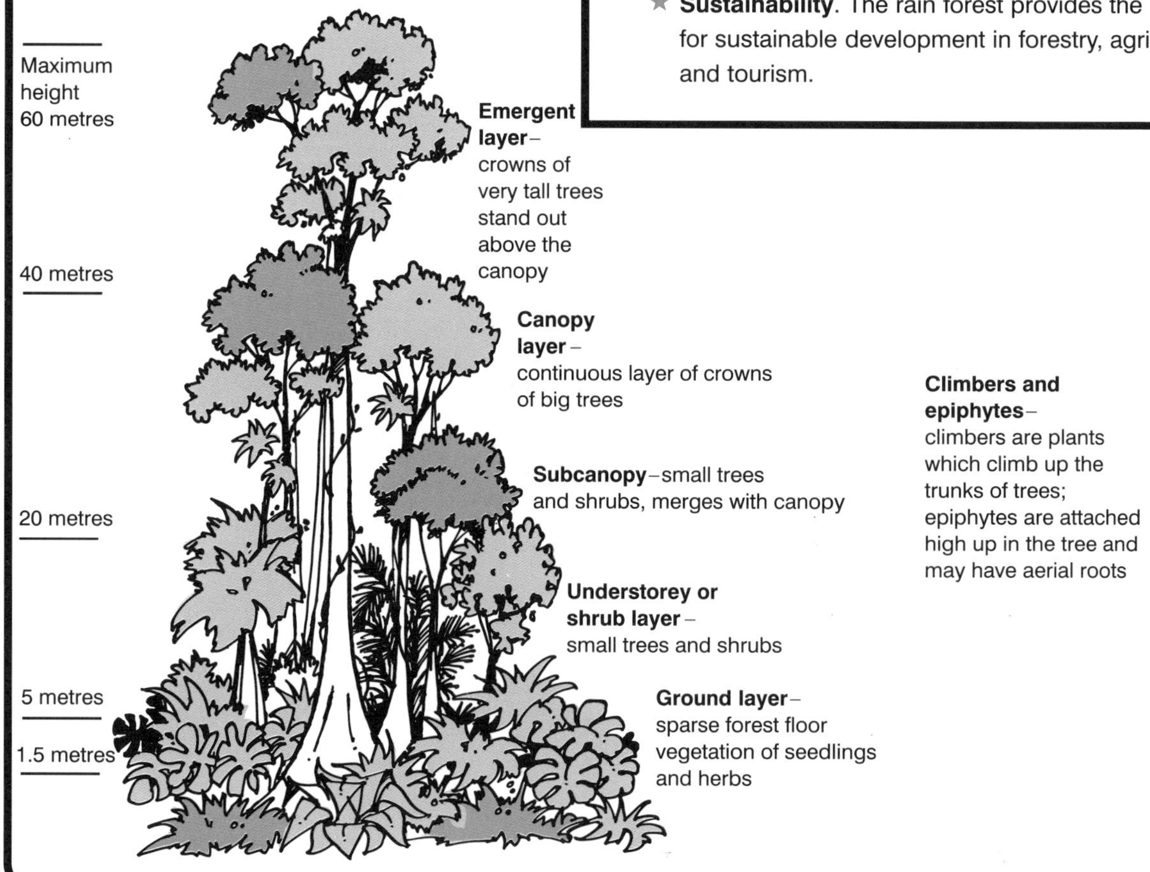
Maximum height 60 metres
40 metres
20 metres
5 metres
1.5 metres
Emergent layer – crowns of very tall trees stand out above the canopy
Canopy layer – continuous layer of crowns of big trees
Subcanopy – small trees and shrubs, merges with canopy
Understorey or shrub layer – small trees and shrubs
Ground layer – sparse forest floor vegetation of seedlings and herbs
Climbers and epiphytes – climbers are plants which climb up the trunks of trees; epiphytes are attached high up in the tree and may have aerial roots

Structure of the rain forest

Removal of rain forests

There are still vast areas of rain forest, but it is being removed quickly. In Thailand alone forest cover fell from 54% of the total area of the country to 29% in just 15 years. However, in some areas on the world map (page 46) there is no natural forest left. In many others there is no forest at all.

The forests are being removed in six ways:

1 **Shifting cultivation** is removing more forest because of population pressures. More people mean that land cannot be left to regrow as in the past.

2 **Peasant farming** encroaches on the rain forest as population pressure increases.

3 **Logging** for timber, since the forests are a valuable source of tropical hardwoods.

4 Forests are cleared, often by burning, to create **grazing** for cattle ranchers.

5 **Reservoirs** forming part of major HEP schemes flood large areas.

6 **Opencast mining** destroys large areas and pollutes and clogs rivers.

The importance of these varies from one region to another. In total 1 and 3 are probably most significant. In particular regions, like parts of south-east Asia, 3 is most important.

Environmental effects

- Soil erosion.
- Flooding downstream of cleared area.
- Silting downstream, clogging reservoirs, irrigation systems and covering farmland.

Figure 6

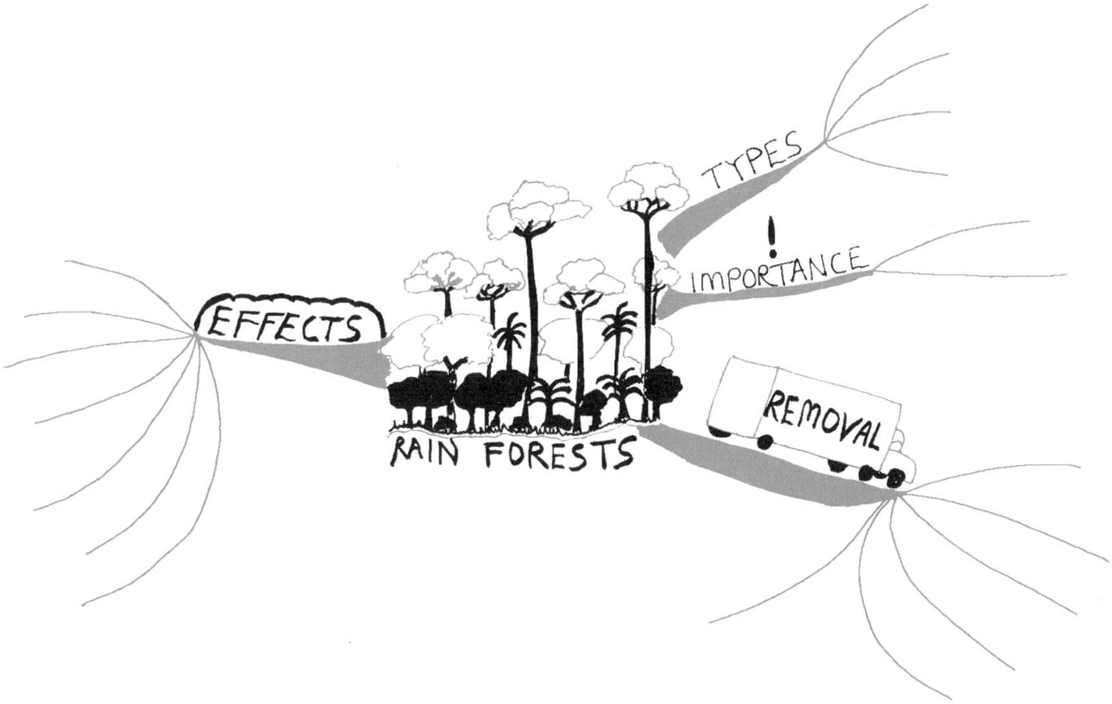

- Loss of biodiversity.
- Loss of human habitat.
- Climatic change locally and regionally due to changes in the hydrological cycle.
- Global climatic changes, as the forests absorb carbon dioxide and give off oxygen. Loss of forest means less carbon dioxide is converted and world temperature rises (*see* page 148).

Task

Complete the Mind Map (Figure 6) using the information in this unit.

Sustainable development

There are many examples of **sustainable development** in rain forests.

Case study

Sustainable forestry in Papua New Guinea

A community project run by local people manages their forest so that they receive a steady income and do no long-term damage. Conservation means they can take timber year after year. The diagram below shows the difference between the clear logging done by the timber companies and the sustainable logging.

Clear logging	Sustainable logging
Removes *all* trees	Takes a *few* mature trees
↓	↓
Destroys young trees, wasting future resources	Allows young trees to grow to maturity
↓	↓
Causes widespread damage to the environment: soil erosion, flooding	Allows other activities to carry on, e.g. hunting, fishing, farming, because the environment is unharmed
↓	↓
Provides work for a short time before the area is cleared of timber	Provides long-term income for the local community

Test yourself

Answer these questions. Check your answers yourself from the text or from the diagrams after you have done the test.

1. Name the continents with tropical rain forests.
2. How many layers are there in a typical mixed rain forest?
3. Name one of the layers.
4. Name two other types of rain forest.
5. What is biodiversity?
6. Name four other ways that the rain forests are important.
7. Which two causes of rain forest loss are due to population pressure?
8. The others are all related to primary products or energy supplies. What are they?
9. What global problem could rain forest removal make worse?
10. What are the other problems affecting rain forest areas themselves?
11. What does sustainable development mean?
12. Name a sustainable development project in a rain forest area.

review

This unit breaks down into very clear separate blocks.

Spend a few minutes on each section and summarise each one into a list. Use as few words as possible – one is best. Learn those key words.

Remember: You need to go over it all for five minutes tomorrow, then two minutes next week, then one minute next month and one minute after another six weeks. By then you will really know the work. Check that you do by using 'Test yourself'.

Add this to your major revision plan.

Conserving landscape

There are **pressures on landscapes and habitats** everywhere. The causes are different but the issue is the same. Should areas be protected and how can they be protected?

Pressures on landscapes

Population pressure means that there are competing and conflicting **demands on land**:

- spreading urban areas, whether major cities or medium and small towns;
- industry seeking greenfield sites rather than redeveloping derelict sites in old industrial areas;
- large retail parks seeking similar sites;
- changing farming methods which affect the landscape;
- resource development, such as quarrying or reservoir building;
- road building, especially major projects like by-passes or new motorways;
- tourist projects, like holiday villages or ski developments;
- forestry;
- military training;
- general recreational activities and sightseeing.

Task 1

Do you know examples of the pressures listed above? They may be near your home, somewhere you have been on holiday, or you may have read about them or seen them on TV. If you do know examples, pencil in their names. Better still, make a Mind Map of the pressures and develop it to include more details of the examples.

Figure 7

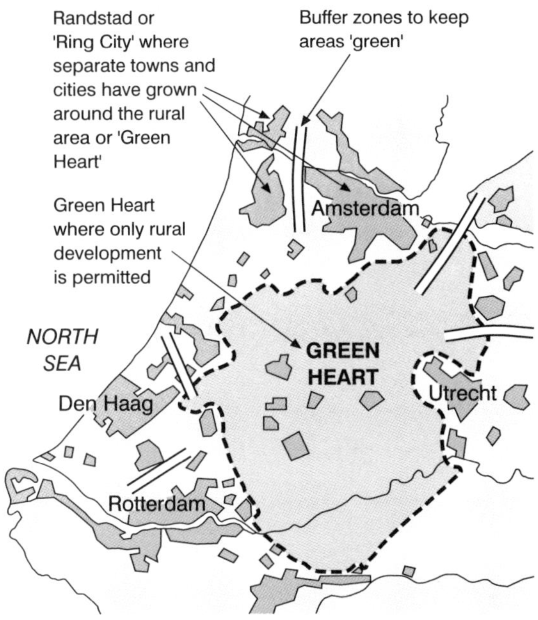

Planning controls to conserve the landscape between towns and cities of Randstad in the Netherlands

Land around cities

In the Netherlands the government creates 'buffer zones' between certain cities to stop them growing and joining. The major cities form a ring surrounding a rural area that is called the 'green heart'. Controls on building limit growth in the green heart (Figure 7).

In Britain the growth of cities has been limited by **Green Belts**. These are areas forming rings around cities and conurbations in which building is tightly controlled. However, as in the Netherlands there are exceptions and certain building is allowed.

Exam tip

Questions are often asked about specific issues or places. They ask you to put forward the likely views held by different people or groups, so you need to think about the views of opposing sides where there are conflicts of interest.

Alternatively, or as well, they ask you to describe an example you have studied and give the views of different groups of people in that example.

Protecting areas of scenic value

National Parks in England and Wales

The purpose of **National Parks** is to conserve the landscape and to improve access to areas of particularly great scenic beauty. In England and Wales National Parks are not owned by the nation. Most of the land is privately owned and used for farming, forestry and quarrying as well as tourism. It follows from this that the areas are not necessarily wild and not completely natural.

Multiple land use is common in the upland areas. The uses may include:

- hill farming
- military training
- forestry
- recreation (especially hill walking).
- water supply

Conservation and access create conflicts.

Access brings more tourists, especially to particularly well-known places. These are called 'honeypots'. Large numbers of visitors mean large amounts of traffic, especially cars. The result is congestion and the need to create extra facilities for the increased numbers. This destroys the very features of the area that first attracted people. The problems of congestion are made greater by the more rapid road access by motorway from distant parts of the country. The planning authorities for National Parks are able to prevent developments or allow them with strict conditions. However, as with Green Belt controls, these rules can be by-passed if the Secretary of State for the Environment wishes.

Other areas of protection

Areas of Outstanding Natural Beauty (AONBs) have a distribution different from the National Parks. They are mainly hilly rather than mountainous areas, and have attractive rather than rugged landscapes.

National Nature Reserves and **Sites of Special Scientific Interest** (SSSIs) are mostly small areas and are scattered around the country. They are protected for many different reasons, such as their wildlife, their special habitats like marsh, or their geology.

The **National Trust**, a charity, owns many areas of land, mostly in quite small acreages. However, it does own large areas of coastline and about 20% of the Lake District National Park.

National Parks in other countries

National Parks are common in many countries. In some, like the USA, they really are owned by the nation. There they also have just the two functions, to conserve and to give access to the public, but public access is tightly controlled. The USA is a large country so the pressures of other land uses is less. However, the more popular parks, such as Yosemite in California, still have problems with numbers of visitors.

In developing countries National Parks have also been set up to conserve natural habitats and wildlife and to act as a major attraction in the tourist industry. Pressures from numbers of tourists can damage the environment and pressures from population growth result in farmland spreading right up to and sometimes into the National Park. The conflicts can be more complicated where the rights of local people to use the land are taken away as with some of Kenya's National Parks.

review

Write a checklist of differences between National Parks in different countries.

Make a Mind Map to summarise what you have read in this unit.

17 Issues and Problems

preview

What you need to know

- Pollution of air, water and land
- Causes of pollution
- Effects of pollution at local, regional and world scale
- The environmental issues linked to the exploitation of resources
- Acid rain
- The complex environmental systems of major city regions
- Global warming
- Greenhouse effect
- Possible effects of global warming

Pollution

This unit summarises the general points to do with pollution. It also includes some case studies. Use them in addition to those you do in school.

Look through the unit quickly to get an idea of the plan. It will be easier to remember the material if you know where it fits.

Pollution is generally divided up into:

- air pollution
- water pollution
- land pollution
- noise pollution
- visual pollution.

In reality they overlap each other. For example, sulphur dioxide and nitrogen oxide pollute the air but also pollute the land and water by dry deposition and as acid rain.

Air pollution

This is produced by:

- the burning of fossil fuels, producing sulphur dioxide, ash and soot;
- road vehicles and factories producing carbon monoxide, nitrogen oxide, lead and other pollutants.

These have an effect locally and regionally depending on atmospheric or weather conditions. Anticyclonic weather in summer and winter produces temperature inversions (Figure 1). They trap pollution in the surface layer of the atmosphere. This used to be a bigger problem in winter than in summer. Now, with more road transport, nitrogen oxides and hydrocarbons from exhausts react with strong sunlight to produce ozone. This can trigger asthma and other breathing problems as well as damage crops.

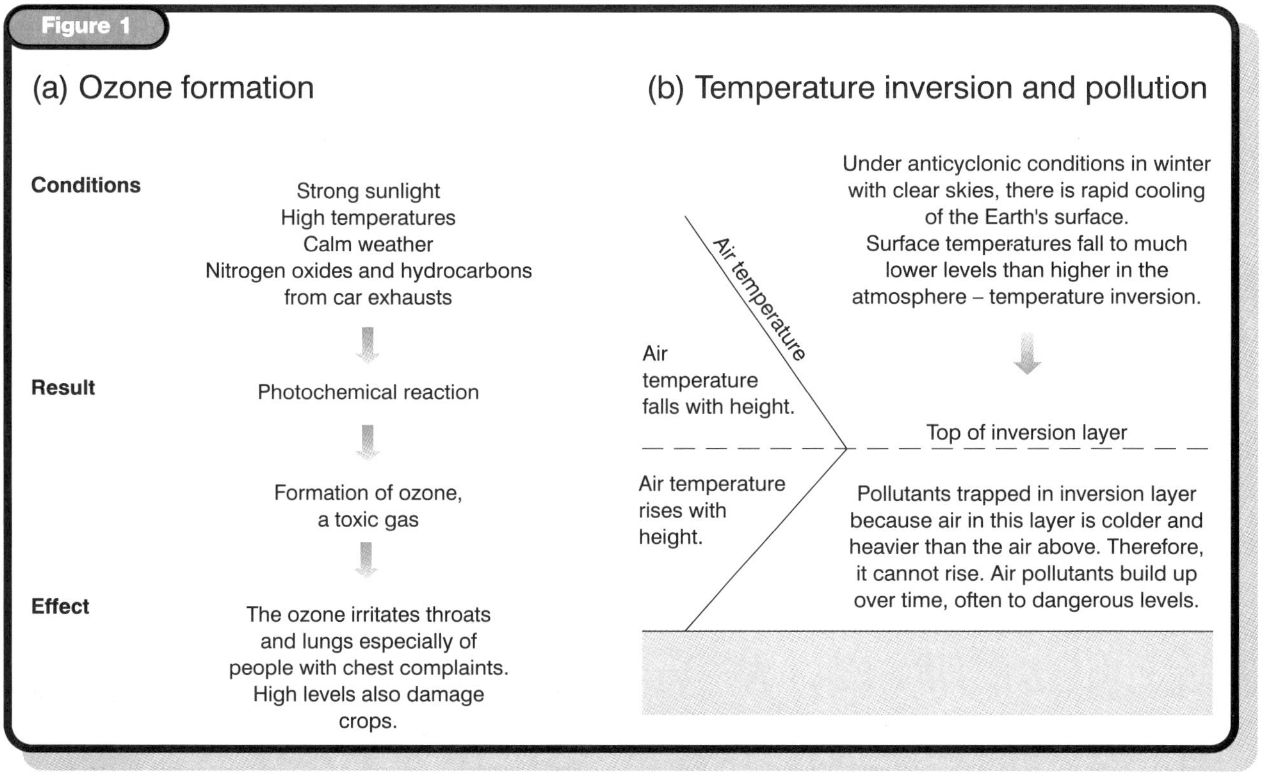

Figure 1
(a) Ozone formation
Conditions
Strong sunlight
High temperatures
Calm weather
Nitrogen oxides and hydrocarbons from car exhausts
Result
Photochemical reaction
Formation of ozone, a toxic gas
Effect
The ozone irritates throats and lungs especially of people with chest complaints. High levels also damage crops.
(b) Temperature inversion and pollution
Under anticyclonic conditions in winter with clear skies, there is rapid cooling of the Earth's surface. Surface temperatures fall to much lower levels than higher in the atmosphere – temperature inversion.
Air temperature
Air temperature falls with height.
Top of inversion layer
Air temperature rises with height.
Pollutants trapped in inversion layer because air in this layer is colder and heavier than the air above. Therefore, it cannot rise. Air pollutants build up over time, often to dangerous levels.

Air pollution

Other sources of air pollution can be nuclear power plants, factories dealing with toxic substances or waste incinerators.

Scale of air pollution

The scale of pollution varies. If the source of pollution is a small one, like a local factory, only the immediate area is likely to be affected. In the case of a city in summer, the air pollution caused by traffic drifts downwind and affects surrounding rural areas just as badly. In some places in cities, of course, pollution will be trapped by the high buildings and will rise to very dangerous levels.

Water pollution

Rivers, underground water, lakes and the sea are affected by water pollution. Some of the sources are:

- effluent from sewage systems
- waste from factories (including chemicals and hot water)
- fertiliser and pesticides sprayed on fields.

Pollution can occur indirectly. Toxic waste dumped on land can percolate into the ground and pollute underground water. Eventually the pollutants reach rivers. The same applies to fertilisers and pesticides.

Pollution of underground water also means pollution of drinking water in areas which depend on borehole supplies.

All pollution reaching a river eventually ends up in a lake or the sea. There is also direct pollution of lakes and sea. Figures 2a, 2b and 2c show sources of pollution of rivers and sea.

Land pollution

Pollution of the land damages the natural environment. It is a hazard to plants and wildlife and a health hazard for people. Land pollution is also a cause of visual pollution.

Types of land pollution include:

- derelict buildings and land
- badly managed refuse tips

- contamination by dumping chemicals
- litter
- killing of vegetation by toxic solid waste and by fumes
- scars and waste tips of old quarries and mines.

One of the problems of reclamation is the disposal of material. Toxic material needs careful handling and is difficult to dispose of. Large quantities of any material are expensive to handle partly due to the lack of disposal sites.

Noise pollution

In densely populated countries there is never total silence. In cities there is always traffic noise. In the countryside noise from a motorway is heard over a considerable distance.

There are specific sources of more localised noise. Airports are examples of intense concentrations of noise but so are major power stations.

Pollution of the air, land and water can be shown to have direct harmful effects on people and the environment. There is now evidence that noise pollution does too.

Visual pollution

This is partly a matter of individual taste and attitudes. Generally, there is some agreement on what kinds of development causes visual pollution. For example, during the 1930s there were many billboards along roads, in the countryside as well as in towns. Restrictions were enforced to limit these because of the way they intruded into the landscape. Brainstorm to think of your own examples of visual pollution.

Air, land and water pollution also have visual effects. Their results are regarded as visually offensive. Dumping rubbish into a river or canal is visually damaging as well as being directly harmful to wildlife, people using the water course and possibly water supplies.

Figure 2a

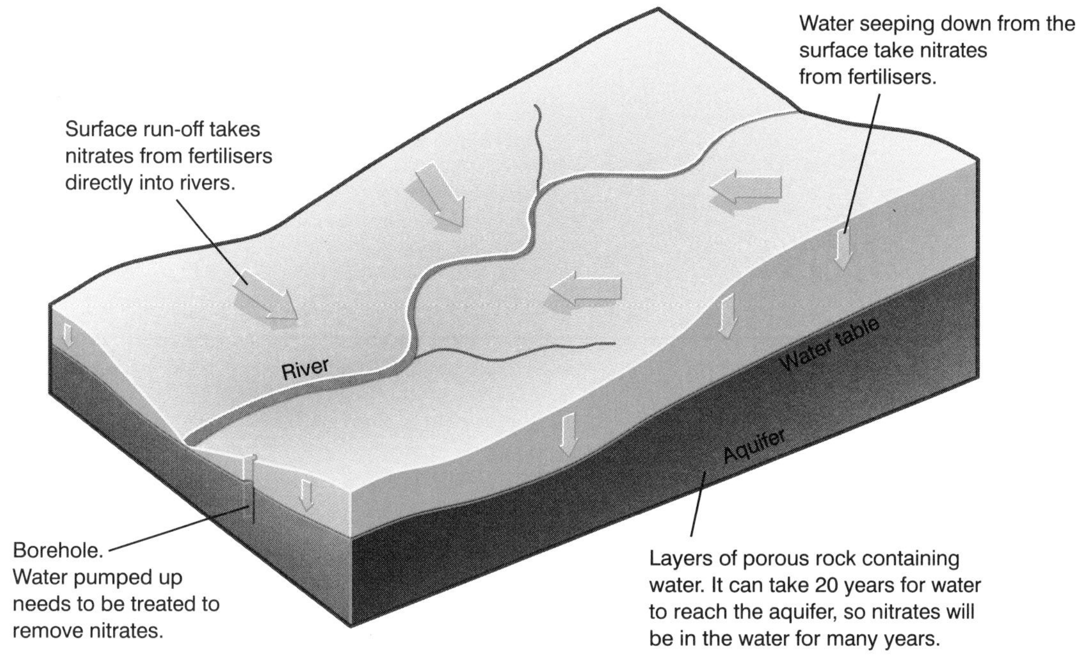
Water seeping down from the surface take nitrates from fertilisers.
Surface run-off takes nitrates from fertilisers directly into rivers.
River
Water table
Aquifer
Borehole. Water pumped up needs to be treated to remove nitrates.
Layers of porous rock containing water. It can take 20 years for water to reach the aquifer, so nitrates will be in the water for many years.

Ground water pollution

Figure 2b

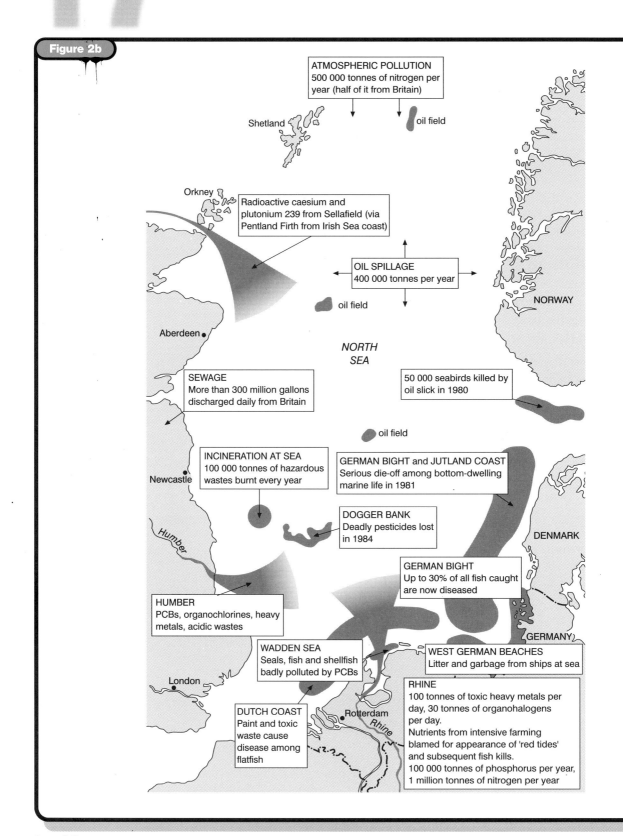

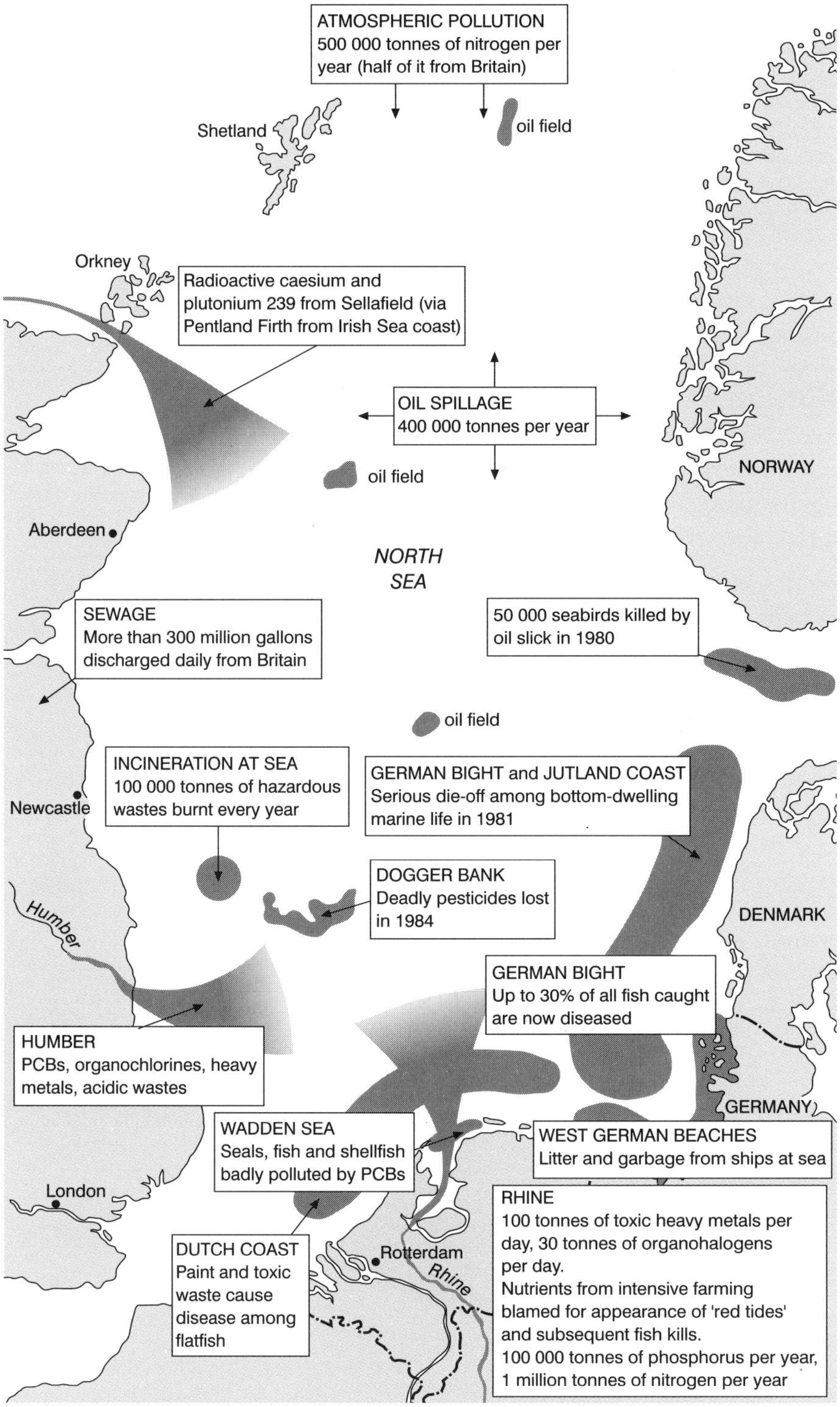
ATMOSPHERIC POLLUTION
500 000 tonnes of nitrogen per year (half of it from Britain)
Shetland
oil field
Orkney
Radioactive caesium and plutonium 239 from Sellafield (via Pentland Firth from Irish Sea coast)
OIL SPILLAGE
400 000 tonnes per year
oil field
NORWAY
Aberdeen
NORTH SEA
SEWAGE
More than 300 million gallons discharged daily from Britain
50 000 seabirds killed by oil slick in 1980
oil field
INCINERATION AT SEA
100 000 tonnes of hazardous wastes burnt every year
GERMAN BIGHT and JUTLAND COAST
Serious die-off among bottom-dwelling marine life in 1981
Newcastle
DOGGER BANK
Deadly pesticides lost in 1984
Humber
DENMARK
GERMAN BIGHT
Up to 30% of all fish caught are now diseased
HUMBER
PCBs, organochlorines, heavy metals, acidic wastes
GERMANY
WADDEN SEA
Seals, fish and shellfish badly polluted by PCBs
WEST GERMAN BEACHES
Litter and garbage from ships at sea
London
RHINE
100 tonnes of toxic heavy metals per day, 30 tonnes of organohalogens per day.
Nutrients from intensive farming blamed for appearance of 'red tides' and subsequent fish kills.
100 000 tonnes of phosphorus per year, 1 million tonnes of nitrogen per year
DUTCH COAST
Paint and toxic waste cause disease among flatfish
Rotterdam
Rhine

Sea pollution

Figure 2c

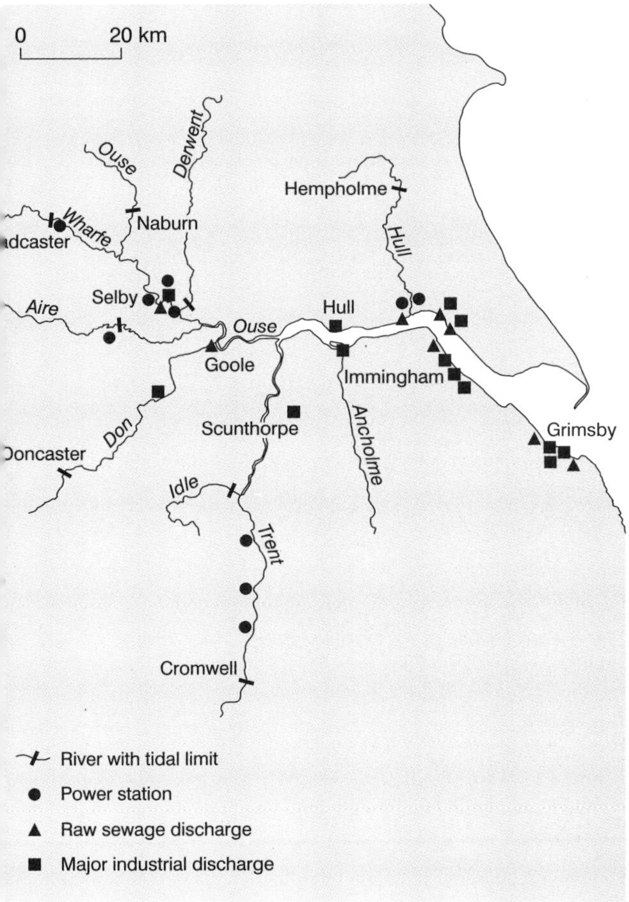

River pollution

Case study

Local environmental conflicts

Many local environmental issues centre on pollution. One example is that of the Rechem plant at Pontypool in South Wales. It incinerates wastes including PCBs. There has been and still is considerable public concern over possible health risks in the local environment. In fact, the local pressure group managed to stop the import of PCBs from Canada which were being sent to Rechem for disposal.

review

Pollution overlaps many topics in geography. There are references to it in many units throughout this book. As you come across them, pencil in the page number on this page.

Regional problems

Syllabus check

Check your syllabus for a specific case study of the environmental issues linked to the exploitation of resources.

Treat each section separately.

First, look through the Alaska case study, below, and complete the task.

Figure 3

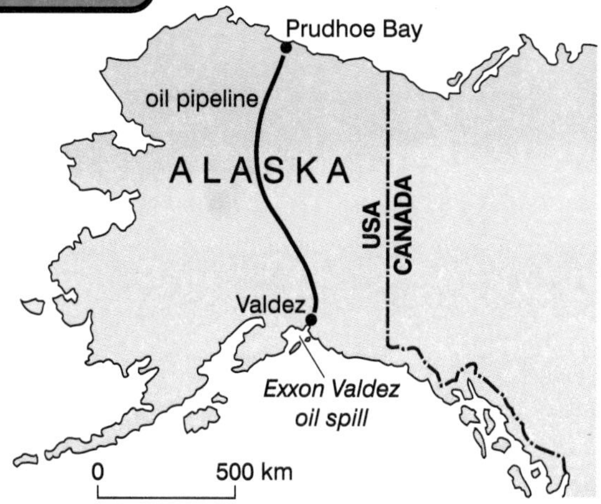

Alaska and oil

Case study

Issues and oil in Alaska

Oil deposits were first found in Alaska during the 1950s, with more in the early 1960s. In 1968 the biggest oilfield in the USA was discovered at Prudhoe Bay on the North Slope (Figure 3). The oil discovery was the start of a major conflict between environmentalists and developers.

The arguments of the environmental lobby

1. Alaska is a unique environment with a fragile ecosystem. It should be kept as one of the last real wilderness areas in the world.
2. The pipeline from the oilfield to Valdez on the Pacific coast would bring the danger of oil spillage as a result of either earthquakes or permafrost zone movement.
3. The construction scars would last for a very long time in the permafrost region.
4. The traditional migration path of caribou would be disrupted and other wildlife would be disturbed.
5. The risk of oil spillage off the coast of British Columbia worried the Canadian government.

The arguments of the developers

1. Prudhoe Bay was needed as a safe source of oil for the USA.
2. Construction methods would ensure safety and preservation of the landscape, even though they would be expensive.
3. Most Alaskans were in favour of a reasonable level of development.
4. The oil would bring a large new source of income to the state.

The result

The result was that the scheme went ahead, although the pipeline construction was delayed for four years.

The effects

1. Alaska moved up from 26th to joint 1st for the lowest percentage of poverty in the USA.
2. Alaska became the first state in terms of average income.

Task

Summarise the Alaskan oil issue using a Mind Map. The three main arms are For, Against and Effects. You will have to go through the material very carefully.

Acid rain

This is a major regional problem in industrialised parts of the world.

Look through this section quickly then concentrate on Figure 4.

Test yourself

1 What are the main pollutants in the acid rain cycle?

2 How do they change as a result of chemical reactions due to sunlight and chemicals in the atmosphere?

3 Where does dry deposition happen?

4 What is acid rain?

5 How far from the source is acid rain likely to fall?

6 Complete Figure 5 by filling in the column headed 'Problem'.

Controlling acid rain

Acid rain can be controlled. However, areas already affected will probably take many years to recover.

Figure 5

Feature	Problem
Soil	
Trees	
Lakes and rivers	
Wildlife	

★ Sulphur dioxide emissions can be reduced by:

- using fuel containing less sulphur;
- reducing emissions of sulphur by mixing coal with crushed limestone during burning;
- cleaning gases after burning using lime to absorb sulphur dioxide from the flue gas.

Figure 4

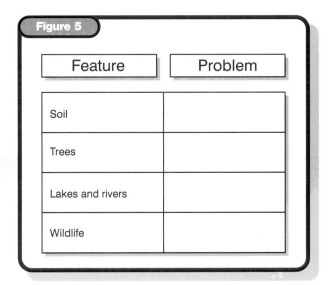

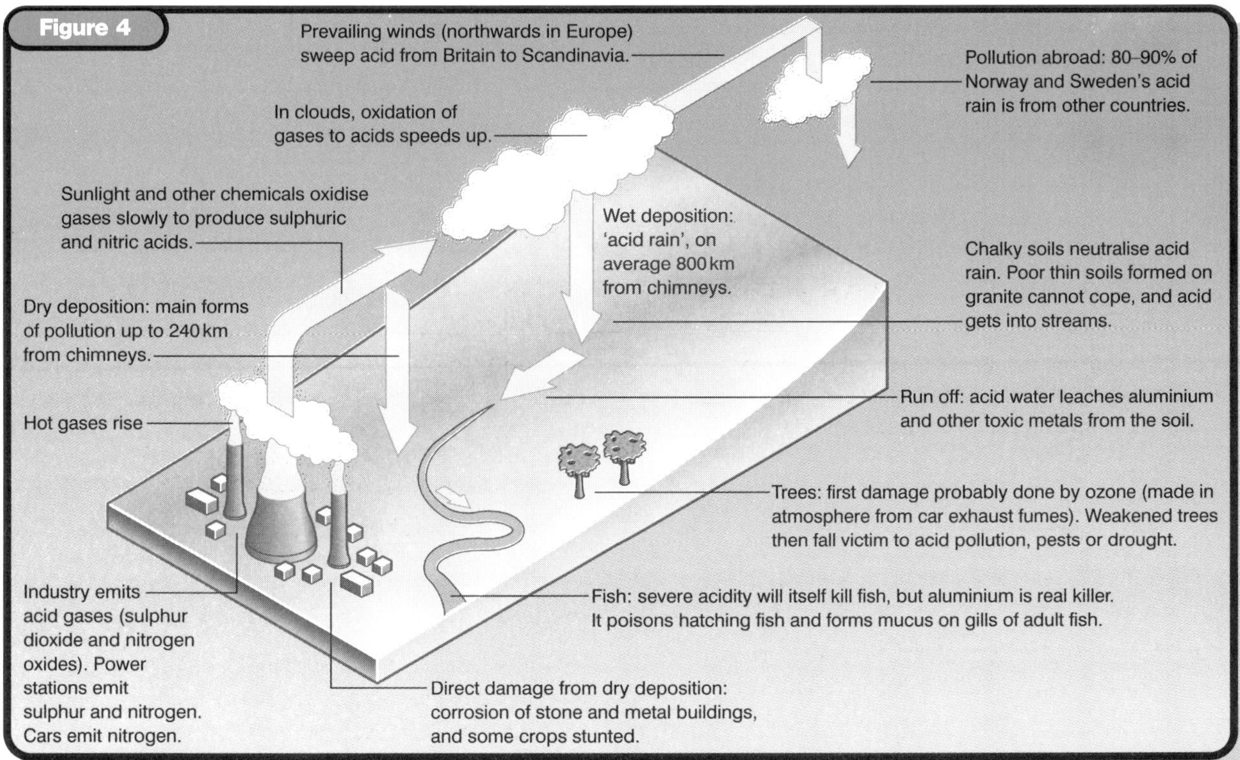

Prevailing winds (northwards in Europe) sweep acid from Britain to Scandinavia.
Pollution abroad: 80–90% of Norway and Sweden's acid rain is from other countries.
In clouds, oxidation of gases to acids speeds up.
Sunlight and other chemicals oxidise gases slowly to produce sulphuric and nitric acids.
Wet deposition: 'acid rain', on average 800 km from chimneys.
Chalky soils neutralise acid rain. Poor thin soils formed on granite cannot cope, and acid gets into streams.
Dry deposition: main forms of pollution up to 240 km from chimneys.
Run off: acid water leaches aluminium and other toxic metals from the soil.
Hot gases rise
Trees: first damage probably done by ozone (made in atmosphere from car exhaust fumes). Weakened trees then fall victim to acid pollution, pests or drought.
Industry emits acid gases (sulphur dioxide and nitrogen oxides). Power stations emit sulphur and nitrogen. Cars emit nitrogen.
Fish: severe acidity will itself kill fish, but aluminium is real killer. It poisons hatching fish and forms mucus on gills of adult fish.
Direct damage from dry deposition: corrosion of stone and metal buildings, and some crops stunted.

Acid rain

★ Nitrogen oxides can be reduced by:
  - altering burners in power stations;
  - reducing motor vehicle emissions.

★ Liming streams and lakes and catchment areas. The long-term effect of this on plants and animals is unknown and it is only a partial solution.

Affected areas

In Europe almost all upland areas are affected. Eastern Europe is badly affected by pollution from power stations and heavy industry. Scandinavia is particularly hit, even though it produces hardly any of the pollutants that cause acid rain, because:

- the prevailing winds from the south-west carry much of the UK's pollution to be deposited as acid rain over Scandinavia;
- the wind patterns over Europe are such that much of Europe's pollution ends up there, too.

review

This unit has looked at some regional problems. The possible problems are innumerable but in most cases they are combinations of the different issues covered in this chapter of the book.

Check that you can use a case study to describe the kinds of issues involved in the development of resources.

Global problems

All environmental issues are really global problems because of the links between different elements of the environment. However, global warming is a problem on a different scale. The causes lie mainly in the more developed world, but the effects will be felt everywhere.

Global warming

The greatest environmental issue is what will happen as global temperatures rise.

The greenhouse effect

Earth's atmosphere is like a natural greenhouse. This is why temperatures do not vary wildly from extreme heat to extreme cold during every 24-hour period. Figure 6 shows how it works.

Task 1

Write down, as briefly as you can, a description of how the greenhouse effect works. Is it easier with a diagram? If so, use a diagram and remember to use diagrams in your exam!

Greenhouse gases

Water vapour is the most important natural greenhouse gas. Carbon dioxide is the second most important one. Both of them absorb some of the infrared radiation emitted by the Earth.

Problems are occurring because greenhouse gases produced by human activity are increasing. These gases include carbon dioxide. It is released through the burning of fossil fuels.

More carbon dioxide in the atmosphere has resulted in increased temperatures. Figure 7 shows what could happen to average world temperatures. The evidence now is that average temperatures will increase but the amount and rate of increase is unknown.

Figure 6

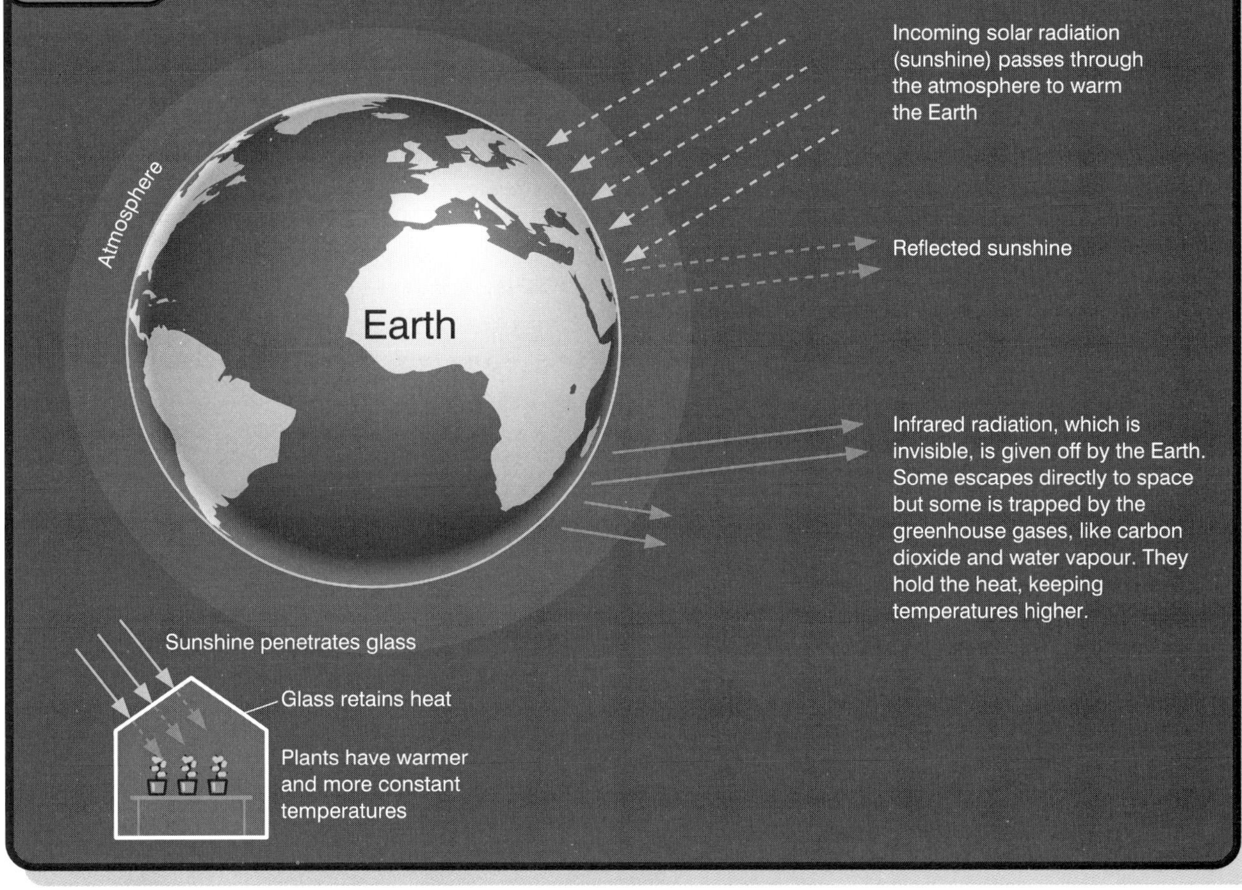

The greenhouse effect

Climate change

Temperatures will not increase evenly everywhere. The world's climate system is more complicated than that. Some areas will become warmer, some will stay the same. Some may even be colder.

There will be changes in rainfall, too, so that areas will become drier or wetter.

As time goes by more sophisticated projections are being made. (Figure 8)

Figure 7

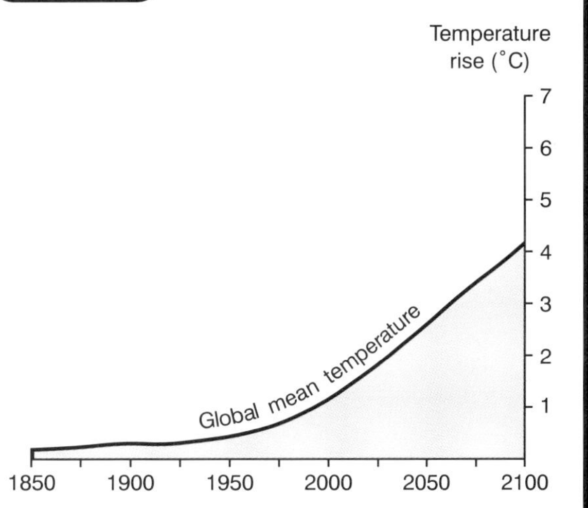

World temperature increase (estimate)

Task 2

The list in Figure 9 is in a random order. Rearrange the items into the following sections. You may need to use some items more than once.

Sea-level changes

Natural disasters

Temperature changes

Rainfall changes

Agricultural changes

The best way to show this is as a Mind Map.

What needs to be done?

1 Cut global carbon dioxide emissions by:

- energy conservation
- alternative energy sources.

2 Reduce deforestation where trees are not already replaced.

Figure 8

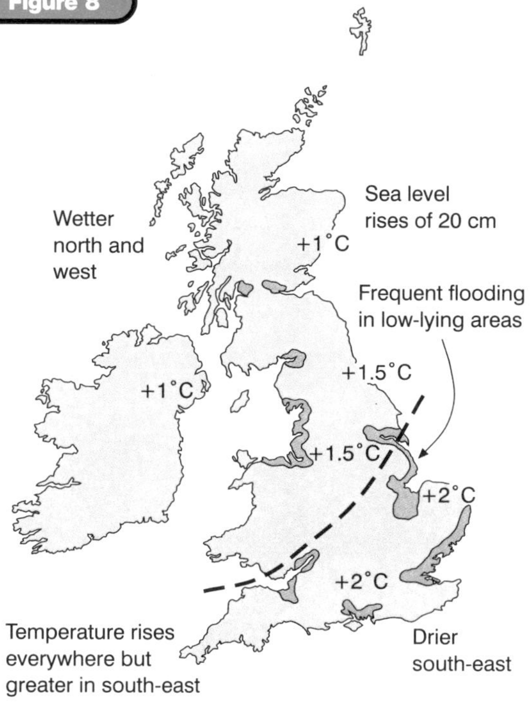

Projected changes to Britain's climate

review

Check that you are now able to:

- Explain the greenhouse effect and the effects of changes in the amount of greenhouse gases
- Describe the observed changes in global world temperatures and the possible global climate changes that could result
- Describe how carbon dioxide emissions can be reduced

Figure 9

- Rising sea level
- Break-up and possible melting of parts of the polar ice sheets
- Small island states at great risk
- Changes in the distribution of species of plants and wild animals
- Increases in the length of the growing season in some regions
- Drier climates will limit agriculture in areas important for agriculture at the moment
- More hurricanes and more powerful ones
- More and worse coastal flooding
- Droughts with deserts spreading
- Higher sea temperatures killing coral reefs and affecting fish populations
- Rainfall changes will affect river flows, underground water and water supplies for all uses
- More forest fires
- Diseases spreading from hotter regions
- More insect pests

Expected worldwide climate changes

Sample question 6 — Higher

a) Study Figure 1 showing pollution of the Tagus estuary, Portugal.

- **(i)** Name the three main sources of pollution. [1 mark]
- **(ii)** What natural process was relied on to deal with pollution of the estuary? Explain how it worked. [3 marks]
- **(iii)** What activities are directly affected by the pollution? [3 marks]
- **(iv)** Suggest measures which would reduce pollution levels. [3 marks]

b) For a place you have studied that experiences pollution problems (other than the Tagus estuary):

- **(i)** Give its name;
- **(ii)** Describe and explain the causes of the pollution;
- **(iii)** Describe the measures that could or have been taken to reduce the pollution. [10 marks]

Figure 1

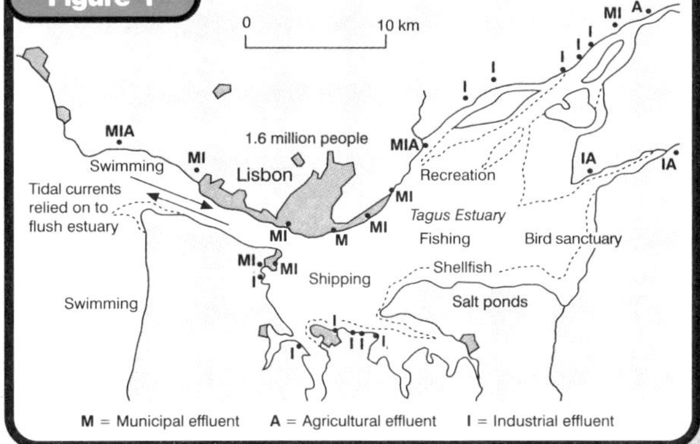

Suggested answer

a)

- **(i)** Municipal, agricultural and industrial effluent.
- **(ii)** Tidal currents through the narrow neck of the estuary, to flush out the polluted water.
- **(iii)** Swimming and recreation generally, fishing, wildlife (bird sanctuary).
- **(iv)** Treatment plants for municipal and industrial effluent; controls on industrial effluent; monitoring rivers for levels of agricultural effluent and establishing treatment plants.

b) For example, air pollution in Athens. Caused by very hot summers, heavy and congested traffic and a concentration of industry in the city. Temperature inversions trap pollution in surface air layer. Measures taken include relocation of industry, major development of public transport, controls on cars, abolishing long lunch break to reduce travel home, and using air conditioning to reduce effects.

Sample question 7 — Foundation

a) Many raw materials are non-renewable. What does 'non-renewable' mean? [1 mark]

b)

- **(i)** Name a raw material which is produced by mining or quarrying. [1 mark]
- **(ii)** Describe the effects on the environment of mining or quarrying in an area you have studied. [2 marks]

c) Name one renewable type of energy and describe how it is produced. [3 marks]

d)

- **(i)** What is meant by alternative forms of energy? [2 marks]
- **(ii)** Explain why alternative forms of energy are being developed in many countries. [4 marks]

Suggested answer

a) Cannot be replaced/will run out.

b)

- **(i)** Gravel, coal, limestone, copper, etc.
- **(ii)** Effects on landscape (scarring, waste tips, subsidence); effects on natural environment (destruction or damage to habitats); effects on human environment (noise, heavy traffic, dust).

c) Wind, solar, tide, wave. For example, tidal barrage built across estuary and movement of tide through the barrage drives turbines which produce electricity.

d)

- **(i)** Source of energy other than fossil fuel like coal.
- **(ii)** Lack of fossil fuels; flexible use of alternative sources on a small scale; reduction of pollution; to meet reductions in fossil fuel use due to global warming.

Sample question 8 — Foundation

a) Study Figure 1 showing the pattern of land use in a British city.

(i) What do the terms residential and open space mean in the key to the map? [2 marks]

(ii) What are the two main groups of businesses found in the Central Business District? [2 marks]

(iii) State two reasons why businesses are concentrated in the central area of a city. [2 marks]

b) Look at the locations of the heavy engineering works and the electronic engineering factory on Figure 1.

(i) Describe the location of the heavy engineering factory and explain the advantages of its location. [3 marks]

(ii) Describe the location of the TV and video factory and explain the advantages of its location. [3 marks]

c) Location A on Figure 1 is in the inner city; location B is in the suburbs.

(i) Describe the typical features of location A, using these headings:
Age
Types of land use
Population
Changes [4 marks]

(ii) Describe how location B differs from location A. [4 marks]

Figure 1

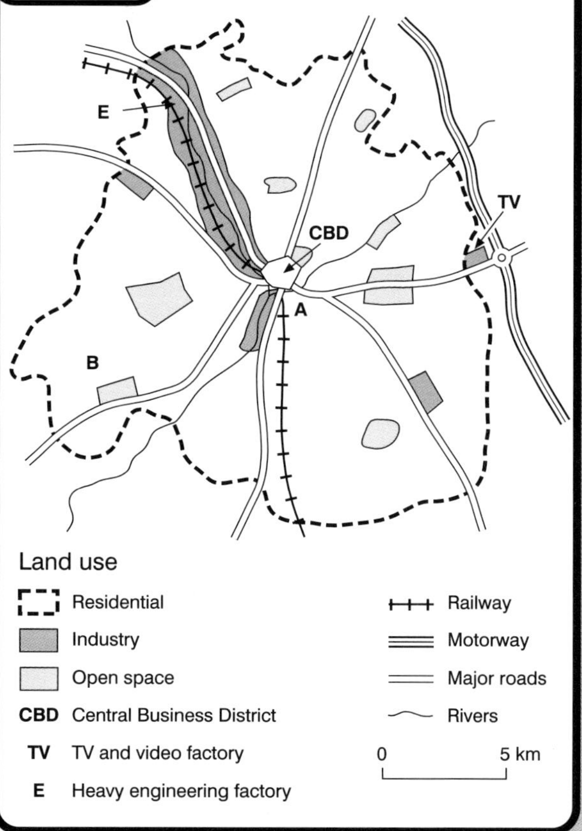

Suggested answer

a) (i) Residential – housing; Open space – parks, playing fields.

(ii) Shops and offices.

(iii) Central location is accessible to population from a wide area; near to other businesses of the same type so able to compete with them directly; high-status location for business.

b) (i) Heavy engineering factory. In the valley bottom; next to river and railway; in suburbs. Level, large site on land previously unused due to poor drainage; cheap land; river water for production use; road and rail transport adjacent.

(ii) TV and video factory. On city edge; on industrial estate; near motorway access. Easy transport of finished goods and components; in pleasant environment; low land costs; room for expansion.

c) (i) Location A
Age – originally Victorian or 19th century; now with post-1950 housing and industry.
Types of land use – mixed housing and industry with derelict land; housing mainly terraced.
Population – falling population due to clearing of old housing; ageing population; greater proportion of ethnic minorities.
Changes – redevelopment since1950; much terraced housing removed, replaced by high-rise developments; some of these now removed; closure of factories; demolition of many; small housing and industrial development in some places; derelict land where cleared buildings not replaced.

(ii) Location B
Lower-density housing; mainly detached and semi-detached houses with large gardens; more open space; industry separated from housing on industrial estates; varied styles of houses according to age; purpose-built shopping centres in some more recently developed areas.

Sample question 9 Foundation

a) Study Figure 1 showing unemployment rates in the United Kingdom.

(i) Name one region which is in the highest unemployment group. [1 mark]

(ii) Name one region with the lowest level of unemployment. [1 mark]

(iii) Describe the pattern of unemployment in the United Kingdom. [3 marks]

b) (i) Give an example of an area where the decline or closure of industries caused unemployment. Name the industry or industries involved. [2 marks]

(ii) State two reasons why industries decline or close down. [4 marks]

Figure 1

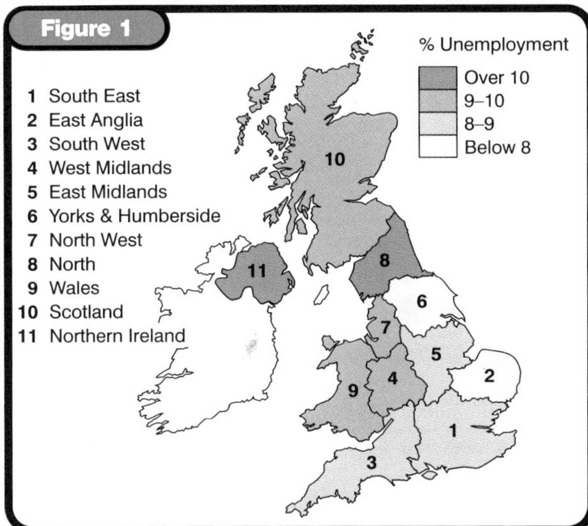

c) (i) Name an area in the United Kingdom or elsewhere in the European Union where new industries have reduced unemployment. [1 mark]

(ii) Describe the new industries and explain their growth in that area. [5 marks]

d) Study Figure 2, a sketch map showing the location of two major stores.

(i) State four advantages of this location. [4 marks]

(ii) What problems are thought to be caused by out-of-town shopping developments? [4 marks]

Figure 2

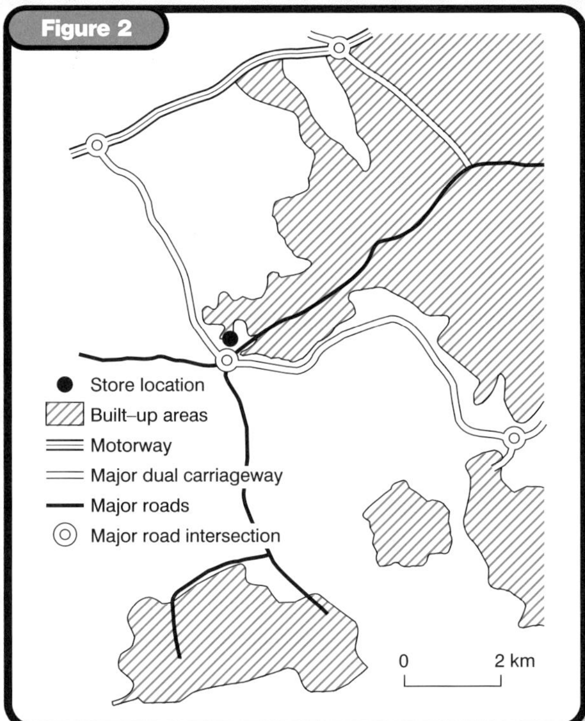

Suggested answer

a) (i) North or Northern Ireland

(ii) East Anglia or Yorks and Humberside

(iii) General south-east to north-west decline in employment.

b) (i) For example, the Ruhr, Germany; coal, steel, textiles and chemicals.

(ii) Exhaustion of coalfield; outdated factories and production methods; environmental problems; distance from alternative raw materials.

c) (i) Grenoble in the French Alps.

(ii) Electronic and high-technology industry generally; attracted by existing research centres and the advantages of the region itself – rapid access to other parts of Europe, excellent transport links and superb quality of life. Multiplier effect (or snowball effect) keeps it growing.

d) (i) Plenty of space for large buildings and parking; close to a major urban area with its population; at a central location on the road network where major roads meet; roads give rapid access to people from a very wide area avoiding urban congestion.

(ii) Using up open land with effects on agriculture and wildlife habitats; taking business away from city centres; causing closures and unemployment in city centres; rundown city centres present a poor image and makes the city less attractive to new businesses; out-of-town locations are often difficult to reach for people without cars or unable to drive.

Sample question 10 — Higher

a) Figure 1 shows the climatic conditions of different types of vegetation regions.
 (i) What are the climatic features of deciduous forest regions? [1 mark]
 (ii) What does the diagram suggest about the distribution of coniferous forest compared with tropical rain forest? [4 marks]
 (iii) Explain how deciduous forests are adapted to the climate of the regions where they are found. [2 marks]

Figure 1

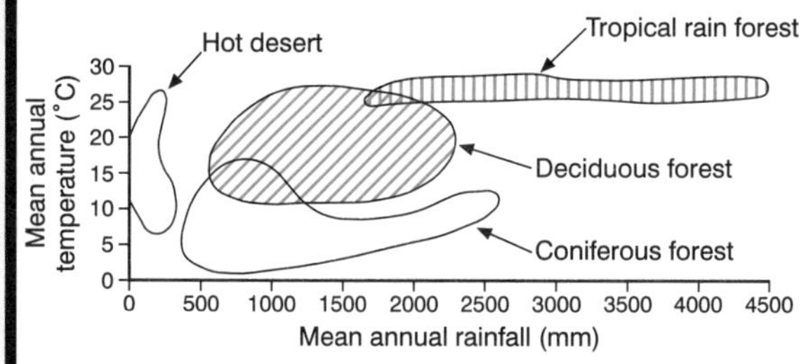

b) Rain forest removal is regarded as a major environmental problem. In your answers to the following questions refer to areas you have studied.
 (i) Describe the ways by which tropical rain forest is being removed. Refer to areas you have studied in your answer.
 (ii) Explain the effects of rain forest removal. [10 marks]

Suggested answer

a) (i) Rainfall between about 600 mm and 2300 mm a year; temperatures ranging from about 10°C to 28°C.
 (ii) Overlap at the warmer and drier end of the coniferous range, but generally coniferous forests are found in colder regions than deciduous. Coniferous forest is restricted to a narrow temperature range in areas of heavier rainfall.
 (iii) Cool winter temperatures restrict growth and leaf buds are dormant; roots are unable to take up moisture in the cool season so trees shed their leaves to cut water loss by transpiration.

b) (i) Peasant farmers; clearing for grazing land; timber; firewood.
 (ii) Soil erosion; flooding; loss of biodiversity; loss of human habitat; regional climatic changes; global climate change.

Sample question 11 — Higher

a) Study Figure 1 showing estimated world urban population changes.
 (i) Describe the trends illustrated by Figure 1. [3 marks]
 (ii) What does urbanisation mean? [2 marks]
 (iii) Using an example you have studied, explain why many cities in more economically developed countries (MEDCs) are losing population. [4 marks]
 (iv) Give reasons for the rapid growth of cities in less economically developed countries (LEDCs). [3 marks]

Figure 1

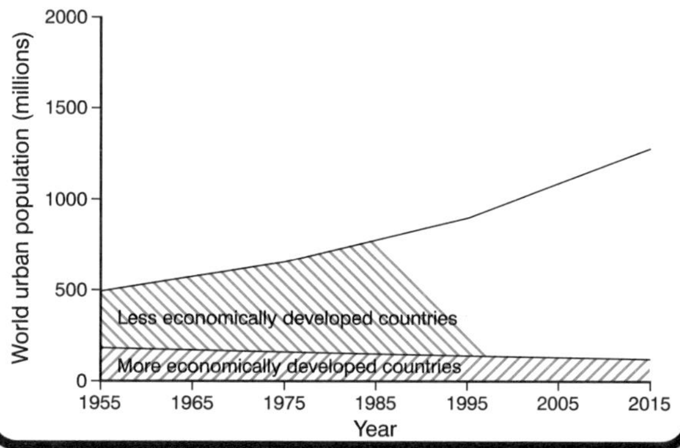

b) The patterns of land use in cities in MEDCs and LEDCs usually have clear differences as well as similarities. Describe the differences and similarities in land use patterns. Refer to cities you have studied in your answer. [8 marks]

Suggested answer

a) (i) Gradual decrease in urban population of MEDCs; marked increase in LEDCs; specific figures or proportions for extra mark.
 (ii) The proportion of the population living in towns and cities or the growth of towns and cities.
 (iii) Name of example. Redevelopment of inner cities; movement of overspill to places outside the city; attraction of small towns as places of residence and employment; increased mobility.
 (iv) Migration from rural areas to escape poverty, lack of land and lack of services and opportunities; attractions of the cities with greater opportunities.

b) Similarities – CBD at centre, industrial sector, distinct zones of high- medium- and low-quality residential areas. Differences – squatter areas around ring of LEDC cities as well as elsewhere, low-quality housing around CBD, high- and medium-quality housing occupy smaller area than in MEDC city.

Index